ENJOYING ARCHIVES

Enjoying Archives

What They Are · Where to Find Them

How to Use Them

David Iredale

Phillimore

First published in 1973
Reissued in 1980

This edition published by
PHILLIMORE & CO. LTD.
Shopwyke Hall, Chichester, Sussex
1985

ISBN 0 85033 561 2

Printed and bound in Great Britain by
REDWOOD BURN LTD.
Trowbridge, Wiltshire

CONTENTS

ACKNOWLEDGEMENTS

In the course of compiling this book I have visited, or corresponded with, many archivists, librarians, museum curators and administrators in Britain and Ireland. Their patience and kindness in providing me with information is much appreciated.

To my colleague at the Moray District Record Office, John Barrett, I am grateful for reading the manuscript and for his helpful comments and suggestions. He also provided me with the excerpts from his unpublished typescript of the memoirs of the preacher, James Allan, and details of his study of the murder trial of Alexander Gillan.

Forres
31 August 1984

DAVID IREDALE

INTRODUCTION

'And the Archives hold my great-great-grandfather's will, all written on vellum and in the Latin tongue.' The retired village postman paused for my comments. I hesitated so he continued, 'You can't see it because it's locked away but my mother once visited Lambeth Palace and was shown a copy. She always insisted he left a lot of money which Lord Russell took after he got a copy of the will . . .'.

How could I explain that the ancestor, a tenant farmer of the Duke of Bedford, left no will? His inventory, hastily scrawled in English round hand, almost illegible but entirely legal, lay open for all to consult at the county record office. Documents, archives, muniments are still a mystery to many people.

This book deals with the great heritage of documents in Great Britain, and with a few of the archives where documents are stored. It aims to describe, in outline, the work of the county record office, the repair of manuscripts, and the method of reading old records.

A document is something written to provide evidence or information upon any subject under the sun. Coins, gravestones, films or Brueghel paintings are documents, though this book will refer mainly to manuscript (handwritten) or printed papers and parchments such as maps, correspondence and deeds of title. When a document is drawn up or used in the course of a public or private transaction and preserved in the custody of the people responsible for the transaction, it becomes part of an archive. An archival document is frequently no longer in current business use but set aside for permanent preservation. Thus a letter written to the Earl of Derby concerning estate affairs, and held at Knowsley since 1764, forms part of the archive or family muniments of the Earls of Derby; but a single love letter from Frank to Emily or the haphazard purchases of an antiquarian cannot form an archive.

The archives is the office or repository for the storage of documents of all types, whether archival or not. Many archives are now known as record offices because here are found parish, legal and official records. Any document created as authentic evidence of legal importance is known as a record: a marriage register at the church for example. A muniment is a document preserved as evidence of rights and privileges. Families and boroughs therefore own muniments.

Documents have varied uses. Books cannot supply all the answers. Is your family tree in print? Has someone written the history of your house? Can the origin of the local smithy be traced? Do you know the names of all inhabitants of your town in 1851? Which London livery company did great-great-grandfather join? You may almost certainly answer these questions by going to the archives, and in no other way whatsoever. Library, local soothsayer, Citizens Advice Bureau and historical society will generally yield disappointingly small amounts of information.

Documents are stored in several thousand different buildings in Britain, ranging from the British Museum to the local solicitor's office, from country mansions to factory cellars. Obviously only a few dozen buildings are in any sense adequately planned and staffed as archives offices. Visiting the remainder can be disheartening. Fortunately many documents have been printed, and are thus obtainable in libraries, saving visits to archives themselves. Many records in print are listed in E. L. C. Mullins, *Text and Calendars* (1958).

The following chapters attempt to describe those archives accessible to professional and part-time historians alike. The term historian to my mind includes all individuals interested in reading documents about the past; and includes, therefore, the genealogist whose work is regarded so often by other students with the condescension that rock climbers reserve for fell walkers; includes the retired ICI worker leafing through a vestry account book; the housewife following the history of her cottage? the sixth-former examining an 1842 tithe plan; the social scientist reconstituting families in the Stuart village. There is no reason to leave out occasional historian including the solicitor tracing deeds, the civil engineer following the track of an old road, the architect or landscape gardener studying Georgian building plans and estate surveys.

Most people visiting archives are indeed part-time amateur historians and my advice takes this into account, leaning heavily on title deeds, wills and inventories, parish registers and quarter-sessions records. For this reason, such record centres as the royal archives at Windsor, not readily accessible, do not appear here. Original Anglo-Saxon charters at the British Museum are a specialised study, a wide knowledge of diplomatic, old English, palaeography and history being called for. Many historians will turn to edited and translated versions, whose commentaries adequately replace my kind of guide. Domesday Book, a most difficult source to translate and understand, is discussed because it does figure in histories, where much of its information is ignored or maltreated. My book is obviously biased towards documents most commonly studied by the majority of historical researchers. With exceptions, the chapters aim to report on types of documents you find in archives once you arrive there, not with individual documents, apart from a few exceptions like Domesday Book.

Following this recitation come hints on how to use documents. It is all very well to requisition land taxes of Bucklow Hundred for 1790–1820, but without guidance you may not realise how to turn land taxes into means of plotting the history of every parcel of land in your village. General remarks on research methods are in the opening chapter. These are intended for the local historian, as, obviously, the professional is more than capable of using source material to best advantage, and his research students lean on their professor for advice. The local historian should also read the chapter on county record offices which discusses the use of manuscripts. It is of course just as important to know for what purposes various kinds of document are being employed by historians nowadays. You may broaden your own field of interests as a result. A friend of mine, an avid peruser of old wills and inventories, was led by such suggestions to extract information on 17th-century cottage interiors. The historical significance of this type of record has only recently begun to be appreciated. People have in the past been content only to copy down names, legacies and lands from probate documents. Obviously without a sound historical sense — common sense as much as book learning — you may easily overlook the wood for the trees and end up with a garbled knowledge of both archives and history.

So I seem to have returned to my retired village postman. 'Why they can't give me the will I don't know. No one else would want it', he told me, his mind only on the supposed fortune mentioned therein, presumptuously ignoring the needs of historians who do use probate records for other purposes.

CHAPTER ONE

ARCHIVAL RESEARCH

'I WAS VERY sick & sore distressed all the time I was in ship which was six dayes haveing got only one stool but many vomites'.

The writer's constriction of the bowels was but one of several bodily afflictions, though tiresome enough for a preacher moving about country, doubly troublesome for one tossed in a tempest on the Moray Firth.

Laughter echoed around the vaulted Scottish baronial record room of the burgh tolbooth as the lecturer warmed to his theme. Although the subject of that morning's talk had been dead these two hundred years, his memoirs stirred us still. Tonia, a vivacious teenager and certainly no academic historian, sympathised with that young man, seventeenth-century presbyterian though he was. The more mature listeners at first hesitated to exhibit their amusement at the naive candour of the author of this little book of memoirs, but before long found themselves unable to restrain their merriment. They relived the occasion of James Allan's sermon in Inverness when, suffering a severe stomach upset, and 'so oppressed with wind that I could hardly pray or praise or do any thing except to look up, wait, beleive, depend, & submit. Hereby I was kept humble, emptied & fitted for receiveing aneother fill'.

One night sometime afterwards Allan believed he had wrestled with Satan himself.

'After venting of much wind out of my stomack (this has been occasioned by trouble of mind & melancholy) I suped with peace . . . the next day, was sore disquieted in sleep wherby I was shortly awakened & thought I found something severall times stirring the cloaths, which I apprehended to have been the devill ready to appear to me in a bodily shape'.

Tonia dissolved in gales of helpless but knowing laughter. I suppressed my chuckles only with difficulty, reminding myself that a too obvious expression of amusement might seem inappropriate. I wondered what James Allan, a dour Scot, the pedantically serious follower of a stern deity, would have made of the hilarity that was generated by these readings from his spiritual memoirs. For he was a man with no very highly developed sense of humour or irony, intended no jocularity, and found no cause for mirth, whilst, convinced of his own 'gracious' state as one of the saved, he traversed the hostile episcopalian lands 'twixt Spey and Dundee . . . ye Devills bounds . . . wherein he reyns with great power without any controll'.

*   *   *

1

I enjoy archives because here I may gain access to the cultivated wit of the Augustan age or the earnest ingenuousness of the Scots covenanters, the uncompromising seriousness of the Victorian paterfamilias or the strident tones of the Irish nationalist. I can consult household correspondence of Elizabethan women, the secret policies of famous statesmen, confidential opinions of counsel, documents about my own forebears, my house, village, school or favourite mountain glen. More often than not I journey to an archives office with a specific purpose in mind, perhaps to discover the dimensions of an ancient church, the origin of a railway company's schemes, the reasons for decay of a medieval community, the documentation of an estate forfeited for religious recusancy. My manuscript notes from original documents facilitate the satisfactory completion of a lecture, the writing of a book or article, and the answering of a correspondent's query. But on occasion I requisition archival material in a record office for the pleasure, pure and simple, of reading old documents and, through the words of people long dead, establishing an empathic appreciation of the life of past centuries. But really I should refrain from defining archival pleasure as pure and simple, because Georgian countrymen, medieval dowagers, regency bucks and naive young clerics encountered in the sources rarely appear simple — and not infrequently are far from pure.

This book, concerned with the heritage of documents in these islands and with a number of the repositories in which this heritage is preserved, is dedicated to anyone whose curiosity may be aroused by the mysteries of the past in which our present is rooted. This book is dedicated to the housewife following the development of her village women's institute, the schoolgirl examining a tithe plan for field names, the social scientist reconstituting family relationships of Stuart times, the civil engineer seeking the line of a Victorian sewer, the landscape gardener studying Georgian estate plans, the litigant seeking ownership of a disputed apple orchard, the maiden aunt pursuing a stolen inheritance, the secretary of a footpath preservation society searching quarter sessions road closure files, the genealogist seeking an illusive baptismal entry.

Archives may prove intensely enjoyable through the patient sifting of original documentation, a thoughtful approach to the implications of their contents, and subsequent considered organisation of information extracted. The historian requires a sympathy with the foibles and complexities of human nature, a knowledge of the political, moral, social and religious preoccupations of the era under scrutiny, an imaginative creativity in reconstructing the story of his period — and a capacity to endure both the drudgery and the disappointments of fruitless searching.

Local history research reveals the actions and words of ordinary folk rather than the notables whose decisions fill the history books. A stray item of correspondence records the personal background of the man actually pressed to fight at Trafalgar; a court book recounts the story of the woman who cursed the monarch's religious reformation; a private diary relates the feelings of the yeoman forced to pay the land tax in support of Pitt's wars; a business archive introduces the name of the girl whose calloused hands greased the purse of the capitalist and the wheels of the machines of the industrial revolution. These ordinary folk — the men who fought the wars, paid the taxes, wasted their strength in the hard labour of the fields, crippled their bodies in the dim and dangerous work of mine and mill — the unsung anonymous men and women of Exton and Ambridge, of shire and borough, form the base of the social pyramid which supports at its apex the great and famous names of history, who otherwise could rant and rave unheeded, their pockets unfilled, their policies unfulfilled. The study of the origin, growth, periods of stability, times of depression, perhaps the decline and decay of communities of men and women all over these islands comprises the main theme of the local historian's research.

Researchers are human beings, not computers, and their choice of subject or historical period reflects their own interest and bias, because few historians escape entirely from their environment or upbringing. The sympathies of the Victorian antiquary, perhaps the squire or clergyman, might remain with the workhouse master or ratepayer in his strictures about parochial poor relief whereas the twentieth-century social scientist, imbued with a more radical turn of mind, may identify more readily with the unfortunate recipients of village charity.

Written by fallible human beings, original documents themselves may exhibit errors and prejudices. Inventories of the goods of deceased men and women, containing perhaps hundreds of priced items, do not always accurately add up. The Scottish landowner's correspondence on estate improvement during the early decades of the nineteenth century ignores the plaintive cries of the cottar and petty tacksman about the burning of habitations to clear the straths for sheep farming.

A history gains in vitality and significance through the inclusion and explanation of the extraordinary rather than in the reiteration of the commonplaces and of the much studied generalisations common to the majority of communities. Significant subjects might include the commutation of tithes in 1736, a century before legislation facilitated commutation nationwide; the survival rather than extinction of a Roman Catholic landowning family through the period of the Protestant ascendancy in Ireland; the community which escaped plague during the black death of 1350 in Scotland, which escaped crippling poverty during the dark war years of 1809–1813 in England, which escaped famine during the potato blight of 1846–1849 in Ireland.

The canny historian distinguishes intuitively between the significant aberration and the comical or meaningless monstrosity. The story of a child with two heads and the legend of the sprouting of a giant marrow are probably historically irrelevant beside the study of infant mortality rates, annual crop yields, religious bigotry, or capital investment. Description of the religious procession in wakes week 1905, repetition of annual reports of the tennis club, praise of performances of the drama group, all tend to clutter a history and impede the flow of the narrative. The compiler doubtless laboured hard and long to accumulate these facts and figures but should firmly sift and ruthlessly ditch before getting down to writing, because there can hardly be anything more boring, or unpublishable, than a history choked with historically insignificant detail or apocryphal stories.

For the earliest history of a village or town the researcher must consult the archaeologist not the archivist. Visitors to archives cannot expect to locate very

ancient papers referring to local communities in Britain; indeed the documentation of most communities stretches back no more than four or five hundred years.
Similarly, although papers may be in existence to elucidate the happenings of
the recent past, the material is unlikely to be deposited yet in the archives, while
owners of the documents, and people mentioned therein, do not always willingly
permit access. A. J. P. Taylor completed his *English history 1914–1945* in July
1964 'that is, exactly fifty years after the first events which it records, and was
thus entirely within the compass of the fifty-year rule'. This rule restricted access
to official archives, at that time for half a century after their creation, a practice
followed by some private owners of historically significant material. 'The
unofficial historian can only register his protest [and] make do mainly with
printed sources', leaving the exploitation of the papers for future generations
of historians.

Research must be confined within manageable physical bounds and for this
reason normally relates to such ancient topographical units as the Scottish laird's
estate; English manor, parish or hundred; Welsh mining valley or holiday resort;
and Irish townland or barony. But too parochial a view isolates a community that
was always subjected to outside influences, however remote, and fosters the
illusion of local autonomy in times gone by. The industrial township of 1820
leaned on the conurbation around and the nation at large for its investment,
expertise, markets and administration while the economic development of the
monastic manor five centuries earlier may have depended as much on the policy
and personality of a distant abbot as on the labour and rents of resident villagers.
The parish priest must have seemed a powerful figure to medieval villeins but he
received orders, like any minion, from his superiors and patron, ultimately also
from Rome. Village life cannot but have been profoundly stirred by decisions
from beyond the horizon at such periods of national crisis as King John's excommunication or King Henry's religious reformation. Similarly, the civil parish
looked to quarter sessions, the seaport to hanseatic forces overseas, the sheriffdom to the royal administration in Edinburgh, the Ulster plantation to landlords
in Scotland, the kirk session to the presbytery, the sparsely peopled glen to a
London estate agent. This survey, by setting the region under scrutiny in its
proper relationship with the wider historical and geographical context, ensures
that no local activity, whether burning a heretic or digging a coalmine, becomes
exaggerated or diminished in significance without sound reason.

But unfortunately there remain those for whom 'history is bunk', historical
characters as dead as the dodo, archives a hotchpotch of rubbish — and dirty old
books. For such people the past is not merely defunct but never really existed,
people from ages gone by figments of a schoolmarm's imagination, records of
times past as expendable as a packet of cigarettes but not half as costly. For such
closed minds archives are not to be trusted to speak for themselves. Failing to
appreciate the true value of documentary evidence and, perhaps fearing the
discovery of their own ignorance, such people will advise 'ask old Bill, he knows
everything about the church' or 'Grandma's the only person who can tell you
about the building of the workhouse'. In 1935 A. G. Cockburn, factor to the
Laird of Pitgaveny in Moray, required to discover the history of a particular road

and ditch at Caysbriggs. Mr. Cockburn wrote to the county clerk, 'I do not want to put you to the trouble of looking up the old Minute Books if this can be avoided, and if you can find the old gentleman living in the County who has knowledge of the subject . . . the information to be obtained from him might satisfy Capt. Dunbar'. And this attitude breeds a curious fatalism that we are always too late to rescue the past from oblivion because old Bill, grandma and their like are dying every day. To suppose that we in our generation may research the archives and learn more of significance about the past than Bill or grandma ever knew seems incomprehensible.

Archival definitions

Documents may be stored in a building and department known to the man in the street, certainly in countries with a European or American tradition, as the archives. Many of the new Scottish local authority centres bear that very title, as in Strathclyde Regional Archives or Argyll & Bute District Archives.

The term 'archives' implies also a collection of documents, *any* collection in some writers' definition. To the archivist bred in the tradition of Sir Hilary Jenkinson, deputy keeper of the public records and erstwhile president of the society of archivists, the term is much more specific. In Jenkinson's view an item forms part of an archive when *drawn up* or employed in the course of a public or private *administrative or executive transaction* and thereafter preserved in the *custody* of the officials responsible for that transaction, or their successors, *for their own information*. Administrators created archives for practical and contemporary purposes, certainly not for the benefit of future academics, or historical researchers, though archival documents, once retired from daily administrative use, may be set aside for permanent preservation for the benefit of posterity in the repository, for instance of a bishop, kirk session, county council or police commission.

That archival item, whilst providing evidence or information, may be in the form of a coin, film, painting, printed pamphlet or illuminated parchment. Accumulations of ostraca, consisting of ordinary potsherds employed as writing tablets and thus undoubtedly three-dimensional objects, nevertheless perpetuate authentic summaries of important historical happenings and therefore appropriately find a home in the British Library's department of manuscripts. The archives of ancient kings in Mesopotamia were, before the introduction of parchment or paper, composed of such tablets. Indeed the biblical ten commandments inscribed on stone were also archival items, though the material itself broke into pieces at an early stage and the text survived only in folk memory and on leather or papyrus.

Archivists include in the definition 'records' such series as proceedings of parliament, court order books, marriage registers, correspondence files, financial abstracts of accounts, quarter sessions petitions, solicitors' letter books, indeed all documentation created to preserve a permanent authentic record of legal, administrative or business transactions. Although the larger part, perhaps 95 per cent., of certain series of records consists of ephemeral material—printed circulars, multiple copies of letters and plans, newspaper cuttings, printed reports available elsewhere and similar documentation — such series are preserved intact for terms of 10, 25 or 50 years to serve the immediate purposes of the administrators who accumulated them, and thereafter are 'weeded' by the archivist exercising his historical judgment and the skill born of long experience to select for permanent preservation a core of archives for the enjoyment and illumination of future generations. County record offices established during the 20th century perpetuate in their name not only this definition of the word records but also their antecedents in the strongrooms established before the present century where quarter sessions records were stored and which assumed the title 'record office of the clerk of the peace'.

The word 'muniments' is used by archivists when speaking of family or municipal collections. The word implies authentic evidence about obligations, rights and privileges, for instance, title deeds or contracts contained in 'muniments of the earls of Derby' or 'of the burgh of Stirling'.

Research practices

When entering the searchroom of a record office, the researcher will usually be required to register his name and address and to study the office rules before being invited to consult catalogues, card indexes or documents. Smoking, eating, drinking and other discourtesies are not permitted in the well-conducted searchroom, nor may unique and priceless documents be borrowed for study at home. The use of ink, especially ballpoint, is forbidden because damage caused through carelessness may prove irretrievable, beyond the help of even skilled conservationists. It is, in most instances, advantageous to write with a pencil because mistakes in notes can be readily erased. Record offices normally maintain a perpetual memory of requests for archival material by means of special requisition forms or registers.

Memoranda, transcripts, photocopies and other information from each documentary collection should be preserved by the researcher in a folder clearly labelled, as for instance:

SOURCE 74

location of archive	Moray District Record Office, Tolbooth, Forres, Moray
owner	J. & W. Wittet, architects & surveyors, Elgin
type of document	architectural plans and specifications
covering dates	1828–1965
subjects	farmhouses, steadings, schools, public buildings, private dwellings
record office reference	DAW

The researcher with a definite purpose generally extracts from any document only the details required for his immediate study. I myself prefer to allow the scent of other trails to tempt me into turning from my charted course. I permit myself to be sidetracked into bypaths which sometimes lead me to my desired goal but by a tortuous unexpectedly scenic route. But I do not lose sight of the beaten track and become bogged down in the charming trivia or intriguing irrelevances in which many sources abound. As a family historian, therefore, I should seek names, ages, relationships and residences; as an economist I follow wages, prices, trade cycle or industrial depression; but as a local historian I cannot ignore the rules of the poorhouse, the madwoman's plea for pity, the workman's defence of rickburning, an architectural survey of the church, a medieval marriage contract, a perambulation of the marches.

Occasionally the researcher considers an exact word-for-word transcription of a document essential, and certain editorial standards should be imposed in order to maintain the spirit and meaning of the original.

The following transcripts from a Latin charter of about 1180 and Scots documents of 1393 and 1592 preserve punctuation, capitalisation and spelling as in the text. Words within parentheses ( ) had been deleted by the original scribe. Wherever the writer employed abbreviated forms of words, the modern editor extends but encloses additional letters within square brackets [ ]. Angle brackets ⟨ ⟩ indicate a tear in the manuscript with letters suggested by the modern editor, following the spellings and practices employed by that particular scribe or, so far as can be guessed, the conventions of the age in spelling, capitalisation and punctuation.

Charter of William the Lion, about 1180

W[illelmus] d[e]i gr[ati]a Rex Scott[orum]. Om[n]ib[us] vicecomitib[us] [et] Baillijs toti[us] t[er]re sue salut[em]. Sciatis me hanc lib[er]tate[m] dedisse b[ur]g[e]n-sib[us] meis de Morauia ut n[u]ll[us] scil[icet] i[n] t[er]ra mea eor[um] namu[m] capiat p[ro] alic[uius] debito n[isi] p[ro] eor[um] debito p[ro]p[ri]o. Q[ua]re p[ro]hib[e]o firmit[er] ne q[ui]s in t[er]ra mea eor[um] namu[m] alit[er] capiat sup[er] meam plenariam defensionem. Test[ibus]. Will[elm]o de Haia PHilippo de Vallon'. Ricardo cl[er]ico m[e]o de p[re]benda. ap[u]d Bonekil.

The clerks in 1393 and 1592 attempt to preserve the letter thorn for *th*, although writing only the contemporary *y*. This is transcribed as y in 1393, [th] in 1592, to illustrate two methods of overcoming this problem in vernacular documents once thorn itself had disappeared. Some scribes employ y for *th* and dotted y (ẏ) for the vowel sound *i*, but the 1393 clerk was not consistent. The latter also writes his *w* very large, as if a capital letter, though this has been transcribed consistently only as a normal *w*. In both documents traces of the letter yogh remain in the initial letter of the word for 'year'. The 1393 scribe's letter in 'ẏhere' is indistinguishable from dotted y while the 1592 letter in 'ȝeir' more closely resembles yogh, hence the difference in transcription.

Grant of Thomas Dunbar, 1393

Be it knawẏn tyl al men. thrw ẏis p[re]sent[is] lettr[e]s. Vs Thomaẏse of Dunbarr[e]. Erẏl of murreffe. for tyl hafe grauntẏt'and gẏfin' tẏl ẏe aldirman. ẏe baẏlis. of wre Burgh

of Elgẏne. and to ẏe burges. of y[at] ilke al ẏe wol. ẏe Clathe and al vthir[is] thẏng[is].
ẏ[a]t gais be schipe owte of wre hafine of spee. vncustomẏt. ẏe qwhilk[is]. we hafe
[con]saẏvit. hurtis gretlẏ ẏaire fredome ẏe qwhẏlke oẏsẏt It wald Rẏn vs to p[re]iedẏce.
and to ẏaire fredome befornemẏt. and ẏis as before wyt al men we wil nocht thole. In ẏe
wẏtnes of ẏe qwhilke thẏng[is]. we gerit put wre seel to ẏis p[re]sent lettr[e]s
At Elgyne xxiij day of ẏe moneth of Iule. i[n] ẏe ẏhere of Grace. m°.C°C°C°. Nynetẏ
and thre

Portion of charter of James VI, 1592

...lykewayis with tuo mercat dayis oulklie vpone Weddnisday and sett⟨ird⟩ay in our
said burgh of Inuernes, Togidder w[i]t[h] aucht frie fairis auchtymes in [th]e ʒeir
To witt The first fair vpone palmesunday, The secund of [th]e sai⟨dis⟩fairis vpone the
sevint day of Iulij callit Sanctandro the boyis fair Quhilk was haldin of auld at ⟨St
Mairtyniskirk in ardmanoch now lyand waist,⟩ the Rudec⟨astle⟩ now dimolisched and
abolisched, The thrid fair vpone the fyftene day of august callit the Mariefair, The fourt
fair callit [th]e Ruidfair in hervist, The fy⟨ft⟩ fair vpone the Tent day of November,
callit Mairtimes fair quhilk was halden of auld at Sanct Mairtyniskirk in ardmanoch now
lyand waist...

As appropriate to the research undertaken, I myself card index the subjects,
place-names and personal names mentioned in my notes in order to bring together
references from a variety of sources. Numbers on the right-hand side of the card
refer to my sources.

MILLING : GRAIN	date	source number
will & inventory of flour miller	1587	15
dispute in manor court	1380	27
mill recorded	1086	84
rental	1712–1756	127
petition on price of milling	1622	164

STONEY HEYS FARM	date	source number
tithe assessment and plan	1843	17
insurance policy	1710	29
title deeds	1686–1924	57
hearth tax	1666	86
household & farm expenses & income	1774–1796	102

McKAY, Mary wife of Thomas McKay, saddler, Kirkton	date	source number
died, aged 57	1847	21
tailoress, widow	1841	72
process for debt	1813	94
admonished for fornication	1816	103

A family unit card for each couple and their children facilitates research on
genealogy, migration and demography. The example here displayed indicates the

age of marriage of three couples, the number of children born to one couple, the death of three out of seven children, the loss in the same year of father and adult son, and the fact that none of the sons eventually inherited the farm. These matters were discovered from the parish register and monumental inscriptions, suggesting that all offspring except Thomas remained in their native place until death. As a contribution to estimating the village population in, for example, March 1731, the Bowyer card adds seven members to the enumeration, taking into account that Philip did not die until October 1731. Obviously the researcher cannot be certain that all seven actually resided in Netherton during March: the husband may have been visiting London, a daughter her aunt in Norwich. Perhaps temporary visitors, vagrants or harvest labourers entered the village during the month but may not appear in documents. Nevertheless the card offers a rough guide in the absence of government statistics on population. The abbreviation m means 'married', c 'baptised', b 'buried'.

BOWYER, Thomas	1695–1757	farmer
Netherton		
husband of Mary (Williamson) 1691–1751		
m. 16 Sep. 1717		
Thomas	c. 11 May 1718	died in London about 1790
William	c. 15 Nov. 1719	b. 20 Nov. 1730
James	c. 16 Apr. 1721	b. 19 Apr. 1721
Mary	c. 22 Apr. 1722	m. 6 Aug. 1748
James	c. 26 May 1723	b. 21 Dec. 1757
Betty	c. 1 Nov. 1724	m. 6 Aug. 1748
Philip	c. 27 Feb. 1726	b. 11 Oct. 1731

Two classic local histories

During the years 1701 and 1702 Richard Gough, a yeoman of Myddle in Shropshire, put pen to paper to discuss the ownership of seats within the parish church. In the course of this excursion from pew to pew, Gough, then in his late sixties, recorded observations on the characteristics of individuals occupying the seats and on their family origins. Possibly Gough wrote only for the interest of his friends and his children, but his novel and unique scheme for producing a village survey and history enabled the author to put together a lively, pithy and informative account of the lives of his fellow villagers and, through this study of individuals, of the history of the community from the 16th century onwards. Gough's manuscript, first published in 1834, provides a source for the historian of Shropshire and of Stuart England but, just as significantly, a salutary reminder for the local historian of the importance of the careful planning of subject matter, the merits of literary style, the telling phase, curiosity about the past and a knowledge of human nature. This *History of Myddle*, the 'most remarkable local history ever written' is an example of a book, based on the author's own recollections and oral tradition, relying on only a limited number of archival documents, and looking back no more than three or four generations.

Montaillou, on the other hand, offers an example of a modern historian's painstaking research into archival material, in this instance the inquisition register of Jacques Fournier, bishop of Pamiers, concerning the Cathar heresy in southern France during the early 14th century. This best seller, a local study of international significance, is a history book that itself made history, in the depth of its penetration into the lives, the most private thoughts, the jealousies and the sexual conduct of people dead these six hundred years. The author, Professor Le Roy Ladurie, brilliantly brings these men and women back to life, the 200 lusty, generous, hardworking peasants of Montaillou, nestling in the foothills of the Pyrenees. Nearly six hundred interrogations took place. The manuscript of the inquisition, in Vatican archives, gives a privileged insight into the homes and minds of medieval villagers. But a document can speak for itself only in a limited sense. It is the historian's lucid and vivid exposition of the words on the page that enables us to enjoy this archival treasure.

CHAPTER TWO

PUBLIC RECORD OFFICE

ALTHOUGH MEDIEVAL ENGLISH monarchs regarded records of the royal court as part of the king's treasure, and presumably meriting extraordinary care, the nascent departments of state preserved documentation in a remarkably careless fashion. Chancery acquired the king's wardrobes at the Tower of London and New Temple, later moving to the chapel of the master of the rolls at Chancery Lane. Exchequer's treasury of parchments and paper festered in decrepit rooms at Westminster, ravaged by rats, insects, damp and souvenir hunters, later sharing with courts of common law the enlarged Chapter House repository. The monks at Westminster, no strangers to the sharp practices of forgery and substitution, even connived at a blatant burglary of the treasury of the king's wardrobe in 1303, and this misfortune seems to have convinced the authorities of the Tower's merits as the safest store for public records, especially for chancery records authenticating royal rights and privileges. However as late as 1674 a scandal about the forgery of official records nearly caused the archivist at the Tower to lose his position and emoluments.

But from Elizabethan times onwards a passion for genealogy and antiquities, especially among certain nobility and gentry desirous of establishing lineage and title to estates, stimulated the quarrying of archival material and even its proper safeguarding. Scholars burrowed into the records. Arthur Agarde, one of the deputy chamberlains of exchequer, compiled a *Compendium recordorum* in 1610 concerning the four treasuries of documentation at Westminster. He it was who wrote, 'There is fower-fould hurte that by negligence may bringe wracke to records; that is to say Fier, Water, Rates and Mice, Misplacinge'. William Prynne, keeper of the records at the Tower after the Restoration, cleaned and sorted his archives but found that civil servants were not eager to touch the filthy bundles 'for fear of endangering their eyesights and healths by the cankerous dust and evil scent'.

In 1708 Thomas Madox, historiographer royal, historian of the exchequer and pioneer of the science of diplomatic in England, drew attention to the storage of exchequer rolls in the pipe office. His description of that archive accompanies an engraving of a nook of the office. Four wooden cupboards or presses with doors and shelves are individually numbered, and the first cupboard provides ten shelves for the earliest rolls, beginning with those of Stephen's reign. The room appears clean and tidy, the rolls stacked neatly, though the amount of timber-work might upset a modern fire officer. Later evidence suggests that the organisation of exchequer and its system of accounting belied the picture.

Both houses of parliament initiated investigations into the problems of preserving state records during the years 1703–32. Members correctly identified the basic causes of neglect, decay, confusion or destruction as lack of space, money, staff and satisfactory buildings. But the solution, though essentially uncomplicated, was not easily implemented, because it entailed expenditure of government moneys.

Parliamentary investigators discovered that records of chancery in the Tower of London 'lye in confused heaps' open to depredation and to forgery, hardly a suitable fate for confidential or sacrosanct legal documents. Officials had not transferred non-current archives from the Rolls chapel to the Tower since 1499 and in fact did not do so even after the commission of inquiry's strictures. Certain papers in 1704 remained under the leads of the White Tower 'and if care be not speedily taken of them are in great danger of utter perishing'. Moreover in 1718 officers reported that 'Wee think it our duty upon this occasion to acquaint your Lordships, that the Magazine of Gunpowder belonging to the Tower is at present under the Rooms where the most valuable Records are kept'. Despite this warning the authorities consigned further archives to the Tower where they languished in perilous juxtaposition to the national powderkeg until the 19th century. Nevertheless a fireproof room was constructed, cupboards installed and various series of papers sorted during this period of spring cleaning.

Legal records in ruinous premises at Westminster suffered from theft, damp and rats, to mention only three problems. The archive of the court of wards in 1709 was discovered under a dilapidated roof 'in a perishing condition, in a Fishmonger's house . . . and the Fishmonger did what he thought fit with the records'. This shopkeeper served the royal family and may have wrapped his goods in paper of a unique and distinctly legal nature. Queen's Bench records were filed above what 'was formerly a Cook's shop and is now partly a Wash-house and partly a Stable, which is a very improper situation for records of such consequence'. Before structural repairs early in the 18th century, archives in the Chapter House remained 'in a great heap, undigested, without any covering from dust, or security from rats or mice'. The documents were exposed periodically to the hazard of kitchen fires.

The state paper office at the Holbein gate in Whitehall functioned as the repository for the government's political and administrative documents as distinct from the archives of medieval departments such as exchequer or chancery. The secretaries themselves provided for the safekeeping of their records during the 16th century. Thus the Cecils transported homewards to Hatfield numerous state papers which they carefully filed in the family muniments, fortunately for historians. Not a few significant documents were purloined by antiquarians such as Harley, Cotton and Lansdowne. These accumulations, now deposited in the British Library, and uncounted similar collections up and down the country testify to the lack of care of past custodians of the national archival treasures.

In 1603 Sir Thomas Lake received an annuity for 'keeping airing and digesting' the papers in official custody. Two 'Keepers and Regesters' were later appointed and from this time, 1610, a much more orderly approach to the archives of the state paper office may be discerned. Indeed Sir Thomas Wilson undertook the storage of material 'in very convenient rooms near the old Banqueting House' in Whitehall and arranged the archive into domestic, foreign, Irish and Scottish divisions, a useful systematic approach that has stood the passage of more than three centuries. Nevertheless these extremely sensitive documents, dating from the early decades of Henry VIII's reign onwards, though normally locked away from prying eyes, only narrowly escaped consuming fires in 1618, 1691 and 1698. Diligent keepers subsequently attempted to arrange the series into logical order but failed to cope with the problems posed by unregulated deposit of further material. Moreover 'Bradshaw, Milton and others at the time of the Rebellion', and doubtless many officials before and after, gained access to the papers, borrowed items and never returned them. Investigations of 1704 and 1705 revealed broken windows, leaking roof, 'rains washing into the turretts', damp documents 'in such Confusion and Disorder that it was very difficult to find any paper that was wanted . . . no body having been employed in this Office, as I am assured, for above 20 years past'. John Tucker, the investigator of 1705 and keeper of records, drew pictorial representations at this date of the cupboards and layout of the rooms, producing for the house of lords a list of documents and a report on restructuring the office.

Although Sir Christopher Wren planned an overflow repository in 1706, many records remained at the Holbein gate until the middle of the 18th century. That the premises housing the privy council registers at that date could be opened and entered only after enlisting the services of a workman with a sledgehammer suggests the appalling decrepitude of the entire building just before its demolition in 1759.

Commissioners appointed in 1764 to arrange, catalogue and index the state papers produced little in the way of published finding aids. Thus it remained for a later commission, of 1825, to print selections of letters of Henry VIII's reign, indexed by person and place. Only from 1852 when the papers passed into the care of the master of the rolls could the publication programme be expanded to finance the regular issue of calendars of domestic, foreign and colonial papers. These published calendars are sufficiently detailed to obviate recourse to the original documentation. State papers moved premises several times, on one occasion to a house that flooded at each high tide, on another to a repository in Great George Street that gradually subsided under the weight of years and documentation.

In 1799 Charles Abbot, member of parliament for Helston and later influential speaker of the commons, indicated his intention to propose the setting up of a select committee to inquire into the state of the public records. Abbot's committee duly investigated by questionnaire several hundred repositories including the British Museum, Tower of London, offices of county clerks of the peace and chapter houses of cathedrals. Abbot noted the conditions in which documents were stored, described the repository structure, furnishings and air circulation, and suggested the preparation of calendars, indexes, guides, lists and full texts of public records. As *a* — but not *the* — 'most essential measure' documents that 'are the most important in their Nature and the most perfect of their kind' should be printed in full or in calendar form.

In 1800 the government, concerned at the deterioration of series of ancient rolls and stimulated, in the course of a patriotic war, by the revival of interest in the nation's heritage which accompanied the romantic movement in art and letters, appointed a royal commission to consider implementing certain of the Abbot committee's recommendations.

The six commissions between 1800 and 1837 attempted to improve the physical conditions where national archives were then stored, in about fifty different buildings in London alone. By reducing the number of scattered repositories, renovating decaying buildings, looking to fireproofing or air conditioning and examining the possibility of one central record office for all departmental papers, the members roused public opinion to favour the establishment of a national archives in London. Unfortunately the commissioners proceeded very slowly and, by adopting expedients such as carting records to more adequate but still temporary homes including Carlton House riding school or Charing Cross mews, contributed to further extensive losses of unique items.

The commissioners felt themselves duty bound to facilitate public access to records by compilation of calendars, lists and indexes; by investigating exorbitant fees charged by rapacious custodians for consultation of records; by obviating the need for historians to sift through ancient rolls unassisted; by sorting, arranging, methodising, repairing; in short by developing the theory and practice of archive administration. But without the services of experienced and trained archivists, the commissioners to a large extent failed in this archival aspect of their work, and produced not a few lists which later archivists found necessary to revise. Several volumes of calendars, however, remain useful for researchers even today, partly because no one can afford to undertake the task of rearranging and relisting, not to mention publication, of the material.

The record commissioners considered, and devoted much effort and money to, the transcribing, editing and printing of important documents or archival series, including parliamentary records of Scotland, the hundred rolls, chancery enrolments, Henry VIII's ecclesiastical valuation, patent rolls, inquisitions *post mortem* and statutes of the realm. In true gothic fashion the commissioners even attempted to preserve the appearance and abbreviations of medieval documents by adopting a distinctive typeface for their volumes. The Scotch rolls published as *Rotuli Scotiæ*, 1814–19, refer to relations between England and Scotland from the time of the disputed succession following Margaret of Norway's death in 1290. The rolls continue through the period of Edward I's intervention in the dispute, Bannockburn, border forays involving garrisoning and fortifying strongpoints, and the slaughter of Flodden in 1513.

But while the commissioners talked and reported, government departments continued to create records and to requisition storage space. When in 1823 the chancellor of the exchequer visited one of the repositories, the Tower of London, his horror knew no bounds and nothing would persuade him to recommend expenditure of public moneys on piecemeal improvements to such a dilapidated ruin. He averred strongly, 'a proper building ought to be immediately erected in some more *accessible* part of the metropolis, capable of uniting and containing all the national Records'.

In 1831 the master of the rolls, the officer in charge of chancery records, preferring to inhabit a more fashionable district of the metropolis, offered his official residence in Chancery Lane as the site for storage of archives. The record commissioners agreed to the establishment of a single 'General Record Repository'. Unfortunately they parsimoniously decided to finance operations from a fund that turned out to be, to all intents, private money. The scheme therefore awaited an Act of Parliament. The consequences of neglecting proper custody of archives became apparent to legislators with the disastrous losses of records in the conflagration of the Palace of Westminster in 1834. Ironically in the course of that very same year a new building for the state paper office, designed by Sir John Soane, was completed.

Inspired to an extent by the example of provisions for the keeping of Scottish registers and records, the 1838 Public Records Act determined on the centralisation of 'all rolls records writs books proceedings decrees bills warrants accounts papers and documents whatsoever of a public nature'. The government would finance a new repository where the master of the rolls, his deputy keeper (the working head of the office) and assistant keepers cared for the records and defined terms of public access. Westminster seemed a providentially chosen site for the record office because the proposed new houses of parliament were to be embellished with a monumental but functionless tower named for the queen, and legislators proposed to fit this out as a repository. But even when completed, and admired from the exterior for its grandeur, the Victoria tower could not but be condemned as 'a highly improper place for depositing the documents in question'. Indeed officials judged the storage space by no means sufficient for the public records.

In 1840 Sir Francis Palgrave, first deputy keeper of the records, urged the merits of the Rolls estate in Chancery Lane. A purpose-built structure would render 'such a Repository the Treasury, not only of your Majesty's Legal Records, but of the Archives, in the most extended application of the term, of your Majesty's State and Realm'. Palgrave's suggestion was accepted.

Eventually James Pennethorne, surveyor of buildings to the office of woods, was commissioned to draw a plan for a repository. His extravagant ideas clashed with the treasury's parsimonious and 'costive' policies, but foundations were dug on the Rolls estate in 1850, nearly thirty years after the chancellor of the exchequer's scandalised strictures on archival accommodation in London. Fearful of a repetition of the Westminster fire of 1834, the archivists insisted first and foremost on a fireproof repository. It was determined 'to form the floors with wrought-iron beams or girders, securely protected, both above and below, from the action of fire, the spaces between them to be filled in with brick arches of less than five feet span and nearly the whole weight of the floors and records thrown upon the party walls'.

Palgrave asseverated that central heating of the repository would be 'positively injurious to the health of those employed'. Though records, too, had deteriorated from a variety of pests in past times, lack of an office heating system had not previously been proved a contributory factory. Hence, open fires in old-fashioned fireplaces were installed, and Victorian archivists and those members of the public intent on enjoying, or more correctly enduring, archives devised sensible precautions 'to mitigate the arctic cold of the Repository'. Nevertheless there persisted 'excessive amount of mortality among the officers' during the early years of accommodation in the old Rolls House on the site. Indeed archivists complained of their filthy rooms untouched 'with paint or whitewash for 25 years, and the chimnies smoking at times to such an extent as to render it necessary to put out the fires, until a change of wind, however inclement the weather'.

The first stage of Pennethorne's florid gothic pile was completed in 1853 and ancient public records were removed from the Tower of London in 1856. However, as a result of government decisions, official documents were already filling Pennethorne's structure to overflowing. From 1852 officials were required to place in the care of the new establishment most series of departmental records, even though no space was allotted to these voluminous series in the original plan of the repository. Less than a decade later, the state paper office was pulled down and its archives handed over the master of the rolls.

It therefore became imperative to extend Pennethorne's building to accommodate all the official records. Fortunately government and public opinion sympathised, parliament voted money, and additional rooms were completed during the periods 1863-8, 1868-71 and 1892-5. In later years remote storage areas were also pressed into service, including the gaol of Cambridge, the house of correction at Canterbury and a former hutted hospital at Ashridge in Hertfordshire.

Sir James Grigg's committee on departmental records suggested in 1954 improvements to existing arrangements within government departments for the preservation of historically and administratively significant material. The report formed the basis of the Public Records Act of 1958 which transferred the custody of all public records whether legal or departmental to a reconstituted national archives, although responsibility for the choice and transfer of material rested with the departments following an agreed schedule of review and disposal. Historians, however, continue to criticise departmental appraisal as haphazard, overselective, unconcerned with masses of individual case files susceptible to computer analysis, careless of records created by provincial agencies of the central government, and timorous in opening series to public access.

In 1969 the government announced the building of a new record office in suburban Kew to supplement the storage at Chancery Lane. Constructed of reinforced concrete in accordance with the most advanced techniques and designed for eventual extension laterally, the structure offers secure physical storage for unique material. Air conditioning maintains temperature and relative humidity control; air filtering extracts dust and sulphur dioxide; smoke detection and fire extinction systems limit possibilities of destruction of papers by flames. The requisitioning and movement of documents is facilitated by a variety of sophisticated automated processes. Mechanical handling systems such as paternoster elevators, oildraulic lifts and electric tricycles in the wide expanses of the strongroom areas relieve storage assistants of much of the physical toil of manhandling heavy volumes from the shelves to the searchrooms. The researcher can requisition documents through a computer terminal in the catalogue room and is summoned to the issue desk when the material arrives by a personal bleeper unit carried in the pocket. Invigilation is conducted through the use of closed circuit television cameras, though not a few experienced archivists consider that this system cannot supplant or improve on constant personal watchfulness on the part of archival staff in attendance within the searchroom. The five-storeyed building eventually opened its doors on 17 October 1977. Its 69 miles of shelving may suffice for accessions until the end of the 20th century.

With a few exceptions, historical documents more than thirty years old become available to researchers without charge. A reader's ticket is however required for entry to the searchrooms, where a variety of finding aids may be consulted. Many libraries hold the guide to the contents of the record office, published between 1963 and 1968, with the catalogue of maps and plans up to 1860 referring to the British Isles, published in 1967.

The wealth of this treasure house of history can hardly be estimated. In his report of 1852 Palgrave, deputy keeper from 1838 to 1861, and father of the compiler of *The Golden Treasury*, stated 'whether we consider [the archives] in relation to antiquity, to continuity, to variety, to extent, or to amplitude of facts and details they have no equals in the civilized world'.

Exchequer

Functioning as the finance, or more properly revenue, department of government, England's medieval exchequer under the presidency of the monarch or his justiciar met during the 12th century in various temporary premises, before settling down at Westminster. The department acquired its original name of the 'tallies' from the stick or tally, cleft in two, on which officials notched their accounting marks. But these same men, harassed by the use of roman rather than arabic numeration, performed their calculations on a cloth marked in chequerboard fashion, thus providing the more usual title for their department of exchequer. The wooden sticks themselves remained in use for certain purposes until 1826. The official burning of the defunct timber archive in 1834 accidentally also caused an uncontrollable conflagration and destroyed much of the old Palace of Westminster. This destruction incidentally reveals the refusal of administrators at that date to recognise as archives anything except paper or parchment, because the tallies yielded information as significant as that in other exchequer records.

All the leading household officers — treasurer, chancellor, constable, chamberlain — sat at exchequer board, though the treasurer rose to pre-eminence as presiding officer in due course while the chancellor sent only his clerk, known as the chancellor of the exchequer. The exchequer summoned sheriffs from the shires and bailiffs from liberties or franchises to render accounts and pay revenue due to the king from their districts.

The sheriffs and bailiffs, summoned as *computantes* or accountants, carried their financial statements, each written on a rotulet, consisting of two membranes of parchment stitched to form a length of about six feet. All the rotulets were piled one on top of the other, secured at the head with cords and then rolled. This series of records of the audit of accounts known as the pipe rolls continued, though of progressively decreasing historical value, from 1129 until 1832. The payments or 'farm' included revenues from the crown's ancient demesnes with perquisites of shire and hundred courts. The farm would be augmented by casual income such as fines for encroachments on royal land, escheats, forest rentals, feudal incidents, subsidies, aids, amercements for trespasses in the forest, and vouchers from the customs, army and navy.

Exchequer's business grew over the decades and the department even came to control the finances of the wardrobe, the financial office of the king's own household, during the 14th century. Two of the officers of the exchequer, known as king's and treasurer's remembrancers, noted outstanding debts to the crown, proceeded against defaulters, investigated claims for allowances in return for services rendered to the crown and instituted official inquiries on financial matters.

The exchequer department served as a court of law for revenue matters and extended its business to problems touching land, goods or profits belonging to the crown. As in chancery, exchequer developed an equity jurisdiction, notably from the late 16th century onwards. In practice almost anybody might initiate proceedings in a personal action by the fiction of claiming rights as a king's accountant, sadly prevented from paying his dues to the king because of an unsettled legal action.

But the ancient department's cumbersome machinery began to creak. The crown therefore turned to methods outwith the exchequer's control. As early as the 12th century the monarchs, in pursuit of confidentiality, efficiency and expedition, employed servants of the royal bedchamber as financial officials for certain purposes. Chamber finance grew increasingly important following Edward IV's administrative reforms; during the early years of Henry VIII's reign the king's personal retainers controlled many of the crown's revenues.

By establishing his court of wards and liveries, independent of exchequer, Henry VIII's ministers systematically exploited the monarch's feudal rights over tenants by knight service. The king expected to derive some profit for livery of lands to heirs of tenants in chief, for their wardship or marriage, and for caring for the property of idiots and lunatics. The court was abolished in 1660 when Charles II received income from taxation raised by parliament in return for surrendering feudal dues from knight service, wardships, tenures in chief and other ancient revenues.

Henry VIII and his Vicar-General Thomas Cromwell also created three special courts – namely of the augmentations of the revenues of the crown, of first fruits and tenths, of general surveyors of the king's lands – to administer revenues derived from the dissolved monasteries, from the abolition of payments to Rome, and from attainders and escheats. These courts were abolished in 1554.

During the early middle ages the treasurer replaced the justiciar as president of the exchequer organisation, but developed no separate office until the late 16th century. He attended exchequer infrequently by that date, because of pressure of other government duties, normally despatching orders in writing through a secretary. Indeed his office was put into commission in 1635, in effect the duties being carried out by a board rather than one man. The board's records commence from that period, distinct from those of exchequer.

Gradually the treasury took control of the public revenue of the country, especially after the House of Commons began to manage the finances of the kingdom. The treasury became responsible to parliament for placing and managing taxation and for monetary policy. Because the first lord of the treasury served also as the king's first or prime minister, the treasury as a government department headed by the chancellor of the exchequer, rose to pre-eminence in national financial affairs. Under an Act of 1833 the ancient exchequer ceased to operate.

Exchequer records include one of the most renowned of documents, the Domesday survey of William the Conqueror. Primarily an inquiry into those holding land in chief of the king, the book owed its inception to William I's decision in 1085 to despatch commissioners 'all over England into every shire to find out how many hundreds of hides of land were in each shire, and how much land and livestock the king himself owned in the country, and what yearly dues were lawfully his from each shire'. To this end the royal messengers assembled sworn juries in each locality consisting of sheriff, priest, manorial lord, reeve and six villagers, noting the answers to specified questions for despatch to the king. The chronicler wryly comments on the thoroughness of the commissioners' work 'so that there was not even one ox, nor one cow, nor one pig which escaped notice in his survey'.

Answers were condensed, perhaps somewhat inaccurately, on parchment in Latin for permanent preservation, though more extensive versions survive for East Anglia and the west country. Cumberland, Westmorland, Northumberland and Durham do not appear, while Lancashire and Yorkshire are hastily sketched. The surveyors considered the country at the end of five centuries of English settlement when by the sweat of the brow people had cleared woodland or waste and established many of the towns and villages occupied today.

A county entry usually commences with a survey of local customs, administration of justice, taxation, inquests and rights of military service. The survey hints at the extent of Norman penetration, the comparative size of English and Norman holdings, and the location of the country's wealth, industry and commerce.

Frequently the entry for each manor provides the historian with the earliest written record of his district, detailing number of plough-teams, extent of pasture, meadow or woodland, economic assets including mill, fishpond and saltpan, family units specified by social class, value of the manor and name of tenant in 1066 and 1086.

Even in the 11th century it may be postulated that literate men regarded Domesday generally as of symbolic rather than mundane value, a kind of sacred text in praise of the permanency of the Norman Conquest, a bible for fair copying and illumination. Its statements about the land of England resembled judgments following the final trump: unalterable. But because the authorities did not update the book, its information on towns and villages must often have seemed of only antiquarian interest, mainly for evidence on the ancient demesnes of the crown. The considered opinion of a jury of a dozen local worthies, specially convened when need arose, was more to be trusted by government inquisitors during the centuries following the survey.

Domesday may be studied in facsimile prepared by the ordnance survey and in translation in the Phillimore edition due to be completed in 1985.

Records of taxation from the 12th century onwards commence with the ancient levies known as scutage granting relief from military service; tallage required from urban communities and the king's demesne; hidage and carucage, levied from lands not subject to military service.

During the late 13th century the crown initiated the raising of a tax or subsidy, founded on the annual value of moveables belonging to laymen and clerics. Originally based on a meaningful valuation, such as that of Pope Nicholas IV for ecclesiastical estates in 1291, the subsidy in course of time frequently ignored real annual values and fairly computed tax demands. Indeed the hated poll tax of 1377-81 sought a fixed sum from each inhabitant, prosperous or poor. From this period during Richard II's reign the subsidy properly so named was demanded. At the rates of 4s. 0d. and 2s. 8d. in the pound for lands and goods respectively, the subsidy arose from a modest but defined valuation.

Subsidy rolls are arranged by counties and parishes. These medieval taxation documents contain people's names with tax paid: 'de Willelmo molendinario vjs . . . from William the miller 6s.'. The lists provide indications of parish population and comparative family wealth. Surnames of taxpayers may indicate the original settlements from which families travelled and thus the mobility of labour: in the subsidy for a village called Sutton, the name of Gulielmus de Esthame perhaps suggests that the hometown of William, or of his father, may have been neighbouring Eastham. Other surnames indicate the occupation of inhabitants: Skynnere, Fleshewere, Flecher, Mather or Mason (skinner, butcher, arrowmaker, mower, mason); and their colonising activity on the poorer lands of the parish under pressure of population: Atmoor, atten Okes, Attele, Forester, Attehil (moor, oakwood, clearing, forest, hill). There are reliable and useful documents for the periods 1295-1332, 1377-81 and 1524-5.

Hearth taxes, levied between 1662 and 1689 in lieu of the abolished feudal revenues of the crown, return the names of householders liable to pay 2s. 0d. on each domestic fireplace and, in certain years, paupers excused taxation. Although widespread evasion, false returns and downright refusal to talk to the 'chimney men' vitiated the government's efforts to raise money impartially according to this particular measure of people's standard of living, the hearth tax — especially that of March 1664 — yields information on genealogy, parish population (multiplying by 4.5 in rural areas) and size of houses. Some duplicate returns survive in quarter sessions and parish chests.

A tax amounting to one-tenth of the possessions of the church, levied by medieval popes for the recovery of the holy land, was appropriated by the crown in 1535. At the same date first fruits or annates, the profits of a benefice for one year following a vacancy, became a royal perquisite. The valuation of benefices for this purpose was entitled *valor ecclesiasticus* and documentation of the income, almost £50,000 in the late 1530s, from first fruits and tenths belongs to exchequer. However, much of this money fell to governors of the bounty of Queen Anne for the augmentation of the maintenance of the poor clergy in 1704.

As a religious mass chanted at the altar for the soul of a benefactor, a chantry became the most popular form of medieval endowment by monarchs, nobles, merchants and yeoman. Wealthy people, indeed, could afford to found hospitals or almshouses, even to pay colleges of priests to chant daily masses in specially erected chapels. Merchant and craft guilds founded numerous charities, often with an emphasis on education and the embellishment of parish churches. When the government dissolved these fraternities, hospitals, almshouses, guilds, colleges, chantries and other endowed authorities by Acts of 1545 and 1547, commissioners visited the localities to value the lands, jewels, relics and plate confiscated to the crown. Relevant chantry certificates of the period 1545-8, deposited in the court of augmentations, described the purpose and work of each charity, the name of the founder, the annual value of the property, the outgoings on supporting hospitals, schools or religious services, the value of goods and chattels, and names of priests, teachers, manciples and others employed in the chantry.

Expenses of war and the government's financial mismanagement, including a debasing of the currency, encouraged the authorities to plunder what remained of church wealth. During 1552 and 1553 commissioners toured the country to investigate goods, ornaments, bells and vestments in the possession of churches and guilds. The surveyors confiscated much of the treasure adjudged 'superfluous', to the tune of at least £10,000, and exchequer holds records of the process.

During the two decades of parliamentary government, almost all crown lands, 'late parcell of the possessions of Charles Stewart, late Kinge of England', were sold following survey and valuation. Exchequer preserves records of the preliminary surveys, subsequent administrative dealings, arrangements for sale and revisions of the position after the Restoration in 1660.

Between 1592 and 1691 annual accounts prepared by sheriffs concern fines and forfeitures imposed on recusants — dissenters as well as Roman Catholics — absenting themselves from worship in the parish church. An Act of 1559 required a fine of 1s. 0d. for each absence, collected for the benefit of the poor, but subsequent legislation penalised recusants at the rate of £20 each month, or the seizure of all goods and two-thirds of their lands and tenements. Known as recusant rolls, documents are written in Latin, arranged by counties, defining farms, houses, chattels or interests 'seized into the hands of the lord king'. Rolls neglect to reveal the names of all recusants in the shires but indicate the varying intensity of official action in the localities from year to year. The documents relate to sums owing to exchequer rather than money actually paid: few people could afford the monthly fine.

Exchequer officials collected documents in the course of their financial, administrative and legal work. Many of these items must have been taken to Westminster on temporary loan but never returned. For whatever reason the accumulation of deeds, charters, accounts and depositions is enormous, including, for instance, '11,324 Deeds, packed in envelopes . . . 760 deeds with seals taken from Wardrobe Debentures'.

Certificates of the mustering of adult males liable to serve in local defence forces date from 1522 when Cardinal Wolsey inquired into the nation's military preparedness for a French war. That proud prelate particularly demanded an exact valuation of property as an incidental bonus, though comparatively few county returns survive. Later musters of 1544–88 attempt the enumeration of men able, chosen or unmeet to serve in each parish. Musters may be consulted among exchequer records and state papers domestic, while local record societies have published various transcripts or editions.

As soon as Edward I returned to England from crusade in the summer of 1274 he commissioned an inquiry into the loss of crown revenues and abuses perpetrated by individuals during the unsettled reign of his father Henry III, relying, however, on administrative procedures and an assault on franchises already tested by Henry's lawyers. The king's treasure noticeably diminished whenever royal manors were wrongfully disposed of or tenants in chief alienated estates without licence, depriving the crown of the profits of wardship, marriage, escheat and military service. Nobility, clergy and burgesses had for some decades habitually claimed privileges such as free chase, wreck, fishery or warren, collected unreasonable market tolls, exacted dues in the king's name, summoned courts and fined wrongdoers, and generally abused their official positions in county and borough, despite numerous royal inquisitions. Edward's commissioners therefore assembled evidence on the oaths of jurors in the hundreds and boroughs. These documents, returned to Westminster in 1275 and known as the hundred rolls, set out answers to some forty-seven articles of inquiry. For example, the hundredors of Winfrith in Dorset presented that William le Moyne held the assize of bread and ale at Winford and Ogris. This privilege permitted le Moyne to regulate price and quality, doubtless to his own financial advantage. The landowner also maintained a gallows. But the jury professed ignorance as to the warrant under which such things should be allowed.

As a result of possessing evidence of abuses, alienations, usurpations and loss of revenue, Edward I's justices in eyre, when next sent on circuit three or four years later, travelled armed with the authority of the statute of Gloucester to demand by what right, *quo warranto*, men claimed franchises or privileged jurisdictions. Additionally, inquisitors or commissioners appointed in 1279 were to ascertain what of right belonged to the crown and what to others, to distinguish tenants holding in demesne, to identify men rightfully enjoying liberties, parks, fairs or honors, 'and to omit not the same out of regard to rich or poor, nor through Hatred, Malice . . . nor for Reward . . . and not to receive any Benefice of Holy Church, nor Pension . . . '.

The justices itinerant thus summoned the aforesaid le Moyne when they arrived in Sherborne and listened as the landowner asserted he held his tenement in chief of the lord king by serjeanty, that is by rendering some personal service to the monarch such as equipping an armed horseman for the royal host. Le Moyne profited from assize of bread and ale and right of wreck (goods cast upon the seashore), as his ancestors had from time out of mind. Only for the privilege of warren – hunting animals such as the cony and hare – could le Moyne produce written evidence, a charter granted comparatively recently by Henry III, King Edward's father. The justices heard and noted, but continued the case when the king's attorney intervened in court and sought the annexation to the crown of those franchises which no one should exercise without special warrant.

Obviously the majority of people could provide no satisfactory written title or answer in the course of the subsequent *quo warranto* proceedings. But certain stubborn or proud men stood firm even in the absence of documentary evidence, stating that charters, letters and similar parchments were never thought necessary in the good old days of their Norman forebears. The chronicler, Walter Guisborough, recounts how Earl Warenne, summoned into court by the royal judges and interrogated about the warrant by which he possessed his estate, boldly if rashly (considering the threat to the bench), brandished in their midst an ancient and rusty sword. 'Look at this, my lords, this is my warrant! For my ancestors came with William the Bastard and conquered their lands with the sword, and by the sword I will defend them . . . '. Though historians now regard this story as not literally true, the chronicler underlines the valid point that, undoubtedly until the late 12th century, it was the sword rather than the pen which imparted or maintained territorial title.

Occasionally the inquisitors specified the rights and duties of freeholders, villeins and cottars, mentioning highways, parks, mills, markets, the extent of the lord's demesne, enclosures, areas of woodland or waste, payment of money rents instead of services, the descent of estates or manors. The records were drawn up for legal and financial reasons, and not for historians, and therefore must be read cautiously by the economic and social researcher.

A special collection of hundred rolls, archivally arranged in part by Bishop Stapledon as early as 1320-22, complements records of chancery, exchequer and justices itinerant. But the original documents are more readily approached through the three volumes printed by the record commissioners, in an abbreviated Latin, entitled *Rotuli hundredorum* and *Placita de quo warranto*, covering the reigns of Henry III and the first three Edwards.

Chancery

The medieval chancellor, originally a royal chaplain, served as king's secretary for home and foreign affairs. Especially after officials settled down in London, his court of chancery functioned as a rudimentary civil service, even during the royal household's itineraries. He also ensconced himself as one of the leading lights of the king's council to hear petitions addressed to the monarch. As the chancellor's responsibilities multiplied, he employed numbers of officials including clerks of the petty bag, examiners, cursitors, registrars and clerks of the custodies of lunatics and idiots. By Dickens's day the department had acquired its reputation for long, exhausting and costly processes, profiting chancery lawyers rather than litigants, so justly satirised in the case of Jarndyce and Jarndyce in *Bleak House* where legal costs absorbed the entire fortune in dispute. Dickens based this scandal on the actual mulcting by lawyers of the estate of the Birmingham millionaire, William Jennings, who had died intestate in 1798.

The chancellor's basic duties were secretarial. From the reign of John the chancellor began the enrolment of official documents including incoming documents, copies of outgoing correspondence and copy charters. Letters patent, in effect semipublic missives, despatched open, addressed 'to all to whom these presents shall come', solemnised with the great seal pendent, concern grants of land, offices and privileges, crown leases, royal revenue, crown prerogatives, licences or pardons for alienation of property without permission, special liveries, borough charters, presentations to benefices, inventions, denisation and creations of nobility.

Issued folded and securely closed by the wax of the great seal, letters close reflect the administrative activity of the king's government during medieval times. Directed to royal officials and other individuals, the originals were copied by chancery clerks before despatch onto the close rolls. The letters refer to the provisioning of castles perhaps in preparation for a royal visit, restitution of confiscated land, writs of summons of peers to parliament, pardons, subsidies, family settlements and many similar matters. As other means of recording government business became available the chancellor allowed the use of the close rolls for the enrolment of documents in private possession. Indeed as early as the 14th century, deeds between individuals were written out on the dorse or back of the rolls to serve as replacement for muniments lost during the civil disturbance at the start of Richard II's reign. The statutory enrolment of every bargain and sale of freehold property from Henry VIII's reign onwards, the recording of surrenders to the crown of monastic land, the necessity of enrolling trust conveyances of charity estates including sites for village schools, churches and nonconformist chapels, all contributed to the successful business of the enrolment clerks. Until 1903 the dorse of the close rolls also provided a convenient location for the enrolment of copies of documents about bankrupts' estates, annuities, coinage, ships, armed forces, papist property, wills, arbitration awards, enclosures, boundary settlements, naturalisation, and change of name.

Charter rolls for the period 1199–1516 detail grants of land, offices or privileges to corporations or individuals. The rolls include creations of peerages and the confirmation of earlier royal grants, known as the *inspeximus*, literally 'we have inspected [the charter dated . . .]'. After 1516 grants under the great seal appear in the form of letters patent.

Fine rolls concern the receipt by the king of payments in kind or cash for renewal of charters, enjoyment of privileges such as wardship or public office, letters of denisation, pardons for trespasses, halting of trials and similar matters. The king's officers continually harassed wealthy people and prosperous boroughs in order to exploit this seemingly limitless source of income for the monarchy.

Parliament rolls of chancery set out the business of the legislature from the commencement of the reign of Edward III until that of Richard III. From that time the rolls were employed for the enrolment of Acts both public and private while general proceedings gradually disappeared. Including petitions and pleas in parliament, this archive was published between 1783 and 1832 with a comprehensive index as *Rotuli parliamentorum*.

As a law officer settling disputes arising out of his department's own administrative activities, the chancellor followed the normal processes of common law. Such chancery files commence in the 13th century.

From the 14th century onwards the chancellor exercised a jurisdiction following rules of equity and conscience in problems for which apparently no common law remedy existed. Chancery script, legal Latin, abstruse terminology and an increasingly complicated method of creating and preserving records hinder the study of the court's proceedings. However, lists and calendars, either published or in typescript in the record office searchroom, aid the diligent researcher. Chancery heard disputes about estates, goods, wills or debts, and required the deposit of relevant deeds, correspondence or financial accounts.

The chancellor's authority extended to inquiries into problems of royal or public concern. By calling together a local jury, inquisitions *ad quod damnum* were taken during medieval days whenever a grant of fair, market or other right might threaten privileges already permitted to individuals or corporations.

During the 16th and early 17th centuries the courts of chancery and exchequer regularly agreed to hear disputes concerning the enclosure of open fields, moorland and meadow. This common land had for centuries been enclosed in the interests of agricultural efficiency occasionally through agreements between the manorial lord and others interested, occasionally by brute force. Now the new Tudor monarchy refused to permit the depopulation of the countryside. Inquisitions into depopulation, the decay of tillage and the extension of hunting parks were initiated by Wolsey as chancellor in 1517 pursuant to an Act of Parliament of 1515. Whereas an Act of 1489 against enclosures, the 'pulling down of towns', decay of husbandry and consequent weakening of military preparedness failed to prevent the evils railed against, the Act of 1515 had more effect on account of Wolsey's powerful influence. Indeed his commissioners unrealistically ordered improving landlords to rebuild deserted villages, fell newly planted trees and hedgerows, and till sheep or cattle pastures. The ancestor of Earl Spencer of Althorp, a certain John Spencer, was one of those summoned, though he claimed to have purchased an already depopulated manor. As a breeder of livestock for the London market, Spencer fought a running battle with the government to protect his livelihood, ultimately not without success. Wolsey's commissions laboured in 35 counties, and persons found guilty before chancery paid half the issues of the enclosed property. In the long term however the government's policy proved vain in the face of economic reality. Indeed not a few of the magistrates charged to uphold the law themselves favoured agricultural innovation. Evidence to the commissioners continued for many decades, occasionally biased and suspect but essentially authentic. It offers vivid word pictures of a changing landscape and a mobile populace.

Chancery initiated an inquisition *post mortem* following the death of any tenant in chief to ensure that the crown's rights, especially of wardship and escheat, were not neglected. A sheriff's jury relied on the family steward to supply the deceased's name and date of death, an accurate description and value of his lands, services due, name and age of heir, with other appropriate information. A manorial extent might accompany the inquisition. Should the heir be a minor, genealogically useful proceedings concerning proof of age were organised. In normal circumstances the heir performed public homage to the king, paid the customary relief and accepted livery of seisin. Documents refer to such customs as the duty of certain estates to victual the army or entertain the king's court, to the extent of royal forest or manorial waste, harbour, market, industry or mill, land use, place-names and family history. Records survive from as early as the 13th century until the abolition of feudal tenures on Charles II's return in 1660. Unfortunately much of the chancery series became illegible through overuse and the employment of restorative fluids in days gone by. A corresponding exchequer series fills some of the gaps and adds additional material. Published calendars and indexes facilitate the study of these documents.

Medieval kings appointed commissioners of sewers, whenever or wherever needful, to cleanse waterways and drains, to repair seawalls and to raise rates for these purposes locally. Although records may have remained in the custody of the representatives of the commissioners, various proceedings, ordinances and petitions survive from the reign of Edward II onwards in the national archives.

Proceedings of commissioners for charitable uses under an Act of 1597 concern inquiries into abuses of donations with answers, replications and decrees of rectification into George III's reign. In the course of his administration the chancellor acquired title deeds and other material relating to disputed charities dating back to medieval times.

Privy Council

The king's privy council consisted of the chancellor, treasurer, keeper of the privy seal, household officers, a number of ecclesiastics, peers, lawyers and other favoured people to advise on routine problems of governing the country. As councillors more or less permanently by the king's side, in contrast to the peers in parliament, these men considered petitions presented to the monarch and attempted the solution of problems to which the common law offered no apparent remedy. Council minutes, reports, orders, correspondence, proclamations and administrative records date from the 15th century onwards, though sadly scattered among national and private repositories. The council, originally reliant on the secretarial assistance provided by the privy seal office, from 1540 started to maintain its own records. Many of the council's administrative functions foundered during the 17th century, though various judicial powers lingered, especially in admiralty and imperial affairs.

One committee of the council, dating from 1621, which expanded rapidly during Charles I's years of personal rule concerned itself with trade and overseas plantations. From 1660 trade and colonies were administered by a separate council, though a single more influential commission, usually referred to as the board of trade, commenced work in 1695. The board remained in theory a committee of the council though closely linked at various dates with the home, colonial and war departments. Much of the board's documentation from the decades before the administrative reforms in 1782 may be consulted among colonial office records. During the 19th century the board's activities aimed at the regulation of commerce and industry including railways, tariffs, bankruptcy, factories, patents, industrial design and ships' passenger lists.

An informal court of requests to expedite poor men's causes sat from 1483 to 1642. Committee members took cognisance of requests and supplications on civil matters, devising an equitable rather than a common law remedy. A similar tribunal for criminal causes sat in Star Chamber at Westminster to exercise summary jurisdiction in the enforcement of law. The monarchs employed Star Chamber for a variety of politically convenient purposes, for example to oppose the tyrannical behaviour of local magnates where the processes of common law failed or proved too cumbersome. The court did not survive the civil war, partly because of this 'unjust' interference in the affairs of the county establishments.

State paper office

Once no more than a humble clerical officer, the king's secretary rose to prominence during the 16th century as administrator of certain matters of state. This official behaved in a manner perhaps more informal and confidential than chancery would have wished but doubtless responded more readily to the monarch's own whims and desires. After the fall of chancellors Wolsey and More, Henry VIII increasingly turned to his clerical staff for advice. In 1540 he appointed Thomas Wriothesley and Ralph Sadler as the two principal secretaries, with rank and precedence regulated by statute, jointly responsible for home and foreign affairs. The office of secretary, later known as secretary of state, attracted such administrators as William Cecil, Francis Walsingham, and Robert Cecil, trusted advisers to Elizabeth I, and James VI and I.

State papers consist of records of the secretaries of state administering every aspect of home and foreign policy in accordance with the directives of the king's council and, later, the cabinet. After 1540 these records became far more historically significant than those of the ancient departments of state, ranging over such matters as diplomacy, war, army, navy, taxation, education, highways, religion, crime, musters, poor law, industry, agriculture, even heraldry and genealogy, 'an index of nonconformists (1663) . . . extents and valors of the possessions of dissolved monasteries in Ireland . . . proceedings before the King's Council of the Marches of Wales . . . Materials largely for a history of Waterford compiled by Dr. Hanmer, an Irish antiquary, who was born in the year 1543 . . . policing the Debatable Land between the two kingdoms' of England and Scotland, and foreign correspondence ranging from the Barbary states to the Venetian republic.

Records of the activities of the two parliamentary committees for identifying royalists, recusants and papists and for confiscating their estates begin in 1643 and end at the restoration. The committee for sequestrating the property of these 'delinquents' worked unfairly and unsatisfactorily, allowing scope for corruption. The authorities seized four-fifths of the estate, leaving just one-fifth for the maintenance of the royalists' children. The committee for compounding superseded the sequestrators, enabling delinquents to pay in proportion to the guilt. Published calendars of the proceedings are available in public reference libraries, though numerous folio volumes remain for study in manuscript in the archives.

During the 17th century the two secretaries tended to divide responsibility for foreign affairs geographically. This policy eventually led to the title of secretary of state for the northern department and similarly for the southern department, and so to the foreign and home offices respectively. Generally speaking, records before 1782 remain with the state paper office, after 1782 with the foreign and home offices.

Home department

From 1782 a secretary of state for the home department was appointed to supervise the internal affairs of the country, especially the law, popular disorder and police. The secretary liaised with magistrates, government spies and politicians on the penal system, trades unions, strikes, militia, the disposal of regular troops, patents, sanitary matters, charters of incorporation, aliens, naturalisation, police, elections, child labour, civil defence, riots, factories, mines, shopping hours, liquor laws, railway accidents, crops, livestock, and numerous other matters from corn grown in 1801 to vivisection in 1910, Bedlam in 1823 to inebriate reformatories in 1905.

On 30 March 1851 the home office supervised a census of religious worship. Enumerators in each church recorded endowments, sittings and attendances on that one Sunday and average numbers during the preceding year. Criticism of official prying into a person's religious beliefs, the dragooning of squadrons of adherents to swell numbers in certain chapels, the miscounting of worshippers, the attendance of families before noon at the Church of England and in the evening for a rousing sing-song with the Methodists, all discouraged the authorities from further excursions into the deep waters of religious enumeration.

The home secretary's voluminous records during the 19th century include personal details of prisoners awaiting trial or convicted. This information may be most readily assembled from documents known as calendars of prisoners. These set out names, abodes, ages and offences and, by the 18th century, appear in printed form. Provincial newspapers issue the calendars for the amusement of their readers. Complementary documents relate the verdicts and sentences, including transportation to the penal settlements overseas, then follow the fate of the criminals to parole, pardon, prison or the gallows.

General register office

In 1836 parliament established the general register office in London to provide for the centralised registration of births, marriages and deaths in England and Wales. The Act provided that the registrar general compile documented annual abstracts of statistical information in accordance with the early Victorian belief in the efficacy of the science of political economy. From 1840 the registrar general was appointed custodian of non-parochial registers and administrator of the decennial censuses. His headquarters at Somerset House became synonymous with information on population, censuses and surveys, though in fact census returns and non-parochial registers must now be consulted at the Public Record Office.

Non-parochial registers of baptism, marriage and burial, from as early as the 16th century, refer to congregations outside the established Church of England.

With the inception of national registration of births, marriages and deaths in 1837, the authorities stipulated that information from non-parochial registers would be legally acceptable only after deposit of the volumes in the national archives.

Among the most genealogically significant of non-parochial material are clandestine marriage records. Before reforms in 1754, couples seeking to avoid undue expense, publicity or family interference, or intent on bigamy, underwent a clandestine celebration of marriage, discreetly conducted by an ordained man without banns or licence in a lawless church. Such marriage registers date from about 1667 to 1777, though numerous suspect weddings are also documented in Anglican records, from city churches to remote chapels of ease. At St James's Church, Duke's Place, London, tens of thousands of weddings of this type are supposed to have been accomplished between 1664 and 1691 while clergy at Peak Forest, Derbyshire, became renowned for their willingness to perform lawless ceremonies, without asking any embarrassing questions.

Acts of 1696 and 1711 imposed penalties on the performing of such ceremonies. However, fines could not deter penniless priests imprisoned as debtors. In consequence marriage houses or inns proliferated and prospered in the vicinity of Fleet prison, London, in the neighbourhood known as the Rules or Liberties of the Fleet. Indeed it is estimated that perhaps one hundred and eighty thousand couples married within the Fleet up to 1754, many being impecunious seamen, soldiers or labourers hoping for heaven's blessing at bargain rates. After 1754 Lord Hardwicke's Act recognised as valid only those marriages contracted, following banns or licence, in the parish church of one of the parties, or marriages accepted as legal abroad. Many couples therefore journeyed to Jersey, Gretna Green or elsewhere outside England and Wales to accomplish their whim or necessity. Clandestine marriage registers provide names of parties, marital status, residence, occupation and date of ceremony.

The earliest national census in England and Wales was conducted in 1801 and the population has been counted decennially ever since, save only in 1941. Enumerators perambulating the parish house by house collected requisite forms and checked details offered by each head of household. These records become publicly available only when one hundred years old or more.

Census records for 1801–31 concerns numbers of persons, families and houses, but not detailed household returns naming individuals. The 1801 census attempted a division according to occupation, though treatment sufficiently consistent to satisfy the statistician proved impossible. By 1831 the enumerators were instructed to divide the population into seven classes: agriculture, trade and handicraft, manufacture, servants, industrial labourers, capitalists and professional men, and all others. The 1801, 1811, 1821 and 1831 census returns may be consulted in printed form, arranged by counties and parishes, in local libraries.

In 1841 the government agreed to enumerate by households and individuals. Written in pencil on printed forms, the schedules indicate the address, name, age, sex, occupation and county of birth. From this census year onwards only parish and county totals are available in print while individual family entries must be obtained from the national archives, though some local history libraries offer microfilm copies of returns from 1841 onwards. The censuses offer statistics on occupation, birthplace, average age, number of family servants, house building activity, persons in each house or room, mobility of labour and similar indicators of social history.

Courts of common law

Records of the medieval royal courts of common law commence late in the 12th century and continue until the establishment of the supreme court of judicature in 1873-5. Cases affecting the king's peace including the all-embracing trespass by force and arms, *vi et armis,* came notionally before the monarch himself, hence the term *coram rege* or king's bench court. King's Bench also tried titles to freehold property through a nice legal fiction in the action of ejectment. Disputes among the king's subjects especially concerning money or land proceeded to the court of common pleas, which incidentally accumulated as evidential material extensive bundles of deeds, settlements, wills and surveys.

But these courts assembled at Westminster, beyond the reach of the majority of litigants or criminals in the shires. As a means of establishing royal authority and the king's peace, therefore, judges were despatched into the provinces to hear and determine civil and criminal causes in courts variously known as eyre, assize, gaol delivery, trailbaston or general oyer and terminer. The country was later divided into circuits each embracing some half a dozen counties but the crown maintained control of the work of these professional justices as far as practicable in days before reliable daily communication between London and the provinces. In 1586, for instance, the privy council directed assize judges to hear and determine all criminal cases set out on the gaol calendar before turning to civil causes. As men on the spot, the judges recognised that, try as they might, their efforts were often brought to nought by the inefficiency of local justices of the peace and constables in finding and holding wrongdoers, assembling witnesses and evidence, or even summoning a sufficient number of jurors. Constables scurrying around the countryside during the first days of the assizes, attempting to bring in jurors, witnesses and thieves by the final day of the sitting, hindered rather than helped the course of justice.

Reforms initiated by the Tudor government facilitated the administration of assizes from the late 16th century. Certainly the general series of circuit records commence about this period, though portions of the archives of certain circuit courts may be located from as early as the 13th century. The series known as indictment files contain a variety of records such as recognisances by witnesses to give evidence at court or by suspects to attend and stand trial; calendars of prisoners in gaol awaiting trial; inquisitions by coroners; and presentments by grand juries alluding to the inefficiency of parochial policing, the expense of chasing and incarcerating suspects, the wretched state of county bridges and roads, the unruliness of certain alehouses, or the danger to the realm from religious recusants. Formalised and precise indictments of specified individuals were framed, according to strict rules, by clerks of court. These could be based on depositions taken by justices of the peace or other officers, setting out colloquial accounts of the dispute or crime soon after the event. Although the majority of people properly indicted offered no successful defence, influential defendants, paying crafty lawyers, more readily escaped punishment by proving the insufficiency of the legal forms of the indictment. The subject matter in indictment files includes theft, scandalous or seditious speeches, assault and forcible entry, with here and there the rumblings of discontented agricultural labourers or urban craftsmen concerning wages, unemployment, taxation, exploitation by middlemen and farmers, when 'lordes hestes ar holden for lawes, And robbery is holden purchas'. To the dispossessed and powerless mass of the people it must indeed have seemed that the squire's hest or command effectively acquired the force of law, that the aristocracy's seizure of common or church lands counted as legal acquisition. Assize records, especially for the period 1660–1800, permit the researcher to catch a glimpse of the wickedness and worries of provincial men and women. Unfortunately, archival disposal schedules facilitate the destruction of records dating from 1800 onwards, except for cases of treason, riot, murder, sedition, conspiracy and others of extraordinary interest.

Admiralty

During medieval centuries the king in council administered naval affairs through officials referred to as keepers or clerks of the king's ships, usually under the superintendence of the lord admiral. Henry VIII's support of and pride in the Royal Navy, evidenced in such powerful battleships as *Mary Rose* of 1509 and the one-thousand tonner, *Henry Grace à Dieu*, of 1514, culminated towards the close of his reign in testing if not victorious engagements with the French in an otherwise inglorious war.

In 1546 officers, later known as commissioners, of marine causes, assembled into a navy board, responsible for civil administration and provision of material under the authority of the lord admiral. The admiralty, a parallel but independent authority, concerned itself with policy, strategy and naval personnel under the lord high admiral and, later, the board of admiralty. The two authorities administered the navy during the days of the Spanish Armada, the Dutch wars and Trafalgar, until in 1832 the admiralty board assumed the work of the defunct navy board.

Until about 1660 naval records must be sought scattered in the archives of exchequer, chancery, privy council and state paper office in addition to some series preserved in the admiralty archive proper. Other official documents became dispersed among several departmental collections and numerous family muniments. From Charles II's reign, however, the admiralty archive provides extensive volumes and files of correspondence, reports, registers and financial accounts.

Thousands of volumes of musters, some from as early as Charles II's reign, refer to the enlistment and discharge of seamen. Description books offer details of each man's service, birthplace and physical appearance while other personnel series relate to pay and pensions including efforts on behalf of sailors and families at Greenwich hospital. This institution, the home for invalided and retired naval men, was founded by the then lord admiral, James Duke of York, later James VII and II, in 1685. Estate deeds date from 1340, but the archive proper commences in 1685 and the register of pensioners in 1704.

Tens of thousands of ships' log books dating from Charles II's time onwards served as diaries of voyages over the seven seas, at war, on explorations, during blockades or in stations across the world. Records of Britain's naval bases from Tristan da Cunha to China survive, mainly from the 19th century.

The question of victualling may be studied from 1683 and of naval supplies to ships and yards from 1688. Both services offered scope for corruption among suppliers and civil servants, as attested by many a seaman's bitter yarn to his people at home, perpetuated in folklore and literature. The diarist Samuel Pepys, as a navy board and admiralty official, employed dockyard labour to put together some new bookcases for his home. The expanding navy assuredly required large supplies of food and drink, and contracts for victualling stimulated agriculture as far afield as Scotland. In that wild country, cattle were fattened for the trysts at Muir of Ord, Inverness and Falkirk whence drovers guided herds to the south for sale to naval buyers. In some respects this trade, so advantageous until 1815, contributed to the depopulation of Scottish glens where cattle and sheep proved more profitable than people.

High court of admiralty

Concerned with cases of piracy and spoil, the high court of admiralty was established by Edward III. The court assumed wide powers, shared with chancery, in cases affecting shipping and merchandise round Britain's coasts, on the high seas and abroad. Henry VIII further extended the court's influence during his bastard son's years as lord high admiral between 1525 and 1536 when officials considered salvage, wages, collisions, commercial disputes, assault, murder, war-time prizes and a variety of similar criminal, civil and maritime causes. In coastal areas of the country vice-admiralty or related courts deputised for the central organisation in London. Records of the court date from the period of Henry VIII's reforms until amalgamation with the high court of justice during 1873-5.

Customs and excise

National customs duties were levied on imports and exports of merchandise at London and provincial outports according to rates determined by, and for the benefit of, the central government. In the years 1275 the financial ministers of Edward I devised administrative means of raising money through duties on wools, fells and hides with the consent of merchants and landowners. Originally referred to as the 'new' custom, this became a permanent impost, before long denoted 'ancient' to distinguish it from the new or petty custom of 1303 on alien imports and exports.

Customs duties were collected by two worthies, usually chosen from amongst the burgesses of a town, who supervised not only the haven itself but also a desig-nated portion of adjoining coastline. These officials compiled particular accounts for perusal by the crown's port comptroller. Customs positions seem to have been sought after, occasionally for entirely mercenary reasons, but normally as secure and profitable means of advancing the family fortunes. In the year 1310 a certain Robert le Chaucer was appointed one of the collectors in the Port of London of the petty customs granted on wine by the Aquitaine merchants. Robert's grandson, the poet Geoffrey Chaucer, obtained in 1374 the more distinguished and lucrative position of comptroller of customs and subsidies in the same port, on the understanding that he would actually attend at the office and maintain the records with his own hand. In 1382 Chaucer gained the comptrollership of petty customs with permission to exercise his duties by deputy.

The collectors' particular accounts vary in format and information but may record the date of arrival and sailing of a ship, the name of the vessel, the identity of the merchants and master, the port of origin, the quantity, type and value of the merchandise with the date and place of shipment. These documents were sent for audit to London and summarised in exchequer rolls from 1279 until 1547. The summaries show the total trade at each port, with separate figures for goods such as wool or wine from which specific duties arose. The enrolled customs accounts form a comprehensive survey of the country's foreign trade, especially when further information was added concerning the movement of alien goods from 1303; the duties imposed on English and foreign cloth from 1347; the poundage raised on most other home and foreign goods, also in 1347; and the tunnage on imports of wine from 1350.

William Paulet, marquess of Winchester, the treasurer to Edward VI, Mary I and Elizabeth I, instituted reforms in the customs during his term of office between 1550 and 1572. Winchester attempted to restrict trade to 'legal quays' within specified hours and, in 1564, began to despatch biannually 'to every Porte Haven and Creeke' a parchment book 'with Leaves nombred of Recorde . . . in a Tynne Box' for the compilation of daily commercial statistics. These registers, known as port books, number some fifteen thousand for the century 1564–1671, half referring to coastal traffic around Britain, half to vessels plying abroad.

Records of the Port of London have suffered from disastrous accidental fires at the customs house and from an official decision to destroy the voluminous collection of port books for the period 1696–1795. Documentation from the capital as well as from numerous British and Irish coastal towns includes bulky ledgers, showing imports and exports from each harbour, with accompanying port books, compiled in obedience to the exchequer order of 1564 but discontinued in 1799. The customs official, if not bribed to write down fallacious information for his own or the merchant's profit, entered the date of arrival, the name and port of origin or destination of each ship, the name of the master and merchant, the ship's burthen, details of cargo including values and customs paid. Although the majority of entries are in English after 1600, the spelling, abbreviation and handwriting hardly facilitate ready deciphering: 'ffor the marianne of hamburghe of the burden of 1 tonnes tuo tonnes of dutch irone from Brydges Willem Braune m[aste]r . . . '. Nevertheless port books cannot be neglected by the historian of trade and industry or by the researcher into the development of settlements of hardy seafarers which grew up in the creeks and havens around the coasts of Britain. The pattern of activity emerging from these official records must, however, be balanced against indications from other documentary sources about the extent of smuggling and official connivance at irregularities.

In 1671 a board of customs was established for England and Wales, embracing Scotland from 1723 and Ireland following an Act of 1823. Surviving minutes of the board, until 1814 only in the form of notes and digests, cover the period 1696–1885. From 1696 an inspector-general of imports and exports was appointed. His office compiled general trade statistics for the whole country which made exchequer port books unnecessary.

Correspondence and orders despatched from headquarters in London to local officials as well as copies of letters sent to the capital from outport customs collectors concern most aspects of port business, smuggling, wrecks, quarantine and, incidentally, the affairs of town or parish. Much of the headquarters archive perished in a fire of 1814 but letters survive from certain outports, occasionally referring to matters of policy but mainly alluding to the everyday problems besetting civil servants. Many of the letters are of genealogical interest, such as two items from the correspondence of 1813, one 'complaining of the Conduct of Henry Comper, a Boatman in absenting himself without leave from the said Boat through Drunkenness', another reporting the promotion of a tide-waiter, an official who boarded ships at sea to prevent avoidance of duties at legal quays, to the position of coastwaiter, the customs officer who superintended the landing and shipping of goods along the coasts. In this instance, James Sammes 'a competent Tidewaiter', acted during the vacancy 'in consequence of the insanity of Mr. Richard Chiverton Coastwaiter at Ryde within the limits of your Port'. Also of genealogical significance are salary books, commencing in 1675, which furnish the names and ages of officers, adding notes about a man's capacity to fulfil his duties.

Seventeenth-century navigation laws, in giving preference to goods borne in English ships, initiated the recording of the ownership of vessels. This process was formalised under the Act of Union of 1707 which provided for the general register in London of all British merchant ships and further emphasised by an Act of 1786 requiring, in practice, the re-registration of every British vessel, wherever and whenever built. Centrally and locally for many ports in the kingdom, registers survive from 1786, with the name, number, tonnage, dimensions and registry date of each ship, the name and address of the owner, and a variety of descriptive details of the vessel.

Local customs were levied at the ports on behalf of the monarch or other lord in addition to duties collected by the national authorities. Indeed certain towns claimed rights by charters written before the Norman conquest: the monastic owners of Winchelsea and Sandwich both referred to charters of King Canute dating from the early 11th century. This claim to profit from seaborne trade formed part of a town's privilege to exact duties on all merchandise entering or leaving its bounds by road, river or sea, and was memorialised in royal or seigneurial charters, sought or confirmed at heavy cost to the community from time to time. Even ports in the possession of the king might acquire their fee farm for a set sum paid to the exchequer and hence replace royal bailiffs by local burgesses.

Financial accounts and related records, occasionally from the 13th to 17th centuries, indicate the daily activity of ports; the changing fortunes of communities, perhaps left high and dry by a retreating sea; the quantity and nature of goods brought into or taken out of the haven; the names of merchants, shipmasters and vessels; and the dates of entry and exit of ships. Although local records survive for by no means every port, the documentation complements and adds to national archives. For instance, from medieval times local officials recorded coastal traffic in addition to overseas trade and instituted a variety of detailed duties not demanded by the national customs.

Parliament raised the earliest of the excise duties on the manufacture or consumption of goods within the kingdom during 1642 in order to meet army wages. After the Restoration, commissioners were appointed whose voluminous series of indexed minute books date from 1695 to 1867. Hated excise officers began to circulate throughout the country to tax such products as whisky and tobacco. Customs and excise departments were amalgamated in 1909.

Forfeited estates commissioners

When George I arrived from Hanover to assume the crown of Great Britain following the death of Queen Anne in 1714, members of the Jacobite party earnestly believed in the justice of the cause of their king over the water, James Stuart. Supported by nobility and politicians, in sympathy with the conservative mood of some people, the Jacobites posed a seemingly serious threat to the new Hanoverian dynasty. Rebellion and invasion in 1715 led parliament to pass an Act appointing commissioners 'to enquire of the Estates of certain Traitors, and of Popish Recusants, and of Estates given to Superstitious Uses'. The commissioners were to declare the real property of traitors forfeited and vested in the crown, then to survey the lands and interests so affected. By a later Act of 1715 papists were obliged 'to register their Names and real Estates' in England and Wales with the relevant clerks of the peace who in turn despatched details to the commissioners of forfeited estates.

In 1717 parliament vested forfeited estates in trustees 'to be sold for the use of the publick . . . and for the effectual bringing into the respective Exchequers the Rents and Profits of the said Estates, till sold'. Recognised as a court of record, sitting in Preston and London, the commission created an archive which additionally embraces promiscuous title deeds, surveys, rentals and other documents from the 16th century onwards, called into court as evidence but never returned to estate owners.

Crown estate commissioners

George III surrendered the revenues of the crown estates to parliament on his accession in order to secure an annual income from the civil list. Commissioners therefore administered lands and honours anciently belonging to the crown or gained through forfeiture, escheat or Act of Parliament. Among these territories were the three northern palatinates of Chester, Durham and Lancaster, counties with extensive administrative and judicial powers, exempt from many regulations enforced across the remainder of the country, though limited by the overriding authority of the royal prerogative. The Bishop of Durham enjoyed perhaps the most ancient of the palatinates until the loss of judicial powers to Henry VIII in 1536 and palatinate jurisdiction itself in 1836.

The earldom and Duchy of Lancaster comprised extensive possessions in many of the counties of England, including the palatinate of Lancaster itself. The earls and dukes exercised prerogative, and indeed regal, rights within their territories, acknowledged by grants from the crown and evidenced in duchy muniments from early medieval times onwards.

With the exception of private muniments of the bishopric deposited at Durham and current records of the commissioners at their office in Whitehall, crown estate documents are now located in the Public Record Office.

British transport commission

Archives of railways, rivers and canals were scattered in offices throughout the country until the nationalisation of transport undertakings following the Second World War. Minute books of directors or trustees, financial accounts, title deeds, plans with schedules, contracts, reports and related business records then passed into the care of the British Transport Commission, which established a London historical records office but stored certain documentation in branch depositories or local record offices. Archives, occasionally dating from the 18th century, refer to canalised or improved river trusts and to canal companies. For instance, records of the public trust to render the Cheshire river Weaver navigable survive from the first half of the 18th century, while detailed plans of the Trent and Mersey Canal, excavated alongside the Weaver, date from 1778 and 1816. Railway company records for the most part commence only after 1840. Much of the material relating to transport history has now been transferred to the Public Record Office.

Paymaster general and war office

Army records of the paymaster general and war office, commencing about 1660, include muster books, monthly returns, description books, pay lists, pension books and discharge papers referring to a soldier's service from the day of attestation. Soldiers' documents from about 1760 give information about men surviving to discharge. These files, arranged by regiment to 1873, thereafter alphabetically by surname, contain proceedings of regimental boards 'for the purpose of verifying and recording the Services, Conduct, Character, and cause of Discharge', which specify the man's age, height, colour of hair and eyes, complexion, trade, marks or scars on face or body, intended place of residence, birthplace, and date of attestation. The record of service — deducting days in prison or recovering from 'a Corporal punishment' — may be supplemented with medical reports on wounds, weaknesses and vices. The careers of full- and half-pay officers are documented in surveys of 1828-9 and 1847, arranged by regiments.

CHAPTER THREE

SCOTTISH RECORD OFFICE

THE PUBLIC RECORDS and treasury of Scotland were probably first lodged in the stronghold of Edinburgh Castle when William the Lion, King of Scots, regained the town from the English in 1186. The fortress and settlement were to form portion of the tocher or dowry of the monarch's new Anglo-Norman wife, Ermengarde. Grievous mismanagement leading to the scattering and mislaying of the national archives ensued after 1291 when Edward I of England required documents in London to facilitate his legal researches into the question of the succession to the Scottish throne. In 1314, however, Robert Bruce's victory at Bannockburn revived national pride. Bruce's successors attempted to accumulate documentation and to devote some resources to the care and preservation of archives under the superintendence of a royal chancery clerk. This clerical position eventually developed into the office of lord clerk register with far-reaching authority over the framing and safeguarding of public registers and records.

Registers, compiled in obedience to specific government regulations to provide evidence of transfer of land, debts, contracts and privileges, and are exemplified in sasines or deeds registers. Records, produced in the course of normal administrative activity, embrace all other departmental documents.

The Cromwellian capture of Edinburgh in 1650 and subsequent dispersal of documents to Stirling, London and elsewhere, resulted in losses. When Charles II consented to the return northwards of Scotland's heritage of archival material, no fewer than eighty-five hogsheads of papers and parchments perished when the ship *Elizabeth* foundered on passage from Yarmouth just before Christmas 1660.

The remaining hogsheads and chests aboard the frigate *Eagle* successfully accomplished their odyssey. The authorities in Edinburgh transferred certain series to 'two laigh rooms under the Inner Session hous' where cramped conditions, dampness, rats, mice and fire conspired to spoil further material. Twelve of the casks brought from England in 1660 lay unemptied, unsorted and unlisted as late as 1753. Registers too bulky or voluminous for storage in the parliament house sometimes remained in the dwellings or offices of the various clerks. Even an impost granted in 1722 of 2d. Scots on each pint of beer and ale sold in Edinburgh (to be applied in part for the erection of a repository) seems to have benefited the archives not at all.

At length in 1765 the Earl of Morton, lord clerk register, obtained a royal warrant to appropriate money from confiscated Jacobite estates towards building an archival repository in Edinburgh. Designed by the architects James and Robert Adam and Robert Reid, the General 'Old' Register House slowly rose from the ground under the superintendence of Morton's successor, Lord Frederick Campbell, between 1774 and 1827, on a central site in the new town. The Scottish Record Office now maintains headquarters in this palatial old building, proud of the fact that Scotland boasted a fire-resistant purpose-built record office while English medieval chancery archives were irresponsibly and perilously stored in Caesar's chapel above a gunpowder magazine.

In 1806 the authorities agreed to establish the new position of depute clerk register, enabling an Edinburgh advocate, Thomas Thomson, to retire from the legal profession and devote himself to sorting, arranging and conserving medieval records, to listing and indexing documents, and to publishing through the record commissioners such series as the Acts of the Lords of Council and Acts of the Parliaments of Scotland. Thomson served enthusiastically for 35 years, latterly with the assistance of a lawyer from Moray, Cosmo Innes, who years after recalled his colleague's 'passion for accuracy . . . admirable and never-failing common sense . . . But his grand defect was, a morbid reluctance to commit his opinions to paper'. Though Thomson's painfully slow work coupled with financial incompetence resulted in his dismissal from office, his impeccable standards of documentary scholarship remain a challenge to later archivists.

In 1855 to the other functions of the depute clerk register was added the registration of births, marriages and deaths, though from 1920 the government appointed a separate registrar general. From 1948 the keeper of the registers of Scotland was charged with the maintenance of the various legal registers while his colleague, the keeper of the records, superintended the preservation of the public records.

By the middle of the 20th century the national archives had outgrown the old premises, and it was decided to convert the disused but architecturally splendid St George's Church, Charlotte Square, into a repository. From 1971 the new office, known as West Register House, provided storage for modern records, plans, microfilms and court processes. Unfortunately for the future of the documentary heritage of Scotland, an officially commended statement on archives in 1981 admitted to the necessity to 'tailor holdings to suit present accommodation', rather than the converse. An official also confessed to 'difficulty in attaining even basic standards' in the administration of the national archives in Edinburgh. For a record office once in the forefront of archive keeping in Britain, this revelation threatens the interests of all intent on the enjoyment of Scottish archives, because when archivists do not maintain standards, laymen and administrators certainly will not. Indeed there is an acrimonious debate between historians and the national repositories over the 'weeding' policies of present keepers of the records, for example in the case of 'particular instance' papers affecting persons (national insurance, social security etc. files).

M. Livingstone's *Guide to the Public Records of Scotland*, 1905, remains a valuable survey for the older series deposited at the Scottish Record Office. An updated guide to holdings is in preparation. In the meantime various free leaflets such as a 'short guide to the records' and 'sources for family history' provide acceptable substitutes. Accessions to the repository appear in the *List of gifts and deposits*, 1971 and 1976, and in annual reports of the keeper of the records of Scotland. Access to the archives themselves may be gained by reader's ticket issued for the calendar year, and renewable.

Administrative records

The business of Scottish administrative officers is formally recorded from the 12th century, influenced by precedents or archive keeping from Norman lands south of the border. Between 1124 and 1153 David I, known as 'the legislator', issued charters, letters, laws, decrees and other administrative material. This work demanded the employment of clerical officers to serve the royal court. Though King of Scots, David, 'the Saint', also enjoyed the earldom of Northampton and distinguished English ancestry, and was not likely to resist the adoption of efficient and respected Norman methods in government, manifested in departments of state functioning at Westminster. Moreover the majority of magnates surrounding David's successor, the boy king, Malcolm IV, at his inauguration in 1153 at the moothill of Scone were lusty Anglo-Normans and Anglo-Bretons, acknowledging their devotion to the ancient traditions of the Scots, but determined to yield to no man in controlling Scottish affairs.

The series, now in course of publication known as *Regesta regum Scottorum*, 'registers of the kings of Scots', begins with the reign of David's grandson, Malcolm IV, and contains texts of royal charters from 1153 onwards. By contrast, the chancellor's registers and rolls of grants of property and offices date from no earlier than 1306 on account of the loss of documentation during the troubles of the 1290's. That official's archive includes confirmations of grants by feudal superiors. Of interest to family historians, chancery retours and documents known as the service of heirs, concerning succession to heritable property, continue from 1545 onwards.

Together with records of the chamberlain and chancellor, the acts of the kings of Scots reveal a number of the medieval sources of royal revenue from burghs and counties, exemplified and corroborated occasionally in local archives. The monarch's demesne, scattered through eastern Scotland and managed by farmers, yielded income in the form of malt, oats, bear (barley) or money while burghs negotiated for the fixing of a money rent known as *firma burgi*. Tributary taxation levied on the country's inhabitants, known as cain, consisted of payment in kind, usually cattle, pigs, hides, tallow, corn, hides, malt or cheese. Cain included customs duties on trading ships entering harbours. The monarchs, additionally, required hospitality, or else compensation in lieu, called conveth or waiting, accepting board and lodging as was the wont of any other feudal lord of his wealthier tenants. Similarly, the monarch rarely neglected feudal incidents of escheat, relief, wardship and marriage or the profits arising from courts of justice. Royal grants of land in return for knight service in the king's host normally permitted exemption from personal attendance following payments in kind or money. For extraordinary purposes such as war or ransom the monarchs demanded aids or community help.

Medieval Scottish kings turned away from their impersonal and busy chancery to the more manageable privy seal office to conduct routine and private business.

In the course of its development from the 13th century that office undertook the issue of grants of minor offices and church benefices, respites for crimes, and precepts for charters for the settling of Nova Scotia, registering the necessary documentation from the late 15th century onwards.

The royal chamberlain's records expound the country's financial arrangements. This archive embraces exchequer rolls and accounts of royal revenue from Alexander III's reign until 1707; treasury accounts and details of expenditure on the royal household, castles, palaces and armed forces, 1473–1708; taxation papers from 1574; the hearth tax, 1692; poll tax, 1693–8; and revenue of ecclesiastical property following the religious changes after 1560.

After the union of parliaments of 1707 a remodelled court of exchequer and boards of customs and excise retained some autonomy in the northern capital until financial reforms of the 19th century centralised revenue matters in London. Intent on devolving certain powers, the government appointed Scottish trustees to nurture and manage nascent manufactures, especially in the linen industry. Boards were set up to encourage the growth of the fishing industry from 1809, fine arts and inventions as early as 1727, to oversee prisons from 1839 and poor relief and public health from 1845. The process of devolution gained momentum with the organisation of the Scottish office during 1885.

Departmental records include processes in revenue cases for the period 1708–1856, papers concerning the taxation of shops and windows, customs outport documents from 1707, and material relating to estates surrendered by Jacobites following the 1715 and 1745 uprisings. Commissioners of forfeited estates strove to develop the agriculture, fisheries and manufactures of the highlands, especially up to 1784. These wide-ranging departmental sources offer scope for the study of museums from 1878; the school inspection system from 1847; roads, railways, bridges, canals, shipping and air services; the agricultural census and related parish summaries from 1866; crofting; dissolved limited companies from 1856; forestry from 1907; friendly societies; hospitals from 1777; post office services from the 18th century onwards; and ancient monuments and public buildings from 1794. Most departmental records remain closed to researchers for 30 years from their latest date, though prison registers commencing in 1657 are closed for 75 years.

The Scottish board of excise archive dates from the early 18th century onwards. Excise officers whose careers may be followed in the records found themselves heartily misliked because of their prying into illicit whisky distilling in even the remotest glens. Though certain collectors accepted bribes to maintain silence about illegalities, even the honest men occasionally found that magistrates themselves imbibed unexcised spirits and were reluctant to penalise the moonshiners. Prosecution was accepted with equanimity as less costly than taxation. In 1816 John Phinn of the old Waukmiln, Knockando, was discovered malting and distilling privately — the penalty £700; the actual fine only 6s. 0d. Local authorities thus connived at 'the congregations of daring spirits in bands of ten to twenty men, with as many horses, with two ankers of whisky on the back of each horse, wending their way, singing in joyous chorus' openly travelling the roads and patronising rural hostelries. Eventual reform of the law in 1823 at the instigation of the Duke of Gordon led to one of that nobleman's tenants, George Smith, applying for the first whisky licence under the statute for his Glenlivet distillery at Minmore. Even so, Smith had to protect himself against angry smugglers by carrying 'a pair of hair trigger pistols worth ten guineas', presented by the Laird of Aberlour, and the riding officers of the revenue department remained for years 'the mere sport of smugglers'.

State papers

State papers, including copies of the king's business letters from 1505 and privy council records from 1545, emphasise the expansion of the government's administrative and judicial functions during the 16th century. The Scottish Record Office has published a series of edited, transcribed and slightly abridged volumes of the privy council registers.

Records of parliament

Though parliament's official records commence only in 1466, miscellaneous acts, instruments, charters and ordinances of both national and local interest survive from earlier centuries. Between 1814 and 1875 the record commissioners published 12 volumes of *The Acts of the Parliaments of Scotland* covering the period 1124–1707.

Legal records

The archives of courts of law furnish a wealth of historical information. Records include minute books and miscellaneous files of legal petitions, complaints and sworn statements.

The royal court, the *curia regis*, developed during the reigns of Malcolm IV and William I, though devolution of work to local justices obviated recourse to the king's presence in all but the direst emergencies. It was therefore not until the 15th century that a national judicature evolved from a parliamentary committee and from sittings known as session and daily council. Acts and proceedings of the lords of council and members of the legislature indicate similar functions and jurisdiction in hearing causes and complaints. Indeed the council accepted the pettiest of problems. In July 1494, for example, it was reported that 'george blare sone of vmquhile dauid blare in bendachy dois wrang in þe occupacioun' & manuring of þe twaparte of þe landes of bendachy And þerfore ordinis him to desist . . . '. This nascent judicature or court of session received endowment as the college of justice with salaried senators in 1532. The college served as supreme civil court in Scotland with original and appellate jurisdiction. Recorded acts or decisions of the lords of council commence in 1478, processes or documentation of law cases in 1527.

A typical court of session case in 1798 concerns Mrs. Clementina Sharp's efforts to rebuild her top-floor tenement in King Street, Glasgow, and the determination of a neighbour below, a bookseller and printer, to oppose Clementina's dangerous disturbance. Apparently the garrets had originally been raised 'much larger than was necessary . . . from the ignorance of mechanics which formerly prevailed among operative masons'. Mrs. Sharp produced a survey, now filed with the artificially created series of architectural and other maps and drawings known as register house plans, to illustrate her efforts to lower the roof in what she considered modern fashion. The burdensome law case, in the course of much wandering, eventually transports the researcher back half a century before 1798 to the first builder of the tenements, a certain Archibald Allison. The reader requisitions such a court process nowadays for its significant circumstantial detail concerning economics, genealogy, religious life, local history, social conditions and vernacular architecture, as well as for the interest of the case itself.

In the sheriffdoms, king's justiciars exercised authority as early as the 12th century in cases involving theft, sasine, teind, burgh fermes, royal revenue, murder, arson, plunder and rape. The king expected justiciars to furnish law and justice to rich and poor, baron and burgess, in such a way that no plaints should proceed to the royal court except those which could not be properly remedied save in the presence of the king. Justiciars assembled in ayre twice a year in the three main regions of the kingdom, Lothian, Galloway, and Scotia north of Forth. Until the 17th century, Scottish justiciars were not professionally trained and paid lawyers sent out from the royal court, but leading noblemen, skilled, wily and experienced in administrative matters, based in the localities rather than in Edinburgh.

Lack of organisation, personal inadequacies of justiciars and straitened coffers during medieval times may explain any inefficiency and abuse in the administration of criminal justice throughout the kingdom. In 1672 salaried senators of the college of justice were appointed to a high court of justiciary. This statutory body sat in Edinburgh and travelled on ayre or circuit as supreme Scottish criminal court. Minute books including justice ayres begin in 1493, books of adjournal with processes in the high court in 1576, circuit court records in 1622.

A case heard in the Inverness circuit court of justiciary in September 1810 involved one Alexander Gillan, servant to a farmer in Stynie, in the parish of Speymouth in Moray. A young man of 19, Gillan several times assaulted local girls. One fateful day the prosecution alleged: 'having provided yourself with a large Oak stick, or club, . . . and having observed Elspet Lamb, daughter of . . . John Lamb, a girl under eleven years of age, herding her Father's Cattle . . . you, did, wickedly and feloniously assault the said Elspet Lamb . . . did ravish . . . and have carnal knowledge . . . did, barbarously murder the said Elspet Lamb, and beat out her brains'.

The court decerned and adjudged the young man to be detained in prison 'fed upon bread and water', then taken to a 'convenient place on the moor near to the Spot' where Elspet was found, and 'to be hanged by the Neck . . . untill he be dead; and his body thereafter to be hung in chains at the said place of Execution'.

The remainder of the story must be told from local records, because the task of carrying out sentence fell to Patrick Duff, clerk to the town and sheriffdom of Elgin. Negotiations with the Inverness authorities for the loan of their executioner were successfully concluded and the officer, William Taylor, not averse to performing at a hanging, was accompanied on the journey eastwards to Elgin by representatives of the latter burgh named Stronach and Scott. This escort was considered necessary not only to protect the loathed Taylor from 'maltreatment by the mob' but because, as Duff was advised, the hangman 'cannot restrain himself from excessive drinking'. In view of this, Duff was privately warned 'to cause him be confined in Prison on his getting to Elgin . . . supplied with Food but very moderately with Drink'.

Gillan paid the price for his misdeeds and his body was placed in the iron chains designed by the deacon of the hammermen's incorporation. It hung near the spot on the muir of Stynie where the murder had been committed until 'in the course of a few weeks [it] was taken down in the dead of night by his friends in a furtive manner and interred in the Wood'. Gillan's grave was located by the ordnance surveyors two generations later and continued to appear on subsequent 25-in. plans, although no trace now remains on the ground. Perhaps the victim survived in folk memory, but whether as a brutal monster or victimised simpleton cannot now be recalled.

The court of the sheriff grew in stature during late medieval times, in contrast with the decay of the shrievalty south of the border. Although a sheriff might succeed in running his court as the personal perquisite of his own family, royal power and prestige eventually prevailed against private greed and peculation, even if merely to require the provision of 'ane sufficient depute'. When hereditary sheriffs were abolished in 1747, judicial powers in the shire were transferred to an official appointed by the crown. The professional sheriff, bound by statute to hold sittings within the county each year, therefore found himself guardian of an important local court for criminal and civil cases, for actions of damages, rent, poinding, furthcomings, for probate purposes, and for the registration and safe-keeping of legal documents. Sheriff courts assembled in any convenient building in various county towns. A burgh tolbooth was a popular place with magistrates, because offenders could be imprisoned in the cells within that centre of town administration. During the 19th century buildings were erected for the use of sheriff courts.

Records of the sheriffdom may commence during the 16th century, especially in the lowlands. But quantities of significant paperwork perished through inadequate storage arrangements before the present century — and in more modern times by the appraisal of records managers.

The sheriff took cognisance of a comprehensive catalogue of problems affecting the locality outwith royal burghs. In one court in 1723 the sheriff heard about the non-payment 'of five merks Scots money as the pryce of two Busshells of faraigne Solt', cash owing on 'the pryce of three fields of bear', assault, refusal to continue in domestic service, a debt on 'thirty bottles of Claret . . . ane bottle of Cherrie . . . tuelve botles of brandie', unpaid rent, a man's declining to restore 'Ane black Cow about nyn years old or there by', concealing 'ane Contract matrimoniall', unpaid debts on 'three oaken boards', 'Seven Salt Salmond', 'heruast fee', 'a Cow and Calfs', 'a Mair and a Staig', 'two trees wrongeously . . . taken be him out of the house sometime possest be him', victuallers, beersellers and tradesmen acting 'Contrar to the Laws & Statutes of Excise, Leather and Candle Duties by not makeing their due, true & Particular Entries and Payments', as well as assault 'with Strong battons & o[the]r offenceive wappons'.

People found guilty of offences were variously fined, admonished, imprisoned, publicly exhibited in the jougs, branded, beaten, and even 'whipt about the . . . Gibbitt & your Ear nailled therto . . . And to be banished the s[ai]d Shyre'. Criminals could be hanged for comparatively minor offences. A certain James Gray was tried in Banffshire in March 1699 for stealing a cow. He 'was commonly bruted for a Loose man & common thief before'. This reputation did not further Gray's chance of lenient treatment when found guilty. He was condemned 'to be taken . . . to the Clune hill . . . & Gibbitt standing theron, betuixt the hours off tuo & Four acloake in the afternoon & therupon hangd up by the neck by the hand of the Common executioner till you be dead'. Rather different was the sheriff's attitude in Moray to James MackKenzie, possibly a first offender. In 1721 he could have been executed for stealing 53 marks Scots and some items of clothing. But he requested 'ane act of Banishment'. This the judge agreed to, ordering him 'to be transported . . . to the harbour of Findhorn And there to be imbargued . . . for London And from thence to be transported to Barbadoes . . .'. Very little sheriff court documentation survives. Hence we can only speculate on the reasons why the judge listened to – and then accepted – a condemned prisoner's request for a life of 'slavery' in the plantations as an alternative to hanging. But perhaps there were financial considerations.

The sheriff summoned tenants in the legal action of compulsory removal at the instance of proprietors – at one court evicting a widow from her town tenement for not paying rent, at another court dispossessing entire communities of their lands and houses to permit the landlord – 'and others' – to 'Peaceably enjoy the Same in all time Coming'. The process was firmly established by ancient laws, which permitted tenants few safeguards. Sheriff-substitute MacKid, who endeavoured to protect the interests of tenants evicted in Sutherland in 1814, retired a broken man, pursued by 'every malignant influence' of the county establishment. Occasionally sheriff court archives hint at what contemporaries considered to be the advantages of the clearance of straths and farm touns – efficiency of agriculture; the creation of economically viable enclosed farms; the protection of game for sport; settlement of people in new planned villages, where fishing, weaving, shopkeeping and manufactures could be stimulated by injection of capital; the employment of tenant farmers, labourers, craftsmen, domestics and gardeners on the improved estate.

During the removals in the Laigh of Moray in 1766 the sheriff officer gave tenants one week's notice to appear in court. 'This I did,' he reported after visiting one house, 'by Leaving a full Double of the . . . Summons . . . for . . . James Mckrobie in the Lock hole of the Most patent door of his dwelling house in Curglass after giving Three Several knocks thereat as use is, And Calling audibly for admittance The people in said house having Shut the Door on Seeing me . . . ' These families were to be allowed two months – longer than the 40 days specified by law – 'to Flitt and Remove themselves Wives Bairns Family Servants Goods and Gear Furth and From their Possession & Occupation of the said Town and Lands . . .'.

Within the sheriffdoms, magnates and lairds maintained regality, stewartry, bailiary and barony courts, permitted by written grant of the monarch to his tenants in chief. The earliest of surviving Scottish charters to a tenant, of 1093-4, allowed the monks of St Cuthbert, Durham, sac and soc, that is certain privileges of local jurisdiction within specified lands. Tenants claimed other rights such as the collection of toll; holding trials by combat or through the ordeals of water and iron; team, the fees and profits accruing to a baron from his jurisdiction in suits for the recovery of goods alleged stolen; infangthief, the right of trying and punishing thieves apprehended within the regality; and gallows for hanging malefactors. Indeed the grant of ordeal-pit and gallows, *fossa et furca*, became in due course the accepted test of a valid franchise court.

'An Act for taking away and abolishing the Heretable Jurisdictions in that Part of *Great Britain* called *Scotland*; and for making Satisfaction to the Proprietors thereof; and for restoring such Jurisdictions to the Crown; and for making more effectual Provision for the Administration of Justice . . . by the King's Courts and Judges there' restored to the crown's courts and judges power of jurisdiction granted by the monarch over the centuries to justiciaries, stewartries, sheriffdoms, baillieries and constabularies. Heritable sheriffships were at the same time annexed to the crown and all records of minor jurisdictions rested in the reformed sheriff courts in the counties. Very specifically the Act recognised that the day had long passed for the exercise of baronial power in capital cases. Such privilege granted to proprietors of estates erected 'by the crown into baronies or granted cum fossa et furca, or with power of pit and gallows, or with the like words importing such capital jurisdiction, hath long been discontinued . . . as to the exercise thereof'. Although barons could still detain criminals in certain circumstances 'it shall not be lawful to such baron or heretor or his baillie to cause any person to be imprisoned in any other room or place than what shall . . . be so situated and have such windows or grates open to inspection from without as that it may be practicable for any friend of the party imprisoned to visit, see, and converse with the prisoner when he shall be so minded . . .'.

Commissary records

Administering districts roughly corresponding to medieval bishoprics, commissary courts granted confirmation of testaments and exercised jurisdiction in executry affairs, actions for debt and similar processes from the religious changes after the reformation until administrative reforms of 1823. From 1564 Edinburgh's commissary court, whose records commence in 1515, monopolised cases involving legitimacy, separation, constitution or dissolution of marriage, and testaments above £50. The capital's commissariat also registered legal documents such as marriage contracts from 1564 until registration of deeds passed to sheriff courts in 1809.

When a Scots person left a testament testamentary, the executor sought confirmation in administering the estate at the office of the commissary. This officer's clerk copied the will in full into the commissary's books. If a person died without leaving a will, the commissary nominated an executor for this testament dative, recording the names of the relict and offspring of the deceased. Testaments were accompanied by inventories of goods, gear, debts and money, though not of heritable property.

Testaments and inventories of 'guidis and geir' of persons deceased yield clues to the social and economic condition of the country from the religious reformation of 1560 onwards. The documents specify household goods, foodstuffs, clothing, farm implements, crops, animals, stock in trade, debts and luxuries, with approximate valuations, in Scots money until the 18th century. Few more useful personal records of the urban bourgeois and rural tacksman or laird survive. The registers containing wills and testaments, arranged by commissariots, are indexed by testators' names.

Local commissariots were abolished in 1823, in favour of sheriffdoms, though Edinburgh's commissariot survived until 1836. Under the Sheriff Court Act of 1876 the commissary clerk of Edinburgh commenced to issue an annual list of all confirmations granted and inventories produced in Scotland, arranged alphabetically by surnames, printed and thus widely disseminated and available locally.

Registers of Scotland

The Scottish system of registering documents, relating to private property and rights, originated in protocol books written up by notaries public during medieval times. The notaries, legal men whose office derived from Roman law, gained authority from ecclesiastical or royal dignitaries, being permitted to compose, authenticate and enrol civil transactions such as marriage settlements, financial bonds and title deeds. From these books, the notary issued, against payment, an official extract, known as an instrument, authenticated by his own distinctive sign. His most useful and lucrative work was the drawing up of instruments following the feudal ceremony of sasine. This ceremony took place on the ground of the relevant property and involved the grantor giving legal possession by delivering earth and stone to the grantee, normally the feudal superior to the vassal.

As a method of facilitating the recording of the transfer of heritable property and the publication of land rights, a register of titles or sasines was superintended by the secretary of state from 1599 to 1609. This did not prove successful in the short term, but within a decade lawyers devised an efficient system which has endured for more than three centuries. From 1617 the authorities insisted that each district maintain a particular register of sasines in order that writs might appropriately be recorded in the locality where the lands lay. A general register opened in Edinburgh for writs applicable to wider areas or otherwise not locally recorded. Royal burghs continued to rely on protocol books, though a number initiated registration following legislation in the middle of the 16th century. An Act of 1681 established burgh sasines registers, a few of which still remain in local archives. A general national register based on county divisions replaced all local registers following reforms of 1868 and 1926.

Printed indexes of persons mentioned in sasines for the period 1617–1780 prove invaluable for genealogical and property searches. From 1781 a printed abridgment by counties in one chronological series, planned by Thomas Thomson, furnishes abstracts of all recorded writs. The Act of 1868 established indexes of persons and places for all subsequent sasines. This Act additionally organised the the transmission annually to the sheriff clerk in each county of the printed minute book of recorded writs with its statutory indexes.

From as early as 1554 legal documents, such as marriage contracts, bonds, obligations and articles of co-partnership, might be recorded for preservation purposes in registers of deeds, more accurately known as books of the lords of council and session. Documents suitably endorsed could then be returned to their owners. Legislation of 1868 gave to sasines registration the same effect as registration for preservation and execution, though original writs were henceforth to be retained at the record office. Hence numerous legal documents of local interest, dating back perhaps to the 16th century, found their way to the capital after 1868 for registration. Extract registered copies were returned to the localities.

From medieval times prudent folk fearful of losing evidential material chose to record bonds, contracts, leases and other documents in local court books such as those maintained by burghs. The clerk copied out the relevant document and, occasionally, retained the original by request or error in his archives. This may be all that survives of the papers of humbler folk — indweller, residenter, burgess or bonnetlaird. Some local registers were abolished by statute in 1809, others ceased to be kept at various dates during the 19th century.

In order to protect the interests of creditors by providing a record of the outcome of the legal process known as diligence, local courts maintained particular registers of hornings (a complicated process against persons and moveable goods) and inhibitions (restraint on disposal of heritable property). General registers of hornings, inhibitions, apprisings and adjudications commenced in Edinburgh from as early as 1579.

The register of tailzies, concerning the entailing of estates, commenced nationally in 1688.

The various local and national registers rehearse the history of families, lands, houses, legal wrangles and businesses and, despite difficulties of interpretation, are a prime source for researchers.

Church of Scotland

The record office serves as the repository for the Church of Scotland's administrative archive and for those of former free sects which broke away from, but later reunited with, the parent body. The local historian supplements records of the annual general assembly at national level with documents deposited as a matter of policy in Edinburgh by regional synods, district presbyteries and parochial kirk sessions. The centralisation of the kirk's documentation in the capital facilitates research by historians, and has probably rescued certain volumes from inadequate parish storage. However, kirk session and presbytery records are being deposited in approved local record offices.

Presbytery records relate to areas as large as shires, but frequently refer to particular parishes. The presbytery administered certain charities and the distribution of poor relief; examined ordained men before presentation; supplied preachers to parishes or chapels of ease without ministers of their own; decided on repairs, alterations or extensions to manses, outbuildings or schools; executed the excambion or exchange of glebe lands; and collected for worthy objects of public utility such as county bridges. The presbytery heard cases of patronage and titles to church lands, especially the continuing and tiresome problems of property misappropriated or confiscated by laymen following the reformation. In certain instances the presbytery clerk copied out the statements of protagonists, evidence of witnesses and abstracts of relevant documentation. One such case in 1791, involving estates erstwhile belonging to the medieval bishops of Moray, quoted documents over a period of two centuries back to 1590 and occupied 29 pages of the minute book. The members of the presbytery, perhaps to their relief, were not in the event faced with reaching a decision, because the participants adjourned to the civil court. Minutes may variously report on the provisions for religious worship in towns; enumerate the number of souls in a parish, not forgetting 'Seceders, Episcopalians, Methodists & Roman Catholics'; and subjects taught in parochial schools, embracing in one burgh during 1795 modern 'Arithmetic, Book-Keeping and Algebra' for both boys and girls. In 1793 Elgin presbytery expressed a fervent loyalty to the constitution of the 'present Government of this Kingdom as affording more effectual security to the Life, Liberty & property of the subject, than any that has yet appeared, is the chief source, under God, of that high degree of prosperity to which Great Britain has attained'. Such sentiments, a generation after Culloden, typify the unionist leanings in Scottish burghs, perhaps resulting from the general industrial progress and enrichment among merchants, farmers and professional men. The burghers blatantly retained the 18th-century trinity of human rights 'life, liberty and property', ignoring the American revolutionary 'pursuit of happiness'.

Minute books of the episcopal period are frequently missing at all levels of administration, and particularly at times of national upheaval when officials carefully kept their heads and records hidden. For instance, there is a 'blank in the record' of the synod of Moray from 3 July 1661 to 21 October 1662 while the episcopacy was being re-established. The synod's volume four 'is lost' for the period 1687–1702 when presbyterianism again won the day. The memoirs of the preacher James Allan already quoted at the beginning of this book, indicate that a presbytery was established in Forres in 1690, though records survive only from a decade later.

Heritors

The landowners or heritors of each parish were responsible for the payment of the minister and upkeep of church property. From the 17th century the heritors in alliance with the kirk session supervised parochial education, building of schools, support of teachers, the poor law, orphans, idle rogues and impotent inhabitants. The authority of these bodies was circumscribed as governmental agencies took over poor relief and education. Surviving records commence generally only during the 18th century.

Nationalised industry

Records of Scottish divisions of nationalised industries preserve much documentation of earlier gas, electricity, canal, coal, railway and dock companies. As one example, the transport archive embraces minutes, accounts, timetables, and legal documents of former railway companies from 1807, loch and river steamers from 1861, and Caledonian, Crinan, Forth & Clyde and other waterway or dock authorities from 1754. The huge holding of shipbuilding records dates mainly from the second half of the 19th century onwards. It includes such famous firms as John Brown & Company of Clydebank for the period 1852-1970, Alexander Stephen & Sons, Linthouse, 1750-1968, Scotts of Greenock, 1780-1968, and Robb-Caledon of Dundee, 1900-65.

Gifts and deposits

The record office accepts gifts and deposits of family, estate and business papers, together with solicitors' accumulations, dating mainly from the middle of the 17th century onwards. Documents of medieval centuries are found in muniments such as those of the Earls of Airlie, commencing about 1161, the Earls of Leven & Melville from about 1165, the Marquesses of Lothian from 1140, the Clerks of Penicuik from 1373, the Stewart-Mackenzies of Seaforth from 1527. Deposited family muniments from before 1650 relate primarily to lowland areas of the country.

The researcher into Scottish industrial growth from the 18th century onwards studies, archives of Invergarry, 1726-1838, and Carron, 1759-1940, ironworks companies. Early furnaces at Bonawe, Invergarry and elsewhere in the west were established in areas of extensive natural woodland, suited for production of fuel charcoal. However, modern blast furnaces at Carron in Falkirk in 1759, utilising local splint coals fed raw into furnaces, substantially increased industrial potentialities. By 1850 Caron produced over 27 per cent. of Britain's pig-iron, and the revolution cradled at Falkirk had nurtured such enterprises as Shotts iron company whose business records survive for the years 1824-1958, Alexander Cowan & Sons, papermakers, with records for the period 1805-1969, James Bertram & Son, engineers, 1847-1972, and T. & A. Constable, printers, 1859-1956.

Archives of societies and institutions, reflecting a thriving confident nation with energy and wealth for the sustenance of the less fortunate, include muniments of Dean orphanage on the outskirts of the capital from 1733, the Society in Scotland for Propagating Christian Knowledge, 1707-1942, the King James VI hospital in Perth whose legal documents stretch back to 1322, and the British Fishery Society, 1773-1877. Projects to extend fisheries may reflect national concern at rural depopulation and possible political disaffection across Gaelic areas of the west. Each attempt at colonisation, as for example at Loch Bay in Skye from 1792, required local surveys, rentals and maps. The Skye rental furnished details about the original settlement plots, as at lot 112 MacCastrie Street held by Donald Campbel, tailor, showing dimensions, rate, rental, date of original entry and length of lease.

The record office collection of maps and plans ranges from old-fashioned bird's-eye views, beautifully hand-coloured, to comparatively modern ship-building blue prints; from privately commissioned drawings to statutorily deposited surveys of public works. Many of these register house plans, conveniently card indexed by subject and topography, and listed in the continuing series entitled *Descriptive list of plans in the Scottish Record Office*, emanated as evidence before various courts, notably the court of session; or were extracted from estate and family muniments, sometimes merely showing a field or byre, occasionally an entire parish or town; or represent the daily productions of businesses, relating to railways, highways, machinery, ships, public buildings, harbours, canals, gas works and collieries.

CHAPTER FOUR

PUBLIC RECORD OFFICE OF IRELAND

THE HISTORY of archives in Ireland makes sad reading. There was fire at the chancery store in St Mary's Abbey; removal of state papers in the portmanteaux of departing lords lieutenant; keepers of the king's records who did 'inbesell or sufferid to be inbesyllid . . . mynymentes'; 'Rain which came through the Roof'; and numerous other disasters which all contributed to the ruin of archival treasures.

In order to protect valued legal and historical records of the exchequer, justiciar and justices itinerant, medieval authorities eventually provided space within the strong walls of Dublin castle. Officials chose the Bermingham tower, with its heavy door and two strong locks, controlled by the constable and the under-treasurer, 'which . . . it is necessarye be an Englyshe man born'. However as a repository primarily for the royal money hoard, the structure could not accommodate all the public records. Indeed, despite being the seat of English political power in Ireland, the entire ancient castle itself had become none too secure by the 17th century. Much material was therefore lodged in the houses of government officers whose damp cellars or mouse-infested attics contributed to further deterioration. In 1635 it was reported that the dwelling of the officer of the rolls 'having taken Fire, many records were therein burnt, and many more by that occasion imbezzled'.

About 1636 the government eventually assigned money to build repositories for records of the courts of chancery and of wards at King's Inns north of the river. Perhaps the authorities economised in archives construction. Be that as it may, a century later John Lodge, deputy keeper of the rolls, described the chancery repository as 'in a very ruinous state, being supported by Props from Top to Bottom. The Weight of the Pleadings is so great that there is reason to fear the sinking of the Floors, which would fall in, should the props give way. The Roof is shored up from End to End, and in danger of falling in by every high Wind. The Slates are stripped by every Storm, and the Windows cannot be kept in repair, so that the Records daily suffer by Dust and Moisture. The whole building is so shook by Tempests, that the Clerks have quitted their Desks through fear'. Between 1786 and 1796 this crazy ruin was replaced by the brand new Four Courts building, destined to figure as significantly in the struggle for Irish independence as in the care of the national archives.

Meanwhile in 1758 a report on the state of archives in the Bermingham tower particularised about 'ten good Deal presses, containing many ancient Records of the Common Pleas and Exchequer'. The contents of two of these presses were spoiled by rainwater, five 'entirely consumed . . . by the late accidental Fire', and the remainder 'much scorched'. When this derelict repository was demolished in 1775, unique records were stuffed into sacks, stored haphazardly during building operations, then crammed miraculously into one-third of the space previously available. What is more, in 1778 officers transferred 19 dozen rolls of exchequer estreats to these same overcrowded rooms.

As for absence of trained staff in the archives, Archbishop William King probably spoke for other aspiring researchers when at the end of the 17th century he complained 'there are no clerks . . . th[a]t I can find can understand old french . . . not one clerke in the Rolls knew where any thing was or coud read or understand it when found'.

In 1810 the Irish record commissioners initiated their inquiry into the condition of the public records. The inquiry considered storage facilities, availability of calendars and remuneration of archives officials. In general, the commissioners criticised the lamentable state of the records and, among other recommendations, sought suitable premises in Dublin for a centralised repository for records. The government, as usual not blessed with surplus accommodation or funds, preferred to distribute archives amongst several specially adapted existing buildings. The splendid Custom House, for some years already employed as an archival store, was now developed into a record office for the land revenue and numerous related series including census returns and agricultural statistics. But despite the tangible examples of Edinburgh's purpose-built record office of 1774–1827 and London's of the early 1850s, and despite the record commission's pleas, a new building for the public records was not completed until 1867. This repository occupied a site adjoining the Four Courts near the centre of Dublin.

The Public Records Act of 1867 placed the archives under the care of the master of the rolls. The statute authorised the transfer of chancery, common pleas, exchequer, probate and parliamentary archives, with all 'Records and Documents of any Courts, Commissions or public offices which shall have ceased to exist, and are not comprehended under the foregoing denominations'.

In 1919 Herbert Wood, a keeper of records, whilst deploring that the Irish archives 'have undergone great vicissitudes', and suffered 'loss of valuable material for history', recognised that 'the centralisation of the Public Records in one building has been attended with excellent results'. Archivists had been trained to decipher, arrange and index documents, to list and even calendar certain series, and 'thus render them accessible to the public'. The store consisted of one large block, a record treasury resembling an enormous library stack and thus an undoubted fire risk.

But fate in Ireland plays strange tricks. Wood wrote too soon. On 25 May 1921 the Custom House with its land revenue archive was seized during an uprising against the authorities. Armed men ushered out the staff and, pouring petrol on the contents of the rooms, ensured that the tightly packed volumes and boxes burned fiercely. Though the rebels were captured, the archives perished in the conflagration.

Then during April 1922 irregular republican forces opposed to the Irish provisional government occupied Fourt Courts, at that date considered by many the finest building in Dublin and home of the voluminous national archives of Ireland. Packed with priceless records, the documentary heritage of the country, the structure sheltered its garrison until the end of June when the government determined to employ artillery against the rebels. The treasures of eight centuries stored for five decades in the Four Courts were in two hours reduced to ashes. Winston Churchill, an historian of note himself, but then wearing his politician's hat, pronounced that 'The archives of the Four Courts may be scattered but the titledeeds of Ireland are safe'. Of the record treasury nothing remained except twisted ironwork and stone debris, but the bombardment blew numerous papers and parchments into the skies above the city and as far away as the hill of Howth. Picked up as souvenirs by the populace, little of the material was returned to the national archives.

State paper office

Some records survived the holocaust of 1921-2, perhaps because out on loan, perhaps because held elsewhere in Dublin or Ireland at the time. These form the nucleus of the present collections housed in the reconstructed Four Courts, Dublin.

The state paper office archive passed into record office care mainly later than 1922, though documents date from the 17th century onwards. Much of this material represents the accumulations of various chief secretaries, formerly assistants to the lord lieutenants but after 1801 increasingly ministers of the crown, and includes government proclamations, 1701-1875; papers of the poor law commissioners, 1822-75; a small number of volumes of census returns for 1821-51; returns to the religious census of 1766 mostly for the dioceses of Armagh and Cashel; and some school records from the period 1879-1918. The record office also preserves minutes, correspondence, reports and returns of defunct commissions of inquiry, such as those into primary education of 1868 and into famine relief following the potato blight of 1845-7, with schedules of crown or quit rents and of papist estates for the period 1663-1827.

Probate records

The Act of 1867 transferred probate documents more than twenty years old to the record office. Surviving wills date mainly from the two decades before the fire of 1922. Wills and administration papers belonging to the principal registry begin in 1904 but books containing copies of grants of probate and administration only in 1922. Fortunately, local district registries preserved and, after 1922, deposited grant books dating from 1858 onwards. Additionally, volumes of wills copied by registries, the earliest dated 1664-84, with ecclesiastical court grant books, the earliest 1684-8, furnish some evidence for the researcher. Further collections of testamentary material may also be consulted in archives deposited by the inland revenue, London, and by commissioners of charitable donations and bequests.

Court records

Very little remains of the archives of ancient courts such as chancery, exchequer and common pleas. However several collections of transcripts or calendars of destroyed material may still be consulted. These include rolls of religious converts for 1703-1838 and registers of the legal documents known as fines for the years 1511-1835 and recoveries for 1590-1834, which are advantageous for genealogical and property studies.

Parochial records

Parochial records of the disestablished Protestant Church of Ireland, notably registers of baptisms and burials before 1871 and marriages before 1845, were by Acts of 1875 and 1876 confided to the care of the record office unless suitable local accommodation existed. Over one thousand parishes deposited material in Dublin. All but a handful of these registers perished in 1922, though transcripts of some had already been produced before the conflagration. Diocesan registrars had also deposited older portions of their archives in the capital for safekeeping.

Land revenue records

Records relating to the management of crown estates, quit rents and other land revenues, forfeitures by rebels, and settlement in Ireland by adventurers and soldiers are relevant to research into colonisation of the country from Britain and the history of particular properties.

The civil survey of 1654-6 concerned the delineation of forfeited, crown and ecclesiastical lands in 27 counties for the purpose of allotting property to satisfy parliamentary debts. The surveyors noticed the ownership and economy of estates; statements of old inhabitants about ancient tenures, place-names or boundaries; details of properties in 1641; and castles, mills, acreage, value, houses, shops and occupiers. One example from the city of Waterford records that John Lewis's home along High Street measured 81 feet by 23 feet, was worth £120 at 8 years' purchase, and belonged in 1641 to the opulent Pierce Sherlock, esquire. Lewis's dwelling house fronted 'to ye streete oposit to the great conduit stone walls p[ar]t cadge worke and slated'. Cadge or cage work denoted a timber frame with whitened plaster in between, resembling a cage. Habitations of the poor rarely appear, being merely insubstantial cabins, but occasionally the survey relents, as in Leixlip, barony of Salt, County Kildare: 'There is one little Stone house . . . which was built for the poore butt noe other maintenance allowed then the Charity of Neighbours'. The Irish manuscripts commission published the survey from a 1901 transcript of the original.

Original 'down' survey maps of baronies with related records refer to land forfeited following the rebellion of 1641. The survey was not merely a description in words, so usual at that date, but included maps *laid down* in 1654-8 by chain and scale under the direction of William Petty, hence the term 'down'. French men-of-war captured one series of these maps while being shipped in 1707 between Dublin and London. These maps have remained in Paris, though the British ordnance survey in 1908 copied the sheets for printing and sale to the public. Reference books dated 1661 contain names of proprietors mentioned in the civil and down surveys with memoranda concerning land distributed, leased or undisposed by 1659. The crown rental of 1706 emphasises the changes in ownership following a century of upheaval and discrimination against Roman Catholic gentry.

Following the union of Britain and Ireland in 1801, the authorities attempted to survey the countryside, especially the basic civil unit known as the townland, and to levy rates on the people with as much efficiency and fairness as was possible at that time. Parliament required the tabulation of the names of parishes, manors and baronies, and estimation of the 'Contents of each' (1819-24). Legislators then decided 'to make Provision for ascertaining the Boundaries', acreage and financial assessments of various civil administrative units (1825). Information on Ireland's townlands was hopelessly obsolete by this date and so the authorities financed a 'uniform Valuation of Lands and Tenements in the said Baronies, Parishes . . . for the Purpose of the more equally levying of the Rates and Charges upon such Baronies, Parishes . . . ' (1826-32). This valuation required townland maps. From 1824 onwards the British triangulation of the ordnance survey was thrown across the Irish Sea to the mountains of Mourne, the surveyors working to a large scale of six inches to the mile. The survey of John Bull's other island greatly facilitated the devoted work of Sir Richard Griffith, commissioner of valuation from 1827 to 1868.

Taking evidence from local people, Griffith registered and plotted the boundaries of townlands, parishes, baronies and counties, recording Gaelic place-names and social data, delineating borders in relation to fixed and recognisable points. For instance, in 1839 these included 'a Row of houses' and 'the S gable of a house tangent to mearing' at Grange Kilree, County Kilkenny. His accompanying sketch maps prove sufficiently detailed to indicate topographical features in the vicinity of boundaries.

To further his project, the commissioner of valuation ordered the production of documents, known as field, house and record of tenure books. In the townland of Corporation, Killybegs, County Donegal, the official book in 1839 depicted a house occupied by Alexander Wilson as 'a neat little cottage well furnished, has a small garden', rented by the year for £5, though with an estimated value of seven guineas. Details in the commissioner's books vary from place to place but generally provide the name of the occupier of a house, indicating the dimensions and value of the property. Record of tenure books of 1847-51 refer to the legal position of occupiers. In the townland of Crosscannon, in the parish of Killenaule, County Tipperary, Timothy Rochford rents his house and land, extending to over ten acres, at £15 15s. 9d. a year. Patrick Waldron, esquire, the immediate lessor, had granted a lease for three lives in 1811. Acts of Parliament of 1846-53 reported the completion of certain valuations for poor law purposes but provided for the extension of such surveys to all property. The primary valuation of Kilnew in Ballyvaldon, County Wexford, dated 1853, records the names of the of the immediate lessor and occupier, acreage of each property, and rateable annual valuation of houses or lands. The valuation also refers to the relevant townland map. Valuation office letter books and registers relate to wider subjects than financial assessments, such as new roads in County Kerry and removal of the destitute from crown lands.

Tithe records

Under an Act of 1823 the authorities agreed on the commutation of parochial tithes in kind into money payments and facilitated the equable apportionment of charges by allowing 'a Survey and Admeasurement... of all the Lands in any such Parish'. The resulting tithe applotment books furnished particulars of land-holdings, names of tithepayers, the quantity and value of land, and relevant topographical features. Such details enabled compositions to be computed. As one example, the applotment registered on 1 December 1824 for Rathedmond townland, County Sligo, mentioned three properties held by John Farrell, V. Arbuckle and James Davidson, 'Houses Built upon these and Charged as half Acres each'. Unfortunately, accompanying maps were drawn to a small scale merely to identify townland, estate or farm but no individual dwellings.

Education records

The Irish education board furnished registers or minutes of national and district model schools from 1835 and salary books of teachers for 1834-1919. There are registers of teachers competent to instruct in Irish and of those qualifying for 1893-1912. The commissioners of intermediate education have preserved lists of school pupils for the period 1890-1914.

Local authority records

The record office preserves archives of a number of local authorities, including Dublin city and county councils. Dublin corporation's leases, freemen registers, guild rolls, court of conscience records and other series from the 17th century onwards represent the most voluminous and significant of these deposits. The capital's commissioners of wide streets attempted, from the early 18th century, to improve the medieval city and to create a fashionable Georgian townscape. The commissioners were responsible for the demolition of the last remaining insanitary, dilapidated but picturesque cagework buildings in central Dublin. They watched redevelopment closely. In 1811 a builder on the corner of Lower Sackville and Abbey Streets requested permission to place four, rather than three, openings in the terrace elevation when the width of his plot was increased. The board agreed, 'provided the uniformity is preserved in the fronts' to both streets. No detail seemed too small, no ground went uninspected. During that same year, 1811, members approved a scheme for the improvement and widening of 'the Site of the Old Bank' in St Mary's Abbey and Boot Lane, having earlier diligently considered a plan of the ground. Wide paved streets, uniform lines of imposing elegant terraced houses, brick, slate, glass, stone, gas lighting, drainage, all contributed to the facilities of a city renowned throughout Europe for its modernity and urbanity.

Public works and other official records

Correspondence, minutes and accounts of commissioners of public works from the early decades of the 19th century onwards concern roads, railways, canals, harbours, education, relief of distress, public buildings, drainage, lunatic asylums and fisheries. This board of works absorbed the functions and archives of such earlier authorities as the directors of inland navigation and the civil building commissioners.

Among numerous miscellaneous official collections may be mentioned mercantile marine ships' logs from 1922; miscellaneous papers in notable legal disputes such as the Erne fishery case of 1927; police records of County Clare for the 1840s; various prison registers of the 19th century; and the registrar general's census returns of 1901 and 1911.

Gifts and deposits

Nonofficial documents, loaned, given or purchased, include the family muniments of Carew of Castle Boro, Greville of County Cavan, Fitzpatrick, Barons of Upper Ossory and Gowran, Agar, Viscounts Clifden, Sarsfield-Vesey, and Edgeworth of Edgeworthstown. The Edgeworth collection contains an informative volume of documents on estate management, copied and compiled by Maria Edgeworth. She is perhaps better known as an Irish novelist, the author of *Castle Rackrent*, the 'first regional novel in English', published in the year 1800.

The papers of Sir Cyril Wyche, chief secretary and lord justice from 1676 to 1695, refer to administrative, ecclesiastical and military affairs following James II's removal from the throne. The Frazer accumulation seems to emanate from the offices of the solicitors for the crown in criminal causes. Documents cover the 1798 rising, the trials of the ribbon men in 1840 and other crises of the Fenian period.

Genealogical collections of Betham, Thrift, Grove-White and Crosslé preserve transcripts, calendars or extracts from public and private records, including testamentary and other material, now lost. Similar copies furnish information from mislaid or destroyed medieval charters as early as the 12th century, documents illustrative of the history of Dublin and Ulster, and the survey in 1586 of lands belonging to the Earl of Desmond forfeited for rebellion.

Further miscellaneous unofficial material includes extracts of returns in some fifteen dioceses to the religious census of 1766; the census of the diocese of Elphin in 1749 providing the name of each head of household, the person's religion, profession, number of children and of others in the household; a list of inhabitants of Newcastle and Uppercross about 1652; miscellaneous lists of electors, freeholders, and papists for the 18th century; civil parish records of St Thomas, Dublin, 1750-1864; records concerning the relief of distress by the religious Society of Friends in the years following the potato famine and until 1865; and administrative archives of local militia for the 18th and 19th centuries.

CHAPTER FIVE

NATIONAL REPOSITORIES

House of Lords Record Office

MEDIEVAL PARLIAMENTS assembled irregularly and infrequently. Members rarely considered the question of permanent archival storage, and documents tended to survive only while their immediate administrative usefulness lasted. As a result the official records of parliament commence no earlier than 1497 with 16 original enacted Bills preserved by Richard Hatton, the clerk responsible for preparing the parliament roll for chancery.

Clerks in the House of Lords office set an example in the retention of archives, though the limited funds available meant that the conditions in which records were preserved left much to be desired. These officials stored journals, petitions, bills and other archival material in a variety of unsuitable locations until gaining access in 1621 to the medieval moated Jewel Tower of the Royal Palace at Westminster. The records lingered in that repository until 1864, available to the public despite a paucity of finding aids. The fire which destroyed the exchequer's wooden tally sticks stored at Westminster, before consuming the palace itself, spared the Jewel Tower. However, the dedicated records clerk, hearing of numerous bundles of parliamentary documents lying around the palace in a kind of limbo awaiting transfer to the Jewel Tower, rushed to the doomed building and valiantly threw out of the window miscellaneous rolls, registers and papers.

Following this disaster and fearing a repetition, the authorities accordingly directed that the proposed new houses of parliament should contain two 'Fire proof Repositories for Papers and Documents' of the Lords and Commons. In the event, Charles Barry's Victoria Tower, then the largest square tower on earth, offered 12 floors, each sufficiently large for up to eight strongrooms, linked by cast-iron spiral staircases of 553 steps. Here were placed records of the House of Lords.

This refurbished repository subsequently began to receive records of the House of Commons in 1927. Although much of the Commons archive had perished either through neglect over the centuries or in the fire of 1834, journals, committee minutes, election returns and miscellaneous papers survived to enhance the new joint archives centre. This was formally inaugurated in 1946 as the House of Lords Record Office. In line with modern practice the building was in due course renovated, air-conditioned and re-equipped before reopening for the service of parliament and, secondarily, of historians in 1963.

Records of the Westminster parliament concern the governance of England since 1497, Wales since Henry VIII's reforms of 1536, Scotland from the Union of 1707, and Ireland during the period 1801-1922. Archival resources are outlined in M. F. Bond's *Guide to the records of parliament*. Documents are listed, described or transcribed, as appropriate, in the calendars of manuscripts of the House of Lords, a series of volumes in the course of publication.

Journals of the House of Lords from 1510 and of the Commons from 1547 chronicle the daily proceedings and decisions of parliaments, at first in Latin but after about 1620 in English. Though the archive copies are in manuscript, the Commons in 1742 and the Lords some twenty-five years later ordered the printing of all journals from their commencement. This continues session by session. The resulting bulky tomes, indexed with varying degrees of success, suffice for most research purposes. Occasionally the historian must resolve doubts by recourse to the manuscript journals at Westminster. The somewhat terse formalised journals are supplemented by the issue, daily since 1680, of information papers known as 'votes' of the Commons. For activities of the House of Lords there are draft journals for the period 1621-90 and minutes or notes of proceedings from 1610. Complementary but unofficial reports of debates, culled from contemporary memoirs and newspapers – and pure imagination – were collected and edited by William Cobbett as the *Parliamentary history*, ostensibly from 1066 to 1803. On the opening of the press gallery in the Commons during the latter year, Cobbett initiated the *Parliamentary debates* which the Hansards ambitiously developed from 1812. In 1909 both Houses decided to publish their own fully indexed verbatim daily reports of debates.

During 1964-5 a commons committee recommended that a 'complete sound record of the proceedings should be made available to the House to be kept by the Clerk of the Records for a certain length of time'. Subsequently, portions could be chosen for permanent preservation to complement *Hansard*. In 1978 the record office began to accumulate tape recordings in an air-conditioned archive unit with appropriate technical facilities for members of parliament and ultimately, when finances permit, for historical researchers. The historian should thus be able to hear the actual voices of politicians, the tones and nuances of speeches, the interruptions and sparkle of exhilarating debates. However, the extent of the archive will depend on the selection process eventually accepted or, more hopefully, on government finance for digital recording techniques which will reduce long runs of tape to archivally manageable proportions.

Bills, petitions, disputed elections and other 'great businesses' were referred to committees of the two houses from medieval times, though little documentation of proceedings in these meetings survives for the Lords before the 17th century, for the Commons before the 19th century. From 1771 transcripts of evidence by witnesses to committees considering Public and Private Bills refer to such diverse local matters as the Cricklade Election of 1782, Chelworth Inclosure in 1789, Torquay Harbour, 1794, and the Scottish Linen Regulation, 1823.

Originally proposed by ministers and members of parliament, Public Acts normally refer to nationally applicable matters such as poverty, trade, religion, transport, taxation and wages. There is usually some convenient short title for the statute, for example 'Act for the further preventing the Growth of Popery' 1700 or 'Charitable Gifts Act' 1601. Early Public Acts frequently responded to local conditions or pressure, as for instance the 1597 measure 'for the Enlarging of the Statute made for following Hue and Cry ... in some Sort to relieve the Inhabitants of the small Hundred of Benhurst' (39 Elizabeth chapter 25). Acts passed in that same year included one 'against Lewd and wandring Persons, pretending to be Soldiers or Mariners' (chapter 17) and another 'against the deceitful Stretching and Tentering of Northern Cloth' (chapter 20).

Private Acts from as early as 1512 proceeded to parliament through the initiative of an individual, local authority, religious institution or private incorporation. These petitioners requested statutory power to construct a canal or railway, inclose common land, improve the amenities of a town, exploit mineral rights, alter the terms of a charitable trust, secure a divorce, change a parish boundary or gain control of an entailed estate. Subject matter varies from the purely Private Act of 1729 'for vesting all the Lands and Hereditaments in the County of *Tipperary* in the Kingdom of *Ireland*, late the Estate of *Godfrey Boate*, Esq; ... deceased, in Trustees, to be sold for the Payment of the Debts of the said *Godfrey* ... ' to the more Local Act of 1597 for 'establishing of the Lands given by *John Bedford's* Will to the perpetual Repair of Highways at Ailesbury'.

The record office preserves authoritative texts of Public Acts from 1497 and of private measures from 1584. These are accompanied by related documentation, including petitions for legislation, texts of Bills as first introduced and as amended, and minutes of evidence. The provincial researcher, however, with access to a county record office or reference library, more readily locates the Public Acts through printed volumes containing statutes of the realm from 1235 to the present year.

Private Acts before 1798 were printed in very limited numbers. However the commencement of sessional volumes furnishes texts of the majority of local and personal Acts from 1798. Certain legislation not included in the local and personal series, mainly concerning inclosures, tithes and estates, was collected in sessional volumes confusingly labelled 'Private Acts', printed only from 1815. Other genuinely Private Acts about divorce, change of name and naturalisation were not officially printed and, with the unique documentation accompanying Acts, may be consulted only in the Victoria Tower.

There is much historically significant information retrievable from statutes. The Act of 1726 'for better Regulation of the Linen and Hempen Manufactures in that Part of *Great Britain* called *Scotland*' commences with a 'whereas' clause offering reasons for and advantages of legislation. The argument goes that the advancement of manufacturing 'will not only imploy great Numbers of Poor, but will be a general Good to the united Kingdom, by adding to the Wealth of the Realm ... Frauds and Abuses are daily committed ... whereby ... the Credit of the said Manufacture [is] destroyed ... for want of proper Laws and Regulations'. Therefore in the hope of a brighter future following legislation, the Act provides the requisite rules, organisation, standards and penalties in the course of 33 detailed clauses.

Printed guides to Acts of Parliament include a chronological table of the statutes, an analytical index under main subject headings of statutes in force, and an index of local and personal Acts for the years 1801–1947.

Before agreeing to discussion of proposed transport legislation, parliament required the deposit of official documentation. For canal or river navigations the standing orders applied from 1794, but were subsequently extended to other undertakings such as turnpikes, railways, harbours and town improvements. Parliament required promoters to deposit carefully executed plans with schedules, indicating acreage, land use, owners, occupiers and location of the public works. From 1813 the scale of plans had to be at least one inch to the mile but larger scales were later enforced for built-up areas. Additionally there are from about the year 1800 onwards, lists of people consenting to the projects, subscription contracts, estimates of cost and minutes of evidence during investigative hearings.

Parliament functioned as a court of law as early as the 13th century. Judicial records, however, survive mainly from the early 17th century onwards. In 1621 the Lords successfully, but temporarily, resumed abeyant jurisdiction to deal with original causes, usually proceeding by petition directly from interested parties rather than by appeal from lower courts. At the same time the Commons in co-operation with the Upper House attempted to punish delinquents whose activities seemed to threaten the safety of the state. The procedure of impeachment of traitors and other individuals, a normal parliamentary task from 1376 to 1459, gained a new lease of life from 1621 as Crown and Commons commenced their sparring for control of the national polity. The Lords also conducted trials of peers until that of Lord De Clifford for manslaughter in 1935; heard cases of privilege of the peerage mainly between 1660 and 1853; received appeals from subordinate courts until 1873; and accepted cases after 1876 from the newly-established Court of Appeal in England. Until law reforms of 1852 and 1907, writs of error lay to the Lords from judgments alleged erroneous in civil and criminal causes in lower courts.

People petitioned the two houses to seek redress of their own grievances or to pray for a change in public policy. Petitions were not systematically preserved by the Commons until 1950, but significant numbers to the Lords remain from 1531 and especially for the period of reform during the early 19th century. The accumulation covers a variety of matters including recovery of debts, Roman Catholic emancipation, parliamentary reform, trade, factory regulation, education and municipal government.

Sessional papers of the two houses of parliament include returns provided in answer to an order of the house or following an address by the house to the crown; papers presented by command of the monarch; documents such as annual reports required by Act to be laid before the house; material offered pursuant to a committee report, church assembly measure, a house resolution or standing order; and Private or Public Bill papers.

Sessional papers, with information and statistics on an extensive range of subjects, date from the early 17th century to the present. Parliament countenanced the printing of this material as early as the Civil War period, although comparatively few papers survive from before 1801 outside the archival volumes maintained by the two houses. Moreover much of the early Commons documentation perished in the great fire of 1834. Fortunately Luke Hansard had prepared 16 volumes of reports for the period 1715–1801, and these were stored elsewhere in 1834. Equally fortuitously Charles Abbot, Speaker of the Commons, organised the compilation of sets of papers for the period 1731-1800. Many sessional papers are available in reprinted or microfiche form. Investigating committees heard the evidence of individuals. 'Dr. John Makinson Fox, called in . . . What nationalities were those foreigners? – Chiefly Poles and Hungarians . . . their habits were not such as our English artisan population . . . show. Throughout the whole barracks not a single chamber utensil. Arrangements for washing there are none. In one room six men and one woman were sleeping unmarried, promiscuously. I should be very sorry for my horses or dogs to be provided for in that manner. I am bound to say . . . the employer . . . has done everything that he could' (1888).

Parliamentary papers concern the army, navy, trade statistics, reports of commissioners of crown estates, streets and bridges in London, Scottish affairs, ecclesiastical policy, accounts of dock and harbour boards, colonies, crime, local government, poor law and the environment. The archive includes the certificates or returns of the names of those making protestation 'to maintaine the true Reformed Protestant Religion' providing lists of ordinary men throughout England in 1642. The journals of the two Houses refer to sessional papers, serving as a form of index, while for documents from 1801 onwards printed guides arranged by subjects provide the key to research. In addition the historian consults select lists and breviates, arranged subjectively, of papers from 1696 onwards.

Miscellaneous reports, memoranda and contracts refer to the works of the two Scottish Commissions – for the Caledonian Canal and for highland roads and bridges – both established under Acts of 1803.

For the chronicler of the aristocracy, the record office holds pedigrees, petitions, reports and similar evidential material concerning peerage claims. The material dates from 1597 onwards and includes documentation on the election of Scottish and Irish representative peers.

The archive of the complete peerage trust relates to the revised edition of G. E. Cokayne's *Complete Peerage*, offering background documentation and corrigenda to the 14 volumes published between 1910 and 1959. Of similar interest are the four reports prepared by the genealogist and historian J. H. Round, 1854-1928, concerning peerage cases and baronetcies. Two of the volumes are subject to restricted access.

Both houses have accumulated by gift, loan or purchase extensive and varied historical collections. These include personal and official papers of parliamentarians, officers of state, clerks and other servants of the houses; material referring to forests, commons and footpaths, for the years 1720-1931; copies of surveys and valuations of church property and livings prepared by surveyors on behalf of parliament after 1646; and miscellaneous documents such as manorial and estate documents of Burley in Hampshire from 1661, emanating from the Shaw-Lefevre muniments.

British Library

In 1753 parliament passed 'An Act for the Purchase of the *Museum*, or Collection of Sir *Hans Sloane*, and of the *Harleian* Collection of Manuscripts; and for providing one General Repository for the better Reception and more convenient Use of the said Collections; and of the Cottonian Library, and of the Additions thereto'. The new repository or museum, financed by £300,000 raised by lottery, opened at Montagu House in London in 1759.

The Cottonian collection consisted of the papers accumulated by Sir Robert Cotton, who died in 1631. His passion for historical manuscripts resulted in purchases or borrowings of items from many counties for deposit in his library. This material he stored in 14 presses or cupboards, surmounted by busts of classical figures including Caligula, Domitian and Cleopatra. The catalogue remains sectionalised according to these 17th-century locations, such as Nero DII. Cotton's library had been presented to the nation in 1700 but while stored at Westminster was badly damaged by fire in 1731. Yet treasures survive. For example, Augustus I volume I includes a bird's-eye view of the town, harbour, and castle of Dover, a plan of Carlisle, a map of the Isle of Sheppey, a plan of Plymouth town and road 'by some Italian', the course of the River Trent about Nottingham and Newark, mostly undated in the catalogue but generally 16th century. Also in the Cottonian library were the manuscripts of the medieval didactic poems *Pearl, Patience, Cleanness*; the 'best boke of romaunce' in English literature, *Sir Gawain and the green knight*; the Lindisfarne gospels; and the 10th-century manuscript of the heroic poem *Beowulf*.

Humphrey Wanley, the linguist and pioneer of the study of diplomatic in England, served as agent for the Harleys in amassing thousands of ancient charters, rolls and manuscripts. The Harleian collection contains, among its numerous local manuscripts, detailed returns from diocesan authorities for the survey or census ordered by the privy council in 1563. Additionally, there survive returns to the diocesan registration of Anglican communicants, papist recusants and protestant dissenters during 1603. In bundle 4181 there is a 'Note about the Estate of Morgan Prosser along the East side of the churchyard of Lhanvronack, toward the River Uske', undated; in bundle 4252 'A Journal to the East-India, in the Ship Unicorn, 1668. A regular Sailor's Journal'; in bundle 6839 'Meers & Bounds of St. Michael's Parish in the City of Coventry 1675'.

In 1757 George II donated the royal library, including the spoils from monasteries accumulated by English sovereigns since Edward IV. These printed and manuscript books had been stored with the Cottonian collection but escaped serious loss in the fire of 1731. The royal library brought to the museum the privilege of compulsory deposit of all copyright material published in Britain and Ireland.

The two series known as Additional and Egerton manuscripts comprise miscellaneous gifts, purchases and bequests from as early as 1756 to the present. Catalogues and indexes indicate the chronological and topographical range of the thousands of items. Included in the Additional manuscripts are numerous texts of plays submitted by law to the lord chamberlain for licensing between 1824 and 1968.

The Lansdowne manuscripts, purchased in 1807, offer national and local historical material some dating from before the middle of the 17th century. A glimpse of the variety of the accumulation may be gained from two items from bundle 108. Number 29 sets out 'Mr. James Rithers's scheme for a free school, and relief of the poor, in the Parish and Manor of Harwood, Yorkshire'; number 30 'An imperfect description of a project of one Russel, to bring the river of Isleworth to the North side of London'. Lansdowne preserves numerous Hicks family muniments, including documents relating to Michael Hicks, 1543–1612, a financial wizard, secretary to the Cecils and brother to the celebrated royalist Baptist Hicks, Viscount Campden. From the Hickses descended Sir Michael Hicks-Beach, Earl St Aldwyn, a noted chancellor of the exchequer in Victorian times. One of the Elizabethan letters is summarised as follows: 'Sir John Spencer, of Althrappe, wishes Mr. Hicks joy on his marriage; and sends him a fat doe, and twelve Northamptonshire puddings, Dec 13'.

Charters and rolls, some dating from before the reign of William the Conqueror, form separate series, with appropriate catalogues and indexes. The most ancient charters are almost all in print, often also in facsimile, and have been edited or described by historians from Victorian times onwards. In these sources may be found the earliest form of a village or field name, a description of ecclesiastical privilege, evidence of commercial or farming practices, names of landowners, topographical features such as the hollow way, ford or earthwork, mention of invading Viking, location of ancient oak, standing stone or woodland grove.

Local historians exploit Anglo-Saxon charters for the detailed perambulation of estate boundaries, following a hedgerow, stream, ditch, bank, tumulus, ridgeway, copse, standing stone or thorny dean. Armed with a translation of a chosen charter and the relevant one-inch ordnance survey map, the researcher traces on the ground the extent of a landholding offered to a Saxon thegn perhaps a thousand years ago. The property may descend directly from a Roman estate and continue to be represented in the bounds of a later farm, parish or hundred. Place-names of rivulets, woodland, valleys, thickets, fields and settlements, described in the charter in Anglo-Saxon terms, are printed now on maps or recalled by farmers and villagers, doubtless in corrupted form but by no means unrecognisable. Common elements include *ford, hyrst* 'wooded hillock', *hæð* 'heath', *stan* 'a stone', *leah* 'clearing', *wald* 'woodland', *worð* 'enclosure', *þorp* 'hamlet', *ponde* 'pond', *pæð* 'track', *sticolpæð* 'steep path between banks', *æppeltun* 'orchard'.

The papers of Edwin Chadwick, the Victorian sanitary reformer, include local reports to the general board of health between 1848 and 1857. Established by Act in 1848, the board inquired into localities in England and Wales where existing local authorities were failing to regulate water supply, sewerage, shambles, cemeteries, refuse disposal and other amenities of urban living. An inspector's preliminary inquiry dealt with a variety of relevant matters such as population, death rate, bylaws, housing conditions, drainage schemes, lighting, watching, ventilation of tenements, privy accommodation and the health of the populace.

Published catalogues of items of special interest include geographically arranged lists of manuscript maps, charts, plans and topographical drawings; a handlist of music manuscripts; medieval chartularies of Britain; heraldic visitations and medieval rolls of arms; and manuscripts relating to Wales. Catalogues of local interest include the Baker and Cole manuscripts relating to Cambridge town, university and county, the Wolley manuscripts referring to Derbyshire, and Davy's Suffolk collections.

National Library of Wales

Founded during the early years of the 20th century at the Cardiganshire seaside holiday resort of Aberystwyth, the National Library of Wales serves as the repository for ecclesiastical documents, private deposits and certain series of public records relating to the principality.

Edward I had subdued the unruly country by about 1283 and, as a means of anglicising Welshmen, established English administrative and judicial organs of government. The Plantagenet monarch granted charters to towns, encouraged commerce, and divided the newly conquered land into six shires on the English pattern. A further subdivision created twelve counties in the 16th century when Wales was fully integrated politically with England. Henry VIII's reforms provided for a twice yearly court of great sessions acting under the common law in each county. The court acquired equity jurisdiction in 1689 but was abolished in 1830 when Wales came under the modern system of assizes.

The Aberystwyth repository, in addition to being the copyright library for Wales, preserves records of the court of great sessions for the period 1536–1830, various county quarter sessions archives, legal and departmental public records transferred from London, and wills and inventories before 1858. Ecclesiastical documents embrace vestry minutes, churchwardens' accounts, and registers of baptisms, marriages and burials of the former established church as well as records of the influential nonconformist chapels of the principality.

Robert Vaughan of Hengwrt collected the most significant and ancient of manuscripts in Welsh during the 17th century. This material, amalgamated with additional treasures in the Peniarth accumulation, was deposited in the national library.

The intending researcher locates material through the annually published handlist of manuscripts as well as in printed calendars of collections. Other lists and indexes can be consulted only by a personal visit to the library.

National Library of Scotland

Founded in 1682, largely at the instigation of Sir George Mackenzie of Rosehaugh, the library of the faculty of advocates became at an early stage of its history a repository for books on law, history, rhetoric and criticism. From its inception the library served not only legal men but philosophers, authors, lecturers and other researchers. In 1698 the advocates purchased the manuscripts of Sir James Balfour of Denmilne and initiated a policy of collecting family muniments, archives and other documents of Scottish or general interest. The important privilege of receiving a copy of every book published in Great Britain was acquired under copyright legislation in 1710.

After 1700 the library moved from a house in Parliament Close to share the laigh parliament hall with the public records of Scotland. In 1815 the books were stored in the upper hall of the the Signet library until the opening in 1833 of William Playfair's building on a site adjoining George IV Bridge in the old city of Edinburgh. The advocates added further rooms round this original structure in 1901 and 1908.

Under the influence of energetic and devoted keepers such as David Hume, visited by readers including James Boswell, Sir Walter Scott and R. L. Stevenson, the institution expanded its collections of books and documents relating to Scotland and the wider world.

However the administration of a national institution proved ruinously expensive even during Victorian times, despite the donations of opulent supporters. The advocate therefore attempted to shed their burden to the state, but unsuccessfully. Finally in 1924 the biscuit manufacturer, Sir Alexander Grant of Forres, offered a generous endowment to enable the nation to undertake the administration of the institution. In 1925 the national library of Scotland was established by Act of Parliament. The faculty of advocates released well over three-quarters of a million books, many priceless, to the new authority together with manuscripts and the copyright privileges. Sir Alexander Grant donated a substantial sum for a new library building on the George IV Bridge site. This extension, commenced during 1938, was not completed until 1955.

The library holds such accessions as autograph letters of famous Scots, selections of the earliest items produced by means of Scottish printing presses, medieval religious illuminated manuscripts and the results of Alexander Webster's parochial census of Scottish population, distinguishing between protestants and papists, in 1755. The library had by 1978 received through loan, gift or purchase some fifteen thousand volumes of manuscripts with an equal amount of unsorted unbound items. The basic policy of the modern library remains the acquisition of material relating to the history and literature of Scotland, including literary manuscripts, papers of Scottish engineers and businessmen abroad, estate muniments, correspondence, political papers, trades union records, solicitors' accumulations, archives of Scottish printers, maps, plans and charters. National Library holdings are described in various publications including *Advocates library; notable accessions up to 1925*, issued in 1966, and editions of *Catalogues of manuscripts acquired since 1925*.

Scottish Catholic archives

During the religious reformation of the 16th century, medieval treasures of the cathedrals, monasteries and churches of Scotland 'wer spoulyeit and reft frae thame in everie place quhair the samyn culd be apprehendit'. Reliquaries, chalices, charters and registers were looted, burned or embezzled. The archives of the bishopric of Glasgow, however, were transported in the care of Archbishop James Beaton to Paris. There Beaton provided for the refounding of David, Bishop of Moray's Scots College for the education of priests and laymen in the Catholic faith. That institution served also as repository for the safekeeping of rescued Scottish documents, books and precious ornaments.

In 1665 the newly erected Scots College within the University of Paris boasted a spacious library and archive area on the main floor. A few years later the collections included college archives from as early as 1564; a chartulary of the church of Glasgow; James Beaton's diplomatic correspondence from 1557; donations such as William Sinclair's manuscript history of Scotland from 1437 to 1625; and a missionary in Scotland, Gilbert Blakhal's autobiography, the 'brieffe narration' of about 1667. Unfortunately by 1686 documents were reported 'lying in confused heaps or bundles in old trunks, without lock, in a wardrobe exposed to all hands'. This was the period when the brothers Lewis and Thomas Innes of Drumgask first came to the staff of the college. Lewis served as principal from 1682 to 1713 and Thomas, after ordination, as an archivist in the college. Scottish historiography owes a considerable debt to Thomas Innes for his care and cataloguing of the Catholic archives.

Both brothers counted themselves disciples of the French scholar Jean Mabillon whose pioneering study *De re diplomatica* profoundly influenced European historical scholarship. Thomas gained access to the See of Glasgow's medieval royal charters and papal bulls from the 12th century onwards. He reported that 'the Number of these Charters will exceed five or six hundred, all of them almost with seals . . . but all are in a most pitiful condition, thrown without any order in 6 or seven baggs of Linnen, where the seals are crusht one upon another . . . but what is the most Curious is an Inventary . . . of All the Silver work, Reliquaries, ornaments as Chasubles, Copes &c of the Church of Glasgow with a Catalogue of the Manuscripts of the Library of the Churchbooks of Glasgow'. Employing palaeographical expertise Thomas transcribed these medieval documents into two large volumes and then commissioned a storage cupboard for their conservation. Moreover, in timely fashion his diplomatic skills enabled him to authenticate the legitimacy of the medieval Stewart dynasty. This delighted the recently exiled James VII and II. The king deposited his autograph memoirs and political correspondence in the college. It consequently became, during the 18th century, a record office for the care of Jacobite archives and for Catholic family papers such as those of the Erskines of Mar.

Partly through the beatification of the king, partly for political reasons, the college authorities only once granted a researcher access to the original memoirs of James VII. On that occasion the scholar so honoured may well have carried off about twelve volumes of Jacobite letters which eventually were deposited in the Bodleian Library, Oxford.

The French Revolution gravely endangered the Scots College archives which were dispersed, burned, lost, stolen or smuggled to Rome or Britain. The memoirs of James VII, despatched by mail coach into the country, lay hidden in various places, stripped of 'covers and bindings, mostly in red morocco and velvet with gold clasps' for anonymity's sake. However these precautions profited nothing, because fearful of being caught by the revolutionaries in possession of religious or royalist material, the wife of one custodian consigned the entire hoard to the flames. Providentially, two copies of William Dicconson's manuscript biography of James VII based on the memoirs survive, one in the royal archives at Windsor, the other in the Scottish Catholic archives.

Fire and plunderers also impoverished Catholic archives in Scotland, including those of the highland vicariate at Morar in Inverness-shire and the lowland vicariate at Preshome, in Clochan, Banffshire. Until 1829 Roman Catholics lacked the protection of the law, priests operated behind code names, chapels masqueraded as farmhouses, mobs looted at will.

The seminary at Morar, founded in 1714, moved to Scalan at the remote southern end of the Braes of Glenlivet in Banffshire following the upheavals in the west during 1715-16. Though the vicariate archive was 'gutted and demolished . . . toss'd about and destroy'd' by the rude militia in 1746, the Scalan archive continued to accumulate until 1799, protected by the influential Gordon family, a faithful Roman Catholic people, and the wretchedness of the trackways. The seminary building stands to this day beside a clear millstream on a track haunted by the ghosts of whisky smugglers and dispossessed hillfarm cottars. The gaunt dark rooms bespeak a dedicated coterie of converts and clergy adamant in their determination to restore the old faith to Scotland.

Unfortunately documents continued to stray, including the *liber rubus* belonging to the See of Glasgow. This had survived the sojourn in Paris and revolutionary horrors but was loaned in 1798 to the antiquarian George Chalmers, a Fochabers man, author of the historical work *Caledonia*. From Chalmers the volume was communicated to Thomas Thomson, the same deputy clerk register who lost his post in 1841, and so found its way to the Scottish Record Office.

From Scalan the Catholic seminarians moved to Aquhorties on Don in 1799 before journeying to the recently constructed Blairs College on Deeside near Aberdeen in 1829.

The muniment room at Blairs, especially the spacious addition of 1896-1903, served as the home of the itinerant archives until 1958. During this period, 1829-1958, documents and books were deposited in the library relating to the Roman Catholic community. In 1839 the surviving contents of the Scots College library in Paris arrived, and some years later archives from Scottish monasteries threatened with secularisation in Bavaria.

Material collected by James Kyle, the seminarian and vicar apostolic of the northern district of Scotland, arrived at Blairs after the bishop's death in 1869. Kyle had worked for 40 years at Preshome, in the hills above the port of Buckie, the isolated farmhouse and chapel that had remained a centre of the old faith through thick and thin. There in a specially equipped but crowded library he stored archives from continental colleges such as Valladolid, Rome and Paris. Kyle acquired the correspondence of George Hay, vicar apostolic of the lowland district of Scotland from 1769 to 1811, and of John Geddes his co-adjutor for the years 1780-99. He even sought out and collected various treasures of the medieval bishopric of Glasgow such as the *registrum vetus* chartulary and the protocol book of Cuthbert Simson. Kyle, a competent linguist, palaeographer and archivist, sorted, arranged and listed the Preshome papers which furnish important source material for the history of Roman Catholicism throughout the country into Victorian times. In 1870 the first report of the historical manuscripts commission presented a survey of the Kyle manuscripts 'at Buckie' including letters of Mary, Queen of Scots. The second report noticed Blairs College archives.

Between 1905 and 1918 Blairs received the voluminous collection of William Clapperton, who lived from 1821 to 1905, a canon in Buckie and an historian of note. The canon, a Fochabers man, compiled memoirs of Scottish missionary priests between 1615 and 1795 from original records at Preshome.

Facilities at Blairs College, however, proved inadequate for archival purposes. David McRoberts in his history of the Scottish Catholic archives in *Innes Review*, XXVIII, 2 (1977) recalls his own unsupervised visit in 1941 to the muniment room. There the 'musty smell of old documents and the south-facing window, firmly closed, made the place hot and airless . . . the most conspicuous object in the room was an unusually large ash-tray, heaped up and overflowing with ash and cigarette-ends'. Such visits and the consequent published work of scholars, including M. V. Hay, revealed the wealth of material at Blairs. Historians in Edinburgh and Glasgow sought the removal of the accumulation.

Authorities in 1957 decided to seek premises in Edinburgh for archival storage. The Columba Trust offered a grant for the purchase of 16 Drummond Place and in 1958 the documents from Blairs journeyed southwards again. The repository was equipped to modern archival standards during 1972–4. The archivists encouraged the deposit of documentation on most aspects of the history of the Roman Catholic community. The books of Blairs College library, preserving the works, gifts and accumulations of scholars during three centuries, were deposited on loan in the National Library of Scotland.

Trinity College, Dublin

Dublin corporation provided the site for the building of Trinity College in 1592. The ground had been granted by the crown as a reward for Dublin's loyalty during the uprising of Thomas Fitzgerald 'Silken Thomas' in 1534. The college occupied the area formerly belonging to an Augustinian monastery, founded in the 12th century by Diarmait MacMurchada, the very ruler whose intrigues encouraged the initial Anglo–Norman invasion.

Subscriptions from the back pay of Elizabeth I's army in 1601 helped to finance the library as a thank offering for victory over Spanish and Irish forces at Kinsale. Sir Thomas Bodley, the restorer of Oxford's University library, and James Ussher both helped to collect and donate books, and Ussher's own accumulation including the book of Kells was bought for Trinity by the parliamentary army in Ireland. Ussher, from 1625 to 1656 Archbishop of Armagh though Calvinist in persuasion, a royalist but not disfavoured by Cromwell, was distinguished for his chronological research in fixing the creation of the world exactly 4004 years before Christ's birth. This was accepted for three centuries before being overthrown by the new revelation of 19th-century scientific rationalism.

The oldest remaining portion of Trinity dates from about 1700, the central façade from 1759, the library, wherein are displayed on weekdays the treasures of the college, from 1732. As an institution modelled on the colleges of Oxford and Cambridge for the education of men of the reformed faith, Trinity attracted such students as Oliver Goldsmith, Edmund Burke, Swift of *Gulliver's Travels*,

Congreve the dramatist, and Sir Samuel Ferguson, 1810–86, first deputy keeper of the public records of Ireland.

Trinity gained the privilege of receiving one copy of every book published in the British Isles under copyright legislation. The library possesses books from the earliest days of printing and thousands of ancient manuscripts including Egyptian papyri and Greek, Latin or Irish religious texts. Like the John Rylands Library, Manchester, Trinity remains a centre for the layman to admire priceless treasures on exhibition and for the specialist of medieval Christendom to undertake research.

Here the authorities conserve a goodly portion of Ireland's documentary heritage including beautifully handwritten and illuminated gospels, hymnaries, missals and pious lives of the saints; the 11th-century *liber hymnorum*; the eighth-century book of Dimma; the 12th-century book of Leinster; the yellow book of Lecan; the book of Armagh of about 807; and the book of Durrow, the earliest in the library. Visitors marvel at the 'most beautiful book in the world' with its wealth of ornamentation, traceries, colouring and fine detail, a Latin copy of the gospels perfected by the anonymous monks of the scriptorium at St Columba's monastery of Ceanannus Mór or Kells about 760–820.

General register offices

National registration of births, marriages and deaths commenced in 1837 for England and Wales, 1855 for Scotland, 1864 for Ireland. The law provided for the compulsory recording of information at the offices of local registrars who in turn periodically despatched details upwards through district officials to principal registries in London, Edinburgh and Dublin. Registrars-general then compiled national index volumes for public consultation, organising the production and issuing of copy certificates against payment of the statutory fee.

The general register office of England and Wales merged in 1970 with the government's social survey department to form the office of population, censuses and surveys.

A birth certificate normally states the child's name, sex, birthdate and birthplace, the married and maiden name of the mother, the name and occupation of the father, with name, description and address of the informant. The marriage certificate provides the name, age, residence, occupation and marital status of each party; the names of two witnesses; the names and occupations of both fathers, with date, district, parish and location of ceremony including the denomination of the church. A death certificate states the name, sex, occupation, age, place, cause and date of death and may bear the signature, residence and description of the informant.

The registrar-general in London has custody of registers of births and deaths at sea since 1837 and consular returns of births, marriages and deaths of British subjects abroad since 1849.

The Act establishing registration in Scotland permitted registrars to seek more information than was customary south of the border. However, before a year was out the authorities retreated from the burdensome if statistically useful task by simplifying requirements. Even so, Scottish certificates continued to offer genealogically significant morsels. For example, birth certificate forms from 1861 required the date and place of the parents' marriage; death certificates required the name and occupation of the father and maiden name of the mother; marriage certificates recorded the names of both parents of the two parties.

The registrar-general for Scotland holds registers of baptism, marriage and burial of the established Church of Scotland from the 16th century to 1855; more modern registers relating to various free churches; original population census returns from 1841 onwards; and copies of some monumental inscriptions. The office of the Lyon King-of-Arms, in the same building at New Register House, offers a wide choice of recorded genealogies and heraldic records.

The general register office for Ireland organised the registration of births, marriages and deaths from 1864 (Protestant marriages from 1845) until the partition of that island in 1922. Thereafter independent registries served north and south from Belfast and Dublin.

Probate registries

Established by statute from 1858, district registries undertake the filing and probate of original wills in England and Wales. The principal registry at Somerset House in London, functioning within the principal registry of the family division of the high court of justice, preserves copies of wills held by district registries. Somerset House files originals of wills proved in London. Indexes facilitate their retrieval.

Lambeth palace library

The library of the Archbishop of Canterbury at Lambeth Palace in London furnishes research material on ecclesiastical history and law. Although manuscripts and printed books accumulated at Lambeth for centuries, their scholarly exploitation awaited the provision of adequate storage arrangements and the compilation of a retrieval system. A principal activity of one 18th-century custodian seems to have consisted of 'brushing away the Cobwebs, which in that old Building you will find to encrease very fast' but despite his efforts each book, though 'several times wip'd as clean as it could be', was 'in a short time afterwards not fit to be handled'.

Archbishop Richard Bancroft first organised the library for scholars during his term of office, 1604–10, accumulating the miscellaneous manuscripts known as Codices Lambethani. His successors, George Abbot and Thomas Tenison, added to the treasures, including family and political papers, local history documents relating to the diocese and province, oriental and Greek manuscripts, and business records of succeeding archbishops. The basis of the modern library was laid during the tenure of librarianship of A. C. Ducarel during the years 1757–75.

Succeeding librarians have listed the collections, including registers, instruments and papers of the archbishops; Canterbury diocesan records; ancient charters and court rolls of archiepiscopal estates; papers of the commission for building 50 new churches in the metropolis between 1711 and 1759; and records of the incorporated church building society after 1818.

Parliamentary surveys of ecclesiastical lands were compiled during the period 1646-60, when diocesan and capitular estates were confiscated for the support of the army and commonwealth government. As with surveys of crown and royalist lands, the documents comprehend nearly all appropriated estates in the country, specifying manors, demesnes, tithes, customary dues, perquisites of courts, burgage tenements, collieries, commons and harbours. Surveyors took account of real market values, acreage, profits of woodland, state of repair of buildings, certain architectural features of houses, rentals, feudal revenues, details of tenants and the descent of their titles. In 1662 the Archbishop of Canterbury chose to despatch certain capitular and diocesan archives to the relevant chapter or diocese, whence these may now have passed to the county record office.

Diocesan registrars of both provinces received returns to the ecclesiastical census in 1676, but comparatively few papers survive in diocesan or parish chests. Named for Henry Compton, Bishop of London, queries were directed to parochial clergy to count the number of persons 'by common estimation and account in your parish inhabiting', and those attending or absenting themselves from communion. Certain incumbents actually listed people by name, though the majority dealt only in numbers of Anglicans, Roman Catholics and dissenters, probably men and women over the age of sixteen. Lambeth's Compton collection may be supplemented with returns available at the Bodleian Library, Oxford, and William Salt Library, Stafford.

Public Record Office of Northern Ireland

Established in 1924 on the fourth floor of a converted linen warehouse, without benefit of even a passenger lift, the Public Record Office of Northern Ireland statutorily acquired responsibility for the custody of official records of the government of the province of Ulster dating from 1921. The repository accumulated crown court, justice of the peace, probate and parish records, occasionally dating back into the 19th century. Archives of the boards of guardian, defunct canal companies, charities and schools accrued to the repository through departmental channels. From its inception the office aimed to obtain duplicate copies of documents in Dublin and of material held elsewhere but of northern Irish interest. The office also encouraged the deposit of original documents or family muniments relating to the north of Ireland, thus serving as local repository for the six counties. The public records occupied a succession of cellars, semi-basements, castles and courthouses, before adequate facilities including the public searchrooms were opened.

Post Office

Postal records at the Post Office archives, London, commence with account and letter books of Colonel Roger Whitley, deputy postmaster general between 1672 and 1677. The government of Charles II developed postal services based in strategically situated post towns and coastal packet stations. These facilities were improved in the course of the next hundred years by public demand and through the beneficial influence of such innovators as the philanthropist, Ralph Allen of Bath, and John Palmer, surveyor and comptroller general of mails. Although comparatively few documents survive from the 18th century, the general accounts, establishment and order books set out the main course of events in postal history as well as local changes in postmastership or policy. Innkeepers discovered the financial advantages of a part-time postal position in attracting coaches and customers to their premises, and the order books reflect the manoeuvrings for preferment by publicans and a variety of businessmen bent on profit.

Palmer's postal reforms, including the introduction of armed guards, fast, regular, reliable and safe mail stagecoaches, and public investment in road building contributed to the expansion of postal services from 1786 onwards. Ambitious young men sought the adventurous responsibilities of guarding the royal mail. Indeed one of my forebears, a Bennett, whose portrait has glowered down at five generations of visitors, has traditionally been described as a post office coachman and, as one of the six tallest men in the country, presented before the king. The official register of inspectors and mailguards for 1798-1845 follows the career of Joseph Bennett, a Derbyshire man but by the 1820s gamekeeper to Sir Charles Morgan on his Monmouthshire estates. At the age of 25 in 1828 Joseph sought the recommendation of his employer as a suitably strong and honest young man for duty as guard on the Birmingham-Grantham mail stagecoach run. He obtained that position and later transferred to the Bath-Birmingham route. Joseph's brother, Samuel, trained as a cooper in Derbyshire, also persuaded an influential gentleman to support his application for work on the stagecoaches. He waited until 1836, having then attained the acceptable age of 26. His application also met with success and he worked several long distance runs before middle age or, more likely, railway competition forced his move to London in 1857 as letter carrier and second class stamper.

Detailed postal records begin only about 1790 with letters and reports from provincial postmasters, petitions from inhabitants, sketches of local posts by district surveyors, financial ledgers, appointment registers, time bills, postal maps, mail coach minutes, details of pre-1840 local penny post networks, and official order books. From these and other documents the chief secretary composed his reports to the postmaster-general on all policy matters affecting the posts. From 1794 a complementary series of records, known as the secretary's minutes, contain statements on personnel as well as matters of local or secondary importance. Postal records, especially following reforms of 1840, reveal not only the technical problems of delivering letters but also the state of local manufactures, the development of railways, political agitation, salaries, working conditions, agriculture, harvests and the weather.

CHAPTER SIX

FAMILY MUNIMENT ROOM

FAMILY MUNIMENTS, the documents of estate administration, include farm accounts, legal settlements, wills, title deeds, rentals, plans, court rolls, correspondence, photographs, genealogies, diaries and wages books. These relate to the exploitation of the family's resources, to the politics, religious life and educational facilities of the neighbourhood, to housing conditions, police, tithes, employment, transport, charities and similar aspects of local history.

Some families installed record rooms at their country seats for the preservation of the muniments. Occasionally a family librarian or archivist worked to arrange and catalogue the items, as nowadays at Chatsworth and Hatfield. At Hopetoun House near Edinburgh the charter room is fitted with 18th-century wooden cupboards and shelves for the storage of metal trunks packed with family muniments. Less fortunate householders commandeered their attic or cellar, encouraging the local rector or a retired uncle to serve as curator.

By arrangement with the owners, many collections of documents including those at Hopetoun, while continuing to be stored in the family home, are arranged, listed and made available to researchers by archivists. Other collections have found their way into the care of solicitors, libraries, estate agents or record offices. Numerous estates belong not to a family but to an industrial or investment company, university college, charitable institution or local authority.

In 1952 the government forbade the export of nationally significant muniments without a licence. This allowed a period of grace during which money could be raised in Britain to purchase the whole or portions of the collection. Warwickshire County Council, custodian of the Warwick Castle muniments until these were withdrawn from the archives, raised £120,000 for their purchase from the owner. From 1979 any document more than fifty years old required an export licence, regardless of value, and might be purchased with the help of the archives budget of a government fund.

In the 1970s the treasury agreed to accept documents of exceptional historical importance in lieu of death duties. The owner could sell at normal market rates direct to a record office or library with the financial aid of a national heritage fund.

Manorial records

The medieval manor, a landed estate in England and Wales not necessarily co-extensive with the parish, belonged to a proprietor known as the lord of the manor. Manorial tenants as well as the owner and his officers had rights and duties specified in the manorial custumal or in decisions of the manor court. The manor declined in importance from the middle of the 14th century as a result of changing economic, social and demographic circumstances. Further powers were lost during the 16th century to rival local authorities, but manor courts were abolished only in 1926.

Manorial officials supervised the proper management and cultivation of the estate, especially the home farm or demesne, and attempted to maintain law and order. To these ends the steward summoned courts, known as leet and baron, and administered the view of frankpledge, an ancient method of preserving the peace through the mutual responsibility of groups of ten or more adult males for the good conduct of each member of the group or tithing.

From the 13th century it was customary to write down proceedings of the manorial court in documents known as court rolls. A typical entry commences, in Latin, with the title of the court and the date, 'court of Wenintun held on the Sunday next after the feast of St John the baptist in the eighth year of the reign of king Edward the third'. Then the latest manorial problems are stated. 'John Winton is accused of cutting turf from the lord's wasteland, pays 2d. . . . for removing one boundary stone between his own and widow Thorneleigh's strip . . . owes for his tenement three days ploughing a year . . . for stealing a horse . . . neglecting to scour a drainage ditch . . . for being wont to empty his chamberpot into the high street to the public detriment . . . breaking the Westfield with horses . . . '.

Whenever a tenant relinquished his property, or died, his holding was surrendered to the manorial authorities. His successor gained entry following payment of a fine to the lord of the manor. The process was recorded in the court roll. Copies of the relevant entries, written out for retention by the tenant, were known as surrenders and admittances. Such tenants or copyholders formed an important legal class, secure in their tenancy by virtue of the authority of the manor court roll.

Beginning in Latin with the words *extenta manerii*, the manorial extent furnished a verbal survey of the lands held by the free and unfree tenants and, in demesne, by the lord. Perhaps accompanying a legal case or inquisition *post mortem*, this document surveys and values the manor house and curtilage, arable, crops, village meadow, pasture, woodland, mill, game preserve, beasts, rabbit warren, dovecote, fish pond, land of freeholders, customary holdings and miscellaneous court perquisites such as amercements. From such extents it may be possible to calculate the size and type of land in demesne, crop yields, animals held, the relative numbers of free and other tenants, value of land and services, and the acreage farmed out to leaseholders.

Title deeds

A bundle of title deeds contains various documents drawn up, during many years, to prove ownership to property. There is no necessary relationship between the earliest deed in the bundle and the age of any building on the site, because all kinds of considerations govern the location of titles. These documents facilitate the compilation of a list of the owners and occupiers over the years. They hint at a description of the building and its appurtenances including notes on new constructions. They record legal tussles, family settlements, wills, marriages, bankruptcies and deaths. They chronicle schemes of expansion or improvement including laying of field drains, access roads, electricity cables and fences. They mention mills, saltings, paths, lanes, woods, ancient mounds, hedges, moorland, waste, village green, market, cross and gibbet. They indicate the processes by which estates were consolidated or divided.

During the middle ages a man held his estate from a feudal superior on condition of rendering knight, labour or other appropriate service. The superior administered the land whenever a tenant could not perform his service, for instance during his minority, and such incidents of tenure proved profitable. For this reason the feudal lord insisted on public livery of seisin in order to identify the tenant from whom dues were to be exacted. But the conveyance of property through the public delivery, on site, was not necessarily chronicled in writing. Symbolism, however, could not compensate for the absence of evidence about the conditions of the transaction, money payment, names of witnesses, and date, should any disputes proceed to court. Therefore a charter of grant was adopted by prudent landowners during the late 12th century. Provided that an estate was not held in chief of the monarch, property in fee simple might be alienated by its owner with a minimum of formality. Nine or ten lines of writing in Latin on parchment sufficed.

In order to offer a sure record of the conveyance of freehold property in the absence of ancient, or even contemporary, charters, 12th-century lawyers in England devised a feigned suit in the court of common pleas, intended from the outset to lead to an agreement or composition between the supposedly contending parties. The grantee or complainant brought an action against the grantor or deforciant who compromised the action by permission of the justices, admitting the property belonged to the grantee. The process was known as levying a fine and resulted in the payment of king's silver to the monarch, an ancient revenue of the crown. The concord or actual agreement commenced in Latin *haec est finalis concordia*, 'this is the final agreement', hence the term *fine* for this deed. Lawyers, using a single parchment, wrote down the entire process in a chirograph, a manuscript in several copies to thwart forgers. The lawyers inscribed *chirographum* in the margins between the texts and then separated the copies by an indented cut. This produced the requisite three 'indentures' for the querent, deforciant and court archives. The fine barred all claims to the property after five years and remedied defects in the bundle of deeds. Hence astute or dishonest landowners levied fines to avoid the emergence of future problems such as the sudden appearance of a hitherto unsuspected heir. A fine could create a family settlement; was used as a married woman's conveyance, barred the entail of a tenant in tail not in possession of his estate, though not obstructing the rights of remaindermen and reversioners.

A landowner in England and Wales employed the 'feoffment to uses' to escape burdensome feudal services or to alienate land to the church without paying for the legally necessary licence. The feoffment permitted a delinquent to evade confiscation of property for political misdemeanours, allowed friars to escape vows of poverty and facilitated the devising of real estate by will (which was, outside certain boroughs, not normally feasible). The owner conveyed his lands to a nominal purchaser to hold 'to the use of' a third party, perhaps himself, or another person, or even a group of people, feoffees protected thereafter by a court of equity, but unrecognised by common law and certainly unpopular with the crown. Henry VIII's Statute of Uses of 1536 thus executed the use into a legal estate in possession, the third party becoming legal owner responsible for all dues. However, during the 17th century, chancery accepted the use upon a use, enabling a person to grant property to the use of others and their heirs to the use of others.

In reply to the legislation on uses, lawyers developed the process of bargain and sale by which a vendor transferred property to the purchaser but was deemed to possess the estate temporarily to the purchaser's use. The use, however, was immediately executed in the purchaser's favour. Hence this contract, usually in English, effectively conveyed interests in real estate following payment of an agreed price. The document, in the form of an indenture, includes the operative words 'doth grant bargain and sell'. As an added legal safeguard, an endorsement or separate feoffment contained the phrase 'alien grant bargain sell enfeoff and confirm'. From 1536 parliament required such documents to be enrolled with the clerk of the peace or at one of the courts in Westminster, partly as a means of identifying the tenant responsible for paying property taxes.

First appearing in 1614 the lease and release ostensibly dealt with leasehold interests and reversions expectant therefrom, requiring no public livery of seisin or enrolment, though effectively conveying the whole legal estate. Consisting of two documents written on consecutive days, then folded together, and with operative words 'granted bargained sold remised released quitclaimed and confirmed', the lease and release survived until replaced in 1841 by a simple release and in 1845 by a deed of grant.

The estate tail formed an interest 'cut down' from an estate in fee simple, the fullest interest enjoyable in land under English law. An estate in fee tail excluded collateral branches in favour of the landowner's own issue. One held in tail male excluded women until all lineal males died out. But on failure of such issue, the grantor or his heirs reclaimed the property. On the other hand the statute concerning conditional grants, of 1285, confirmed the validity of entails. The Act determined that a tenant in tail could not alienate his estate for longer than his own lifetime, and tied up land generation after generation for as long as the family line continued. Disadvantages soon became evident. Such an estate could pass to a distant relative rather than to daughters. There might be restrictions on selling farms or developing resources such as collieries. Untying the entail then became imperative.

Following Taltarum's case of 1472, lawyers employed the common recovery to bar the entail. The recovery was an assurance of title founded on a court decision in favour of the demandant or recoveror following a collusive action. The tenant in tail was supposed to recover property of equal value from 'a man of straw', usually the court crier. The document may be recognised by its royal portrait within an initial letter. The process is complicated, especially if by double or treble voucher, but the researcher need only extract, from the Latin text, the names of the tenant in tail and demandant, the date and the admittedly conventional and unrealistic description of the property. A disentailing deed enrolled in chancery replaced the recovery in 1833.

Suffering a recovery resulted in barring a tenant in tail's issue and all estate in remainder or reversion. To avoid disentailment by an unscrupulous tenant in tail, an estate might be resettled every generation. The heir on coming of age, through the inducement of an annual income from his father, would be persuaded to join in a recovery, bar the entail and resettle the property on the father for life, remainder to the son for life, remainder in tail to the son's issue. The demandant in such a case recovered to the uses specified in an instrument previously signed.

As an alternative to the recovery, an Estate Act of Parliament could be promoted in the House of Lords between 1512 and 1882, when the Settled Land Act permitted tenants for life to dispose of their property. An Estate Act defined the nature of the problem, detailing farms and manors, names of tenants, conditions of tenancy, charges on the property, dowries, jointures, family history and relationships. The Act sets out the Lords' decisions on the administration of the estate.

The jointure was an estate settled on a woman in consideration of marriage, to be held by her after her husband's death. The arrangement deprived many an heir of the enjoyment of his property after his father's death. Indeed the heir lost out to the stepfather if his mother remarried. The medieval dowager thus attained a significant status in English life and literature; the dowerhouse becoming a centre of power and intrigue.

Mortgages frequently materialise from bundles of title deeds. This pledging of property as security for the loan of money may record family penury, the raising of capital for agricultural and industrial development, or merely the building of a house. But the motive behind the raising of capital in each instance becomes clear only from other papers in the muniment room. Should the family sell mortgaged property and redeem the mortgage simultaneously, their lawyer devised an assignment of a term in trust to attend the freehold and inheritance as a safeguard against irregular demands.

As transaction followed transaction, deeds of title burgeoned into bundles, meet for tying up in red tape. Lawyers began to produce abstracts of title listing all the documents relating to a single property. Additionally, they quoted back to previous titles in a 'whereas' clause within each new deed. For example the earliest deed to one house on the canal side in Barnton, Cheshire, drawn up in 1844, refers to 'all those two Messuages formerly one Messuage'. The 'whereas' clause, however, quotes from a mortgage of 1817 which describes the original building: 'all that newly erected Messuage or Dwellinghouse Shop Oven and Buildings conveniences and erections . . . the Shop and House also fronting to the Northwest and the Towing Path'.

Deeds of title may have been copied into registers known as chartularies, perhaps for security's sake, from as early as the 12th century. Unscrupulous scribes compiled chartularies as a means of 'improving' or 'modernising' documents which were considered to be unsatisfactory evidential material in their original form. But even the most honest and best intentioned copyist may occasionally allow his attention to wander as he transcribes lengthy documents, wrongly spelling place-names or omitting whole lines of writing. Though offering information usually unavailable elsewhere, chartularies must be studied with these considerations in mind.

In Scotland a Statute of 1469 facilitated the removal of feudal restraints on the transfer of land. Following a charter or other warrant the act of giving possession of feudal property was proved in an instrument of sasine. Property rights generally are conveyed by a deed of alienation known as a disposition.

Rentals and leases

During the late Middle Ages, leases for terms of years or for lives replaced customary tenure. Proprietors frequently required payment of a fine at the commencement of a lease and, thereafter, only a modest annual rental. A typical lease for three lives involved John Phillipson, aged 48, James his son, aged 22, and Mary, James's daughter, aged one. The lease, heaven being kind, could endure for perhaps a century, until young Mary's own death, but might expire within the year if plague or famine struck the household.

A landowner's rental sets out the rent paid by tenants for their houses or parcels of land. The document may include the terms on which each property was held, arrears of rent, field names and acreage.

The recovery of freehold land could be attained in a court action of ejectment in the common pleas through the writing of a fictitious lease, entry and ouster. The plaintiff alleged a lease to a certain non-existent John Doe who had been ejected by one Richard Roe. A fictitious well-wisher advised the true defendant to replace Roe in the action. If the defendant was found to have unlawfully ejected Doe, then Doe's lease was adjudged legal. So therefore was the plaintiff's title to the land.

Perambulation

The perambulation of a boundary for the purpose of establishing the property of a landowner, church, manor or village dates from the days of the earliest written documents in Britain. Anglo–Saxon diplomas offer tours of estates, as do medieval title deeds and 16th-century royal charters. Although the earliest perambulations appear in Latin or Anglo–Saxon, more modern versions may be translated into English, Welsh or Scots.

A rural perambulation in about 1173 in Selkirkshire, roughly translated, commenced from Longhope burn as far as the slope on the southern side of the Alne, just as the main road climbs; and from the same side of Haruude burn as far as the nearest watercourse on the western part of Wiuenesae; and on the northern side of Alne from the standing stone between Witeslade and Aunemer as far as the source of Blakeden.

Surveys

A survey or word picture of an estate, usually dating from the period 1540–1720, offers the following kind of information: 'mansion outhouse stables and garden ... one windemillne ... William Horsfeldes close called saltersclose adjoynes north-Easte on the Common, south and west on Hall Fielde 1 ac 2 r ... One pece Lyinge next the more betwixt the Landes of vphall North and the more South 0 acre 2 roodes 7 dayworks 2 perches'.

Maps and plans

During the first half of the 16th century Henry VIII employed master masons as military engineers to design and construct fortifications. The king's warlike tendencies, and his interest in cartography, encouraged his engineers to draw up 'plats' or maps of military installations, including, in several instances, the environs of a fort and its immediate hinterland.

At about the same period, inspired by architectural practice, makers of old-fashioned verbal surveys attempted, by trial and error, to improve techniques of draughtsmanship in the production of maps. Surveyors adopted an early form of triangulation, employing the 'backside of an astrolabe' divided into 360 degrees, a magnetic needle, and a sighting rule. As a result, workshops began to manufacture surveying instruments to meet demand.

Sixteenth-century governments required maps of the country for the sake of becoming better informed and facilitating intervention in local affairs. And, in the shires, estate owners, including the crown, demanded visual knowledge of their properties, frequently for specific reasons such as farm management, changes in agricultural arrangements, settling boundaries, resolving possession of a valuable mill, claiming riparian rights, planning industrial development or enclosing the common. A map of Dewsbury dated 1600 may have been presented to resolve such a dispute concerning the use of the River Calder for driving local mills. The legend reads, 'A plat of the Towne of Dewesbury with the course of the Riuer and waies from Maister Birkbye mill, to the ouer, and nether myllnes of Dewes-burie. Made by Christofer Saxton'.

Surveyors usually drew plan-views of their territory as if looking out from a hill, or from a passing ship in the instance of coastal areas. Their town plans appeared as bird's-eye views, Bristol being so treated as early as 1480. Braun and Hogenberg's book, *Civitates orbis terrarum*, published between 1573 and 1618, offered oblique and bird's-eye views of a number of British towns, drawn apparently about 1560–87 and 1611. In the absence of conventional symbols for topographical features, draughtsmen experienced considerable difficulties with the depiction of hills, valleys and relative height. Surveyors attempted to indicate orientation and scale, though it is not always clear whether distances were measured by the eye or by pacing out, or even by questioning knowledgeable locals. Sometimes they worked in black ink only, sometimes in watercolour. Usually they surveyed only the property of their patron, occasionally the whole parish or manor.

The making of 'a platt of this our Realme' may have been mooted by John Rudd, 1498-1579, vicar of Dewsbury and chaplain to the king, as he listened to Henry VIII's ideas on military matters and cartography. Rudd's apprentice, Christopher Saxton, actually commenced the survey about 1573 under the instructions of Thomas Seckford, a master of the court of requests. In his official capacity Seckford was required to present to Elizabeth I petitions or bills for action in the court of requests, a task he found tiresome on account of the difficulty of securing an audience. However, this Suffolk esquire and member of parliament for Ipswich, known to history for his ready wit, did not permit himself to be downtrodden even by the formidable Elizabeth Tudor. After one long period of delay in gaining access to the monarch, Seckford entered the royal presence wearing brand new footwear, even though the queen hated the smell of fresh leather. To this sauciness the queen is supposed to have said, 'Fie, sloven! thy new boots stink'. 'Madam,' he riposted, 'it is not my new boots that stink, but it is the stale bills that I have kept so long.'

Seckford was thus a privileged man for whom it was advantageous to work. He in turn was responsible to the mighty Lord Burghley, the queen's treasurer, whose insatiable demand for intelligence from every corner of the kingdom could not be denied. Burghley required a county by county survey using the most up-to-date-techniques, and this is what Saxton provided within five years.

It is not certainly known how much of the country Saxton actually surveyed, though a document of 1577 claimed he had 'traveled throughe the greateste parte of this oure realme'. He seems to have mapped Wales, carrying instruments for use on elevated points which could be observed from each other, measuring distance where practicable, accepting reports otherwise.

Saxton's county maps, engraved on copper plates, were printed between 1574 and 1579. Editions appeared until 1611, a revised version in 1645, and updated reissues until about 1770. Saxton's maps form the first atlas of England and Wales, the basis for John Norden's cartographical endeavours in certain counties during the 1590s and residual source of John Speed's maps of the shires in his *Theatre of the empire of Great Britaine*, 1611-12.

The classic estate map of the 18th century, on a scale of perhaps 20 inches to one mile, shows all features of the landscape with conventional symbols. Measurement of every parcel of land relates to an accompanying schedule displaying acreage, crops, annual value, rentals, purchase price, names of tenants, fields, streets or places. Developing urban townscapes were similarly mapped.

A map sufficiently accurate to show every topographical feature to a true scale merits the term 'plan'. In general the term should be reserved for the work of 19th-century surveyors, especially those of the ordnance survey. For the origins of ordnance plans it is necessary to return to the 1740s and to the wild highlands of Scotland.

The army's wanderings through Scottish glens in pursuit of the Pretender during 1746 convinced the authorities of the potential value of a map of that remote land. David Watson, deputy quartermaster-general in North Britain, conceived the scheme for an official survey but the actual task occupied the attention of William Roy, his assistant, between 1747 and 1755. Roy's military surveying parties worked on their 'Great Map' at an administratively and militarily useful scale of 1,000 yards to one inch, sufficient for the delineation of military fortifications, rivers, roads, lochs, settlements, farms, parks, ploughed fields and natural features of the landscape. Roy evinced particular interest in Roman sites, measuring numerous forts and structures nowadays no longer visible on the ground. Indeed Roy continued to research into Roman military antiquities in North Britain for a book which was eventually published posthumously in 1793. Copies of Roy's maps may be consulted at local history libraries throughout Scotland, originals only at the British Library in London.

War and straitened finances postponed Roy's ambitious 'general Survey of the whole Island at the public cost'. However, defeat in America exposed the country's weakness in the face of French bellicosity and convinced the government of the need urgently to plot the 'Nature of the Coast, and the principal Positions and Posts which an Army should occupy'. In 1784 therefore Roy measured a base line, in Hounslow, for a national trigonometrical survey at a one-inch scale. From this line the country was subsequently divided into triangles and in 1791, after Roy's death, the board of ordnance assumed the task of mapping the kingdom for military purposes. The uncoloured one-inch maps of England and Wales began to appear in 1801, covering the whole country south of a line from Preston to Hull by 1840. Original detailed drawings for this survey remain in manuscript at the British Library.

In response to public demand for larger scale plans, the board of ordnance initiated a six-inch survey first in Ireland in 1824, then in the north of England in 1840, finally in Scotland in 1843. Town plans at the extraordinarily useful scale of five or even ten feet to one mile were produced for Britain and Ireland from 1844 onwards. London was surveyed in 1847-52, 1862-71, 1891-5 and 1906-9. Although the one-inch sheets were the best sellers to members of the public, being small enough to carry in a coat pocket but sufficiently detailed to indicate most requisite information, these stood on the shoulders of the splendid six-inch plans, accurate and comprehensive for historical, scientific and administrative purposes.

A survey on a scale of 25 inches commenced in 1853 in Durham, eventually including all except uncultivated land in Britain and Ireland. Between 1855 and 1886 accompanying reference books indicate area and use of each plot of land. The large scale and accurate measurement of Victorian surveyors permitted the representation of every detail of the landscape, every farm steading, castle, mill, hill, escarpment, hedge, tree, shed, house and lane. Indeed before economy measures predominated each bay window, flower bed, path, shrub and hummock appeared in plans of the period 1853-93.

Official papers

Estate owners served as justices of the peace, lords lieutenant, members of parliament, land tax commissioners, yeomanry officers, turnpike trustees. Records of their activities, occasionally with strayed official papers of the various authorities, frequently remain in muniment chests. Additionally, family members gave support to ecclesiastical and charitable organisations. Minutes, accounts, title deeds and correspondence of the local church or almshouse may have found their way to the muniment room.

Historical manuscripts commission

As a means of locating, listing and otherwise making more accessible to the public the wealth of private family and estate muniments scattered throughout the kingdom, the historical manuscripts commission was appointed in 1869. Inspectors were to arrange to visit country houses, castles, legal offices, alms-houses and libraries to list in varying detail the papers of politicians, antiquaries, scholars, squires, peers, parsons, colleges, cathedrals, burghs, authors, societies and others. The experts might, on request, counsel owners on the proper con-servation of their muniments.

During its first half century the commission reported on some four hundred privately owned but significant collections of muniments. Since the initial listing, about forty per cent. of the collections have been dispersed, some *en bloc* to such purchasers as the Huntington Library in California, not a few split for public auction, yet others denuded of ancient chartularies, illuminated manuscripts, maps, surveys or autograph letters. A number have disappeared into thin air. The Bootle–Wilbraham muniments were dispersed through the chimney of the furnace at Blaguegate colliery into which they were fed following the demolition of Lathom House, Lancashire, in 1929.

Calendars, lists and edited texts produced by the itinerant inspectors usually appeared as appendices to published reports. These provide a most significant source for historians, locally and nationally, occasionally sufficiently detailed to obviate consultation of the muniments in the original. Reports are supplemented by indexes of places and personal names mentioned in reports of inspectors for the period 1870–1947. Additionally, the commission issues documentary source lists on various historical subjects, an annual list of accessions to repositories, and an occasional handbook of addresses of record offices in Britain. Researchers may enquire by personal visit or otherwise, at the commission's London office in Chancery Lane, as to possibilities and conditions of access to muniments.

The commission maintains a register of manorial documents, established in 1925 under the Law of Property (Amendment) Act 1924, to record the location, nature, ownership and covering dates of collections of manor court rolls with related muniments. Where possible, the registrar records the name and address of the lord of the manor and his steward. An alphabetical index of parishes refers to manors within each parish. The Tithe Act of 1936 authorised the registration of plans and apportionments following the model of the manorial registry.

The national register of archives, maintained by the commission, commenced in 1945 'to record the location, content and availability of all archives and col-lections of historical manuscripts in England and Wales, other than records of the central government, without limit of date'. Scotland and Northern Ireland operate their own registers on similar lines. Registration depends primarily on reception of calendars, catalogues or lists of documentary collections from local record offices or libraries. These copies, filed in a numerical sequence, are located through indexes of subjects, places, persons and short titles.

British records association

Many people who enjoy the study of archives belong to the British Records Association, established during 1932 to organise the preservation of archives at risk and to represent the interests of custodians, researchers and owners of records. The association's notable achievements include the rescue of thousands of documents in the offices of London solicitors, especially those whose buildings were to be demolished or modernised. Among the association's publications are the journal *Archives* and a continuing series known as *Archives and the user* concerned with indexing, editing and guides to specific types of documents.

CHAPTER SEVEN

CATHEDRAL

BISHOPS IN England and Wales exercised authority over clergy and laity as administrators and judges of their dioceses. They — and their assistants, the archdeacons — granted probate of wills, licensed schoolmasters, supervised charities, visited parishes (perhaps once or twice a year) and organised ecclesiastical courts. They registered documents deposited in obedience to canon law and Act of Parliament.

But the bishop could not act independently with regard to estate and cathedral affairs. His moves were checked by the dean and canons, clergymen corporately known as the chapter, whose meetings in the cathedral chapter house administered episcopal property, the cathedral building itself, budgeting and spending for the diocese, and some aspects of jurisdiction within the cathedral city. Colleges such as St George's, Windsor, were also governed by chapters.

Records of the bishop are termed 'diocesan'; of the chapter 'capitular'; of the archdeacon 'archidiaconal'. Latin was employed until the 16th century, certainly for the more formal documents. A diocesan registrar was given custody of appropriate archives, including parochial registers in 1929, and continues to maintain current administrative files. These include the historically significant benefice papers referring to each parish and a mixed bag of ecclesiastical topics. Older records are deposited in record offices.

Capitular records

Chapter act books, commencing during the 13th century, chronicle administrative decisions of the dean and canons on a variety of subjects, including licences to quarry or dig coal, styles of religious service, probate of wills, lists of lay officials, appointments of chantry priests, leasing of church property and repairs of the minster. The capitular estate archive itself consists of title deeds, surveys, rentals, account books and correspondence.

Bishop's registers

Bishop's registers, beginning during the 13th century, provide an official record of diocesan business including appropriation of benefices to religious houses, ordination of clergy, wills, the bishop's visitations, delivery of criminous clergy, church courts and consecration of churches. From the 16th century the registrar tended to neglect the keeping of the ancient register in favour of maintaining

85

separate files. In certain instances, papers were merely tied together and bundled annually, divided subjectively into such categories as institution, deprivation or collation. In more modern times, files known as consecration papers refer to the process of establishing new parishes and churches in industrial towns or suburbs.

Licence

Perhaps in response to a parishioner's petition, the bishop, from as early as the 13th century, granted a licence or faculty to alter or construct a building, allot seats in church or reserve a burial plot. This type of licence may be accompanied by files of documents and plans from about 1720 onwards.

The bishop issued licences allowing schoolmasters to teach, ministers to preach, laymen to eat meat in Lent, surgeons or midwives to practise, clergy to hold livings in plurality or to remain non-resident. Special registers, certainly after 1803, record licences granted, particularly to clergy absent from their cures.

An Act of 1688 granted Protestant dissenters freedom of worship provided that their meeting houses were registered with the diocesan authorities or at quarter sessions.

The variety of licence most frequently found, that allowing marriage, date mainly from the 16th century onwards. Before issuing the licence, the diocesan authorities heard an allegation or sworn statement averring the lawfulness of the proposed union. Entered into a register, the allegation leads to a bond setting out the names of the two partners and the proposed place of marriage. Only when the bond was lawfully signed and a memorandum written in a special diocesan book might the actual licence be released for conveyance to the relevant officiating clergyman.

Terrier

Derived from the Latin *terra*, 'land', a terrier sets out the endowments of benefices, especially clergy incomes, and the possessions and privileges of a church at the time of visitation by an ecclesiastical dignitary. Drawn up in obedience to a canon or regulation of 1571, this word survey was added to parochial muniments in the vestry chest or filed by the diocesan and archidiaconal registrars as a means of chronicling the furnishings and fittings of the church, the tower, roof, church-yard, parsonage, glebe cottages, meadow, woodland, arable, tithes, mortuaries, Easter offerings, surplice fees, upkeep of bells, provision of the church clock, and payment of the parish clerk. The terrier may obliquely refer to agricultural practices and customs, village ceremonies, location of ancient forts, harvests, famine, weather, place-names, enclosures, imparking, industries, trade routes and markets.

Bishop's transcripts

During the reign of Elizabeth I churchwardens were ordered to despatch to the diocesan registrar transcripts of all parish register entries for the preceding year.

These bishop's transcripts date generally from 1597 to 1837 though the completeness of any particular parish bundle doubtless depends on the personality of incumbent, bishop and registrar.

Parish registers and transcripts were possibly both written out independently from memoranda. Transcripts are thus not necessarily copies of the registers. The register of Walton near Liverpool records the burial on 9 August 1729 of 'Ellin & Anne Bridge of Walton' but the transcript states more fully 'Ellin Bridge Sp. & Ann w. of Jo: Bridge husb.'.

Visitation

In order to maintain ecclesiastical authority, and to correct abuses, the bishop or his representative began to visit his parishes regularly every three or four years, recording his findings in writing at least as early as the 13th century. In 1603 canons standardised procedure for the Protestant established church. The prelate despatched articles of inquiry to the churchwarden before a visitation concerning church fabric, conduct of parishioners, value of ecclesiastical goods and extent of glebe lands. He demanded presentment of parochial abuses and production of licences by ushers, lecturers, preachers, midwives and surgeons. From answers received, the registrar compiled *specula* or surveys of the diocese, parish by parish, in English, of 'things found out' concerning sexual offences, drunkenness, usury, puritanical influence, anabaptists, whores, godless living, swearing, disturbers of religious calm and of the king's peace, non-communicants, charities, schools, church buildings, furnishings, bells, plate, libraries, witchcraft, May-day games and other pagan revels, football, tennis, working on the sabbath and agricultural customs.

Courts

Until 1860 the bishop claimed jurisdiction over clerics and laymen in matters of faith, morals and daily behaviour. His court of summary jurisdiction heard cases and pronounced sentences orally: a man who 'upon the Saboth day . . . did yoke a horse and drawe a boate upon a sled to the great offence of manye', was forced to make a public confession at morning service. More serious cases requiring written allegations and responses concerning adultery, incest, marriage within prohibited degrees, slander, tithes and holy days necessitated the procedure of plenary jurisdiction.

Probate of wills

Diocesan or archidiaconal authorities undertook the probate of wills and related papers from the middle ages onwards. A will dealt with real property and a testament with goods and chattels. Strictly, only the latter type of document was legal before the statute concerning wills of 1540. People with property in two or more dioceses normally looked to the relevant provincial courts in York for northern England and in Canterbury for Wales and southern England.

The prerogative court of the Archbishop of Canterbury claimed supreme testamentary jurisdiction in England and Wales, proving wills or administrations of those who died at sea or overseas, of some Irish people, of people of substance wherever resident. From about 1642 when diocesan courts fell into desuetude Canterbury gained sole jurisdiction over probate, and from 1653 to 1660 was known as the court of civil commission.

Diocesan collections of wills have in the main in recent years been deposited in local record offices, though the nationally significant archive of the prerogative court of Canterbury remains at the Public Record Office.

In 1858 the power of ecclesiastical courts over probate was replaced by a principal probate registry at Somerset House, London, and district registries throughout England and Wales.

A typical will commences with an acknowledgement to the deity, 'in the name of God, amen', and continues with testator's name, residence and occupation. There may be provisions concerning the burial place, 'my body to be buried in ye chirche of Lanthony byside Gloucestr' in ye place wher I have beforn ordeyned and do mad my tombe'. Disposal of the real and personal estate includes such items as 'my Dwelling House lately rebuilt with the work room adjoyneing . . . my silver tea service . . . to the poore of Mellynge . . . to my faithful servant Mary Jenkyns . . . xx^s to pray for my sawle . . . to Marion George Brych wyff my wyffes gyrdyll . . . Item lego Nicholao filio meo optimum equum meum . . . Willelmo Halle optimam togam meam stragulatam . . . lego uxori Iohannis Chamberlen meum argenteum saltseler ycovert . . . a dublett . . . my best kyrtill . . . a ma fille Dangayne mes deux primers et un livre appelle Artur de Britaigne . . . un livre de medycynys et de marchasye . . . j quaterna anglice scripta de proverbiis'.

The testator signed and dated his will in the presence of witnesses. When the testator died, his wishes would in normal circumstances be obeyed, perhaps without involving ecclesiastical authorities, though prudence suggested official probate by the bishop, archdeacon — or testamentary peculiar.

The will was proved following the evidence of witnesses. The registrar recorded particulars of the deceased and his document in an act book, despatching a probate copy to the executors. The original will remained in the diocesan registry for public consultation.

When the deceased died intestate, representatives could approach the diocesan authorities for the issue of an administration bond.

Before the authorities granted probate or administration, officials demanded the compilation of an inventory of the dead person's goods as a means of protecting the heirs and of calculating court fees. As far as time, skill and patience permitted, designated neighbours known as appraisers listed and valued the deceased's goods 'in the hawle . . . the chamber over the Parlour . . . in the seller . . . in my cozen Maries yellow Chambre'. The resulting inventory may have described '2 flockbeds 4 featherbolsters . . . one joyned desk . . . posnett skimmer cresset wetting vat . . . one payre of blacke satin velvet Venetian drawers . . . all the shoppe tooles £9 17s. . . . a nawger 2s. . . . peas in West feilde . . . one harrow a mattock ii plowbeames . . . 4 bowes of Ewe . . . things forgot 15s.'.

Probate records provide a source for the study of household management, including the quality, range and cost of kitchen utensils, larder stores, crockery, bedlinen and family diets. Clothing and furnishing indicate standard of living while books, writing material and artistic ornaments may suggest the family's educational attainments. Objects scattered around, especially in a workroom, probably give evidence of a person's occupation: reams of paper for a scrivener, potions for a barber surgeon, devotional tomes for a teacher. Details of the herbs from the kitchen garden, crops in the fields, animals at pasture, supplies of wool and stocks of timber indicate the family's economic involvement. There is mention of afforestation, terms of leases, value of fields, agricultural finance, drainage, open-field farming, enclosure. The list of rooms in the home facilitates the drawing of a ground plan of the dwelling. A will mentions family and friends by name, the settlement of real or personal property, the foundation of a charity, school or hospital. And from the testator's handwriting the graphologist may reveal some aspects of the deceased's character.

CHAPTER EIGHT

PARISH CHEST

THE PARISH is a unit of ecclesiastical organisation. The earliest parish church may have been sited away from the populated area, on ground with pagan associations, perhaps within a sacred grove or beside a well credited with magical powers, or even inside a henge or circle of standing stones. Chapels of ease were constructed to minister to the spiritual needs of outlying settlements.

Some churches were originally founded by, and continued to be the property of, landed gentry or magnates. In about the year 1100 an Anglo-Norman adventurer, Thor Longus, was granted an area of barren land, known as Aednahem in the vale of Eden, by Edgar, King of Scots. Thor encouraged people to colonise the site. He then erected a place of worship dedicated to St Cuthbert, enriched the building with a ploughgate of land, and gifted the church and its endowment to the monastery of Durham. Numerous churches were similarly placed in the ownership of monastic or educational institutions. These authorities received the profits of the parish and nominated a priest in charge.

A chest in the parish church served as the repository for valued records. Of stout oak with impressively weighty locks, such a 'sure coffer' was required following Thomas Cromwell's mandate in 1538 concerning parish registers. An Act of 1812 demanded a dry well-painted iron chest, stamped with the date 1813.

Almost from its inception the parish undertook civil tasks such as caring for the poor or educating the young. Various Acts of Parliament multiplied the duties to such an extent that the parish became one of the most active administrative units. Reforms in local and national government between 1834 and 1894 stripped almost all authority from officials of the ecclesiastical parish. An Act of 1894 provided for the administration of local affairs through a civil parish. This enabled the parochial church council to confine itself to ecclesiastical matters, as confirmed by a church assembly measure of 1921.

Vestry minutes

The administration of the parish was directed by representative parishioners, known as the vestry, assembled in the vestment room or sacristy of the church. Minutes and accounts, perhaps commencing as early as the 14th century, record vestry business conducted in accordance with traditional practices or in obedience to Acts of Parliament. The activity of the vestry complemented the work of other authorities such as the manor, quarter sessions and diocese, and in certain parishes became the predominant force in local affairs, especially during the 18th century. Substantial householders therefore strove for seats in the meeting, partly in order to keep a tight rein on galloping expenditure and so avoid saddling themselves with heavy rate burdens. By not calling open meetings, such prosperous men arrogated to themselves power in the self-perpetuating oligarchies known as select vestries. In not a few industrial towns these bodies influenced the choice and manipulation of members of parliament to the chagrin of nonconformists and local government reformers. In other urban centres even the open vestry meeting could be corrupted, cajoled and controlled by rich, sinister and self-seeking men.

Vestrymen dealt with a variety of parochial affairs, including highways, common land, relief of the poor, charities, enclosure of open fields, paving, lighting, watching, education, police, chantry and apprentices, but their most important function concerned the maintenance of the church building, clergy, property and worship. Decisions, agreements and correspondence of this parochial parliament were written out — and perhaps preserved — by the parish clerk.

The vestry clerk recorded reception of each royal mandate, known as a brief, for collection of money in his parish to mitigate the effects of natural disasters in unfortunate communities across the land. The brief itself was passed on to a neighbouring parish together with money collected.

Vestry members also dealt with queries despatched by parliamentary investigators, including the papers on charities of 1816 and 1819-37. Vestrymen, their clerk or the parish priest from time to time compiled lists of inhabitants, males of military age, householders, paupers or taxpayers, as at Ealing in 1599, Stafford in 1622 and Cogenhoe, Northamptonshire, in the years 1618-28. Some documents undoubtedly refer to the Compton Census of April 1676, others to enumerators' drafts for the 1801-31 national censuses.

With a view to raising money for the French war, parliament determined in 1694 to tax births, marriages, burials, childless widowers and bachelors. The Act required an annual list of adult inhabitants showing their status or tax liability. Parish clerks drew up lists and deposited copies in the parish chest. However, the tax was impossible to collect. A further attempt to levy money — by imposing a 3d. duty on entries in the parish registers between 1783 and 1794 — occasioned additional work for the vestry. Special record books for taxation purposes might be written out, excluding paupers and others claiming exemption. Some families refused to register baptisms and so avoided the stamp duty.

Churchwardens' and town officers' accounts

Two or more churchwardens appointed by the vestry undertook a variety of necessary parochial duties. Their financial accounts specify expenditure and income: 'from Matt. Woodesons tenement half years rate . . . from William Andersons mortification for the poor . . . to Dorothy More for washing the Surplice 3s. 0d. . . . for making the alter 2s. 4d. . . . for candles . . . for church ale . . . for chalice'. Vestry accounts refer to the bishop's visitation, almsgiving, the parish plate, misericords, paintings or missals. They emphasise the central place in daily life maintained by the medieval church through its feasts, processions, miracle plays and dances. They hint at the impact of the religious reformations on church furniture and worship.

The vestry appointed various officers in addition to churchwardens as appropriate to the extent or population of the parish. These officials included sexton, molecatcher, supervisor of hedges and ditches, horse pinder, nightwatchman and overlooker of the hayfields. In various large parishes the ratepayers of each settlement or township nominated their own officers and required the compilation of financial accounts in a town book. But the most important of officials were constable, overseer and supervisor.

Originally a manorial officer, the constable spent money on such matters as 'delivering the Traine Band armes and cloathes . . . repaireing the town butts . . . journeying to Liverpool conc. Hannah Westall's bastard dau. 95s. . . . pounding cattle 6d. . . . placeing in Stockes 6d.'. His duties were clarified under the Parish Constables Act of 1842.

The overseer of the poor appeared in 1572 as an almsgatherer and supervisor of rogues or vagabonds. The law envisaged 'convenient houses of habitation' for the aged and impotent, stocks of raw material for setting the able-bodied to work, apprenticeship of children, relief of the sick or indigent and punishment of the incorrigible. Few communities invested in workhouses until, in 1722, the law permitted unions of parishes for that purpose. Hospitals and almshouses offered shelter. Their registers detail the lives — and deaths — of the inmates: 'Mrs. Wright died this day at ¼ to 4 O'clock, of suffocation by a lump of beef. During her stay in the Institution, she has been very peaceable, agreeable and inoffensive'.

In 1662 parliament determined to control the settlement and movement of the poor. This excessively restrictive law was liberalised later in the century, resulting in acceptance of certificates identifying parish of settlement of people in transit: 'Recd Abraham Ball's settlement certificate on his Comeing to the towne'. An 18th-century book of immigrants into Northallerton shows the date and parish of each settlement certificate in order that the parish might swiftly retaliate should non-parishioners demand relief. Without such a certificate a person could, until 1795, be removed, whether chargeable or not. Occasionally a magistrate's examination prior to removal provides full details of age, parentage, successive occupations, various abodes and names of children.

The overseer provided regular or occasional relief in money and kind for parish poor, despatching out of town 'common players of interludes . . . persons pretending to be Egyptians' (gipsies) and, until the change of law in 1743, pregnant women without legal settlement. Reform of the law of 1834 resulted in the transfer of poor relief into the hands of unions of parishes.

Overseers' accounts offer scope for study. Some researchers have concentrated on prices and wages reflected in the level of weekly pensions, house rents, gifts in kind, living costs and tradesmen's bills; others speculate on the impact of industrialisation, unemployment, war, harvests, weather and housing conditions on the poor. Statisticians count the number of paupers as a percentage of the total village population or the proportion of bastard to legitimate births.

The overseer negotiated the apprenticeship of orphans or paupers. Although many boys were set to learn worthwhile trades, other children were consigned as cheap labour to farmers or factory owners. The formal indenture sets out the conditions to be observed by each party; the type of trade; the name, age and parentage of the child; and the master's name and occupation. Large parishes maintained a register of apprentices.

The supervisor of the highways or waywarden maintained parish roads and bridges under Acts of 1555–1835. The officer, though expecting four days labour of each parishioner annually, also hired men and women to maintain communications from village to fields, moor, mill and market. His work was affected by the advent of turnpike road, canal or railway, and Victorian reforms effectively abolished his powers.

Scottish parochial board

From 1574 magistrates might assess Scottish parishioners for the upkeep of the poor as a means of replacing or supplementing parish church collections and mortifications. A levy on heritors and tenants supplemented this magisterial fund after 1672. Elected parochial boards appeared in 1845. Records between 1845 and 1929 include general minute books; registers of paupers, orphans, parishioners and invalids; case histories of deprived families; letter books; and applications for maintenance with ledgers of expenditure on outdoor relief.

Tithe records

From medieval times the church claimed one-tenth, a tithe, of the produce of land, stock or industry as a contribution to the support of worship in each parish. Great tithes of corn, hay and timber supported the rector, often an abbey, college or layman, while small tithes from other sources maintained the vicar of the parish. Tithes seemed a scandal to church reformers and a burden to agriculturalists. Hence many parishes drew up agreements under local parliamentary acts to fix corn rents or allot lands in lieu of payments in kind. An Act of 1836 enabled tithes to be commuted, compulsorily if necessary, into money payments.

A village meeting agreed on the value of tithes based on average corn prices for the previous seven years. Commissioners under the Act then awarded a rent-charge for sharing among all proprietors of property. A surveyor drew a plan on a large scale showing every parcel of land, every house, road, outbuilding or stream, every acre of manorial waste or common pasture, to facilitate the division of financial burdens. Each charge was then written in an official apportionment showing the names of owner and occupier, as well as the description, acreage and state of cultivation of the appropriate parcel of land. Three copies of the award, plan and apportionment should survive: one in the parish chest, another with the diocesan or county record office, and a third at the Public Record Office. When the rent-charge was abolished in 1936, a stock was created to provide compensation, extinction of all payments being envisaged by 1996.

Tithe records often antedate large-scale estate, village or ordnance plans and indicate field names, boundaries, surviving strips of the medieval open field, abandoned house sites, an old river course or earthwork, ancient tracks or industrial tramways.

Parish registers

In 1538 Thomas Cromwell, the architect of the Henrician reformation, issued a mandate to the clergy requiring the maintenance of registers of baptism, marriage and burial in each English and Welsh parish. In October 1597 a provincial constitution of Canterbury, approved in 1598, ordered the parish clerk to write only on parchment and to transcribe earlier entries, if on paper, from the year 1538 onwards but especially since the first year of Queen Elizabeth's reign, 1558. The clerk was bound to store registers securely in the parish chest.

In order to clarify the legal position of marriage, Lord Hardwicke's Act of 1753 specified that banns or licence should precede any ceremony. The reform required the recording and witnessing of the marriage before an authorised celebrant. Printed forms from this date demand the names, signatures (or marks) and places of residence of the man and woman; the date and place of the ceremony; and names of witnesses and minister.

Until the provision of printed forms for baptisms and burials under Rose's Act of 1812, details varied from parish to parish. The clerk may write, for a baptismal entry, no more than 'John Parkes 7 Sept'. An assiduous clerk might, as at Newcastle-on-Tyne, continue at length 'July 15 1801 Edmund Reed born 10th June 2nd son of Edmund Reed miller native of Norfolk by his wife Hannah daughter of John Pile gardener of Norwich'. After 1812 baptismal forms required the full names of child and parents; date of baptism; the father's abode and occupation; and minister's name. Burial entries after 1812 provide name, abode, occupation, age and date of burial.

Though Scotland's reformed church attempted as early as 1552 to organise the compilation of vital statistics, few parishes kept the requisite volumes despite further edicts and canons, partly because of the changes of ministers as the country vacillated between episcopalianism and presbyterianism. Some records may have been carried away among their personal possessions by deposed and departing preachers, destroyed by rabblers, or concealed during uprisings and never recovered. Thus comparatively few registers commence before the middle of the 18th century. Indeed some clerks failed to record burials at all before the period of national registration from 1855.

Numerous registers, mainly for the period before 1837, have been transcribed and indexed by national and local record societies. The parish register society under the inspiration of G. W. Marshall, rouge croix pursuivant of arms, and W. P. W. Phillimore's printing of marriage registers up to the year 1812 were both ambitious enterprises of the opulent late Victorian era, indicating the continuing interest in parochial matters even in the headiest days of imperial pomp. A project of more recent days, the *National index of parish registers*, in course of publication by the Society of Genealogists, surveys archives maintained in parishes or deposited in record offices in England and Wales. There is supplementary information for Scotland.

The late Percival Boyd's index to marriages in printed volumes of parish registers, bishop's transcripts and licences covers the period 1538–1837. It is held at the library of the Society of Genealogists in London.

Parish registers are also available on microfilm in public libraries, mainly through the initiative of the church of Jesus Christ of Latter-Day Saints. Latter-Day Saints – the Mormons – believe that Christ visited America after the Resurrection. During the fourth century A.D. the prophet Mormon recorded the history and traditions of the ancient inhabitants of that continent. His writings, engraved on golden plates, were lost for centuries. In September 1823 a farmer's son, young Joseph Smith, saw a vision in which he was guided by the prophet Moroni to rediscover the book of Mormon. Smith was murdered but his followers established a religious community at Salt Lake City in the desert of Utah.

Latter-Day Saints assert that family relationships are sacred and eternal. They therefore search records – especially parish registers – for genealogical information, and identify ancestors who can be sealed for all time into families by posthumous baptism and marriage. The church organisation copies, usually by microfilming, relevant records from many countries. The master copies of these microfilms are stored in Granite Mountain Records Vault, Utah. In air-conditioned rooms under hundreds of feet of solid rock there is space to store microfilms safe from pollution, vandalism and even nuclear attack.

From microfilms and other copies – as well as from genealogical information deposited by researchers – millions of people's names are extracted. These names are arranged by computer. The result is the international genealogical index or I G I, a continuously updated alphabetical index of vital statistics world wide, divided by country and county. The I G I has revolutionised genealogy and family history. The researcher can now consult records from many lands in the familiar surroundings of any public library or record office with microfiche facilities or at a Latter-Day Saints genealogical library. The I G I is subject to human error in compilation. Researchers must therefore authenticate vital entries by consulting the microfilm copy or the original record. Nevertheless the research value of the I G I may be seen from the simplified extract from one page of the document.

INTERNATIONAL GENEALOGICAL INDEX

Country: England	County: Cumberland			As of Mar. 1981		Page 1,598
Name	Father, Mother or Spouse	Sex M Male F Female H Husband W Wife	Type C Christening M Marriage	Event date		Town, Parish
Blakburn, Sibel	Richard Blakburn/ Ann Dinwoodah	F	C	16 Dec. 1774		Arthuret
Blackburn, Sibil	William Pool	W	M	07 Feb. 1746		Arthuret
Blackburn, Solomon	Joseph Blackburn/ Mary Ann	M	C	20 Aug. 1865		Great & Little Clifton

Parish registers contribute to the compilation of a family history and genealogy. In revealing not a few of the traits of ancestors, this study helps us to understand our own condition and character.

Surnames contained in registers provide tentative evidence of mobility and geographical origins of families. This entails the investigation of the homes of surnames and their meaning.

Historical demography

Historical demography, the study of population trends, yields information about individuals, families and communities essential to our understanding of the past in the absence of 'annals of the poor' for each parish. One historical project, known in the textbooks as aggregative analysis, can effectively commence only during the 16th century when parish registers become available. Registers must cover at least half a century, and preferably the entire period 1538-1837, and contain entries for the majority of inhabitants. Villages with numerous families of papists, dissenters or itinerant labourers, people not infrequently absent from parochial records, prove difficult to analyse in any meaningful way. Aggregative analysis involves the accumulation of population statistics to facilitate the study of the nature and essential features of a community. Demographers must enjoy counting. Their successful conclusions depend on compilation of pages of statistics including total numbers of baptisms, marriages, burials; burials of paupers, of infants, men, wives, widows; baptisms of illegitimate children; and marriages of couples from the same parish, adjoining parishes, and other counties.

The exploitation of information involves crude calculations. The subtraction of all burials during one decade from all baptisms at the same time indicates natural increase. The division of the number of baptisms by marriages shows the number of children produced by an average union. The multiplication by 30 of the annual number of baptisms suggests parochial population. This last figure may be checked against hearth taxes, parish censuses and the researcher's own card index of inhabitants or households. By multiplying the number of country households by a notional factor of 4.5, town households by six, a fair estimate of the total population of a community may be obtained.

Armed with an approximate population and an aggregative analysis of the parish register, the researcher attempts to draw conclusions. The population of the canal settlement of Barnton, Cheshire, reached 280 in 1775. Baptisms numbered 43 during the five years 1771-75, or an annual average of 8.6. The baptism rate amounted to 8.6/280 x 1000/1 or in excess of 30 per 1,000. The birth rate must have been higher, because not all children were baptised in the parish churches. Indeed not all were baptised. Although demographers criticise crude calculations from parish records, the figures may usefully indicate trends from decade to decade. Birth rates fell behind death rates in certain parishes. Analysis indicates periods of famine, economic distress or plague when whole communities suffered serious losses. Such villages may subsequently have enjoyed a spate of marriages and pregnancies as a new generation occupied the deceased parents' house.

Baptised	*christian name*	*surname*
13 Mar	James	BLEE
born 1836	Morriss	

male / female / unknown
bastard / twin
stillborn / abortion

Father

name George

residence Truro t.p. ✓

occupation druggist

Mother	*maiden name*
name Mary Ann	CUMMING

mother's father's name John

residence Truro t.p. ✓

occupation confectioner

Remarks George born 22 Sep. 1810 at Truro

Parish St. Mary TRURO (Cornwall)

E.S. I   viii 64   No.

Form used to record details of baptism, prior to family reconstitution

Family reconstitution entails drawing together references to each family from parish records in such a way that historically significant characteristics more readily appear and the concatenation of events affecting the lives of individuals or members of a family may be suggested. The researcher initially writes down, on specially prepared printed forms, relevant details of baptisms, marriages and burials from parish and other registers, before sorting the slips alphabetically by surnames and chronologically for each surname. The Cambridge Group for the History of Population and Social Structure designs and issues the necessary forms.

Family reconstitution permits the researcher to calculate an average age at which people married during each decade; the age at which women experienced their first and subsequent conceptions; the number of women in each five-year age group related to the total number of legitimate births as an indicator of female fertility; the length of marriage before the death of one partner; the interval between the death of a spouse and subsequent remarriage. The researcher in possession of these and other figures for a 17th-century village may discover that wives were apparently somewhat older than their husbands. This had implications for childbearing. One-third of these villagers married more than once, following the death of a spouse, resulting in the presence in certain village homes of step-parents and step-children. This may have contributed to unhappy domestic relationships. Many families lost a parent before the age at which childbearing normally terminated. But two-thirds of these Stuart households consisted of parents and children, the nuclear family, rather than the legendary clan of youngsters, parents, grandparents, great-grandparents, uncles, nephews, cousins, the three or four generations not infrequently pictured together in prints and stories. The population in general was young, perhaps as a result energetic, noisy, quarrelsome, arrogant and impatient, a force for radical change in society, agricultural practices and industrial enterprises.

Family reconstitution follows the movement of individuals as, on average, five per cent. of males and females died or migrated each year. Half the inhabitants therefore disappeared from a village within 10 years, especially during the 18th century.

Reconstitution reveals the life span of men and women. Even after rejecting from calculations infants below four years old, the researcher discovers an average length of life, in certain urban communities, of only 25 years. Records cannot *prove* the cause of death because even in a plague year a man may perish in an accident or as a result of senile decay. The clerk or doctor may not know the *real* cause of death.

Kirk session

The kirk session, an influential parochial meeting representing an element of lay control over ecclesiastical affairs at congregational level, developed soon after the reformation of the Scottish church during the late 16th century. The reformers attempted to restore a pattern of ecclesiastical order based on the teaching of the new testament, with an emphasis on service in the parishes rather than in monasteries or cathedrals; on preaching the word and administering the sacraments; on qualified ministers superintended by godly bishops sound in doctrine; and on an educated laity sharing in the governance of the national church.

Ministers, chosen by congregations, came together with lay elders and deacons, at first elected annually, in the local kirk session to superintend the moral and religious life of the community. The kirk session followed the practice of European institutions, especially of Calvin's consistory at Geneva, and performed essential administrative functions in each parish. Developing under both presbyterian and episcopal regimes, the session remained the constant in Scottish ecclesiastical life during the 17th century.

However from 1575 onwards Andrew Melville, principal of Glasgow University, later of St Andrews, spoke for a growing number of Scots. He urged the adoption of presbyterian forms with ministers all of equal rank and a kirk session of elders appointed for life, responsible to higher courts of presbytery, synod and general assembly. Melville's seclusion of the laity from a controlling voice in church affairs was opposed by James VI. The royal supremacy in ecclesiastical affairs required bishops as crown commissioners to administer the church, and this became clear when parliament agreed with the king in 1584. Indeed James proposed in 1586 that bishops be acknowledged as 'constant moderators' of presbyteries and synods. The ensuing contest of systems dominated religious history in Scotland for more than a century.

In 1592 parliament approved a modified presbyterian system. The Act of that year 'for abolisheing of the actis contrair the trew religion . . . anent particulare kirkis: gif they be lauchfullie rewlit be sufficient ministeris and sessioun' gave legal standing to the nascent kirk session as well as to presbyteries, synods, and an annual general assembly. The offices of dean, archdeacon and bishop, though not abolished, continued in a merely titular capacity for the next two decades but the kirk session retained the practice of annual election of elders by church members.

Following this statute the kirk session became an effective ecclesiastical meeting, functioning under presbyteries and bishops and in cooperation with town councils, heritors and justices of the peace. This moderate episcopalian polity, as developed by James VI and Charles I between 1610 and 1638, seems to have been not unpleasing to many Scots people, though administrative costs and bishops' stipends were criticised. However the majority of parishioners came into contact only with their own kirk session, and the work of this body remained most significant for the daily life of the local community. The meeting consisted of parish minister as moderator, elders 'men of best knowledge in God's word, of cleanest life, faithful men, and of most honest conversation', and deacons, essentially treasurers to collect and distribute church revenues. Strictly speaking, ministers and elders perform different functions of the same office, the former regarded as 'teaching elders', the latter as 'ruling elders'. Deacons in course of time largely disappeared, although the office was revived for specific purposes, as at Forres, Moray, during late Victorian days when deacons joined the session to speak for the congregation originally only on matters affecting the church organist but thereafter on routine parochial affairs. Congregations of the Free Church following the disruption of 1843 appointed deacons to superintend finances and disburse poor relief. The elders were especially charged to 'tak heid that the word of god be puirlie preachit within thair boundis, the sacramentis richtlie ministrat the discipline intertenyit and the ecclesiastical guidis vncorrupt-lie distributit'. A session clerk held office during the pleasure of the session, even though his salary might be met in exceptional cases by burgh magistrates. The clerk prepared and safeguarded session records, sending minutes regularly to the presbytery for attestation, and usually served as parochial schoolmaster and as precentor to lead congregational singing.

Members of the kirk session reproved, corrected and punished parishioners for vices and offences which the civil authorities might feel unwilling or powerless to consider, such as swearing, fornication, malicious gossip, licentious living, drunkenness, Sunday trading, unneighbourliness, unfair rents, rates and other exactions from the poor, suspect weights and measures, and dishonest bargaining. The session rebuked privately and publicly admonished, perhaps in the face of the entire congregation with the penitent placed on the cutty stool. Excommunication might be imposed for heinous offences.

At some time in the late 19th century the minutes of the kirk session of Dyke in the county of Moray were laboriously transcribed by hand from the volumes covering the years 1663–1761. The anonymous enthusiast tried to preserve original spellings and abbreviations, and the resulting tome provides a glimpse into the work of a session and some aspects of the life of a rural community. On 27 December 1663 'Margaret Gall receaved from the place of repentance having satisfied Discipline for her scandall in fornication & gave the Collector 38 Shill' while one month later 'was delivered to a poor woman 25 shill. of the Collection at the Sessions desyre & to a poor stranger haveing a testificat 5 shill:' In 1664 the presbytery recommended that the session 'see that a schooll wer builded for accomodating the young... [and] injoin the whole heritours & elders to meet among themselves for Designing a place for a manse'. A poor boy was given the whole of a day's collection, £1 9s. 0d., 'for buying a bible', an adulterer and incestuous woman excommunicated, the money for bridges of Dey and Spittall considered, a woman interviewed for striking her mother-in-law and commanded to 'satisfie in Sakcloth befor the congregation'.

Although containing irreplaceable local historical material, the minutes of kirk sessions before the 19th century tend to dwell on the faults of parishioners and especially on those men and women unfortunate enough to be detected in adultery or fornication. It would seem that the prying of neighbours extended not merely to castigation of enceinte females, who might become a charge on the poor rate and thus legitimately require public attention, but also to interrogation of any man and woman suspected of sexual relations outwith the marital couch. This obsessional curiosity, together with administration of poor relief and mortification funds, may occupy the major portion of the session clerk's writing.

A typical example dated 1771 recorded the summoning of a woman great with child, required in public 'to be Ingenuous and tell the truth' about the father of her child. As was her privilege she named a man, confessing to misbehaviour on two occasions, 'Once at his Fireside while his Wife was in Bed in the other end of the House; they having Risen out of Bed to Attend the Whisky pot; and another

time in the Barn while She was Drawing Straw'. Much debate in the session failed
to discover the truth of the matter because of the accused man's firm denial. The
wise elders 'Delayed any Further Procedure in the Matter at present, to see if
God in his Providence shall bring it to light'. The sessioners seem to have concentrated on the sexual misconduct and to have ignored the whisky still, which was
almost certainly illicit, perhaps relying on heaven's more intimate acquaintance
with the one aspect of Scottish spirit than the other.

Some minute books, ledgers and registers remain in the care of the relevant
session, perhaps in the church safe, but many are deposited in the Scottish
Record Office or local record offices. There are many gaps in the evidences
through the ravages of the old enemies of archives. Two centuries ago a session
officer regretted that his 'Labour as Clerk for sixteen years' had been almost
'useless'. He sadly had to record that on 17 April 1783 'his house in Archies-
town, accidentally and unfortunately took Fire from a Neighbouring Chimney,
the three Session Books Commencing in 1712, and ending with the year
1782, were... Consumed to Ashes'. All he could hope for, was that
people would ascertain various particulars to be rewritten in newly published
volumes.

The victory of presbyterian over episcopal church discipline following the
revolution of 1688-9 went unremarked in the Dyke minutes because, perhaps
wisely, the clerk ceased writing in June 1689, after noticing a collection 'for the
Irish & French Protestants', until the dust settled by March 1693. Scribes in the
district were wont to hide their heads in the sands during the years of national
trouble. The neighbouring kirk session of Forres followed the example of town
council and burgh court in attempting to maintain silence during the tiresome,
not to say dangerous, period when the young pretender's army roamed the
country in 1745-6. Just after Culloden however the session met again on 9 May
1746: 'There having been no Session Since the Eleventh of November last untill
now on account of the Rebellion ... '.

Until the 19th century local courts and other governmental authorities
functioned in very rudimentary fashion outside the burghs. Hence the kirk session
represented what became for practical purposes the most accessible meeting
competent to hear and determine problems, even of a secular nature, at a local
level, including improvement of roads and bridges and relief of the indigent.
Following a calamitous harvest in 1782, the government directed the distribution
of meal to the necessitous poor of the highlands through kirk sessions. During the
summer of 1783 the session of Knockando, Moray, reported that 491 persons
'require an immediate supply'. The parochial census of heads of household
compiled at that time was recorded in the session minute books: 'Aeneas
McDonald Day Labourer in Bishop Croft, Kirdels Estate, 4 Persons in ... family
... Distribution of 28th July 8 lbs.'.

The kirk session weathered the blasts of the national covenant of 1638
against 'novations already introduced in the matters of the worship of God'
and 'corruptions of the public government of the kirk, or civil places and power
of kirkmen'. Surviving the abolition of episcopacy in 1638-9, the restoration
of bishops in 1661 when Charles II returned to the throne, the upheaval following

James VII's removal from power in 1688, and the imposition of thoroughgoing presbyterianism in 1690, the kirk session continued to exercise some authority over the morality of parishioners, church services, certain aspects of the upkeep of ecclesiastical buildings and finances of the parish into the 20th century.

CHAPTER NINE

TOWN'S CADJET

BOROUGHS DEVELOPED as administrative, commercial or military centres. People gathered at the market, fair, ford, harbour, manufactory or letter writer's desk to exchange goods, news or contracts. Families worshipped in the minster or sought refuge in the castle. Boroughs did not always develop from, or evolve into, populated communities, even by modest medieval standards, nor were towns all elevated into boroughs. When William I, the Lion, King of Scots, addressed a royal charter to men in the north of Scotland about the year 1180, he thought of the burgesses of 'Morauia' as soldiers, administrators, clerics and merchants, scattered throughout the province, in communities which were developing in the shadow of the royal castles of Inverness, Auldearn, Forres and Elgin, only later to be recognised as independent burghs.

Decisions and deliberations of the mayor, aldermen and councillors are recorded in minute books, perhaps as early as the 14th century. The town council regulated the price of wheat, malt or other staples; determined the trading rights of burgesses; maintained law and order through courts of the bailie or pie powder; appointed liners to fix the boundaries of each rood of burgh bigged land; and forbade encroachment on the common good land or town moor. Councils undertook additional duties in obedience to parliamentary legislation or as a result of agitation by ratepayers, particularly in the 19th century. A reformed council administered the market, fair and shambles; town school and almshouse; harbour, gaol, waterworks, sewerage, burial ground and public edifices. Officials put into effect regulations on public health, police and buildings. This work was financed from rates and petty tolls. Many towns owned 'common good' arable or moorland, a source of money for the community, and could call on income from charitable donations for public purposes.

Councils rarely acted precipitately. Town records provide instances of public works coming to fruition only after three or four decades of struggle. The authorities were reluctant to accept additional burdens. Even an uncomplicated request by a ratepayer — an additional gas lamp for a dark vennel, the scavenger's attention to a noisome gutter, a speed restriction on postboys' horses — might not result in action. In 1835 the respected and aged guardian of Elgin Cathedral graveyard was apparently ignored by the council, when asking for police protection for himself and 'his tender spouse' against unwanted intrusions into his home by the debauched attendants at the 'two establishments for the gratification of the carnal passions' next door to the church gatehouse.

Bylaws — ordinances for the better order of the community — prohibit nuisances. The various activities condemned in bylaws possibly reflect the normal, rather than extraordinary, behaviour of townspeople. The historian may therefore glimpse aspects of life in a 19th-century borough by reading these documents. Bylaws suggest that carters and carriers not infrequently drove through 'the streets, lanes or outlets of the town, without reins' and parked their horses and carts at the sides of streets 'unyoked' and 'longer than is necessary for loading or unloading goods'. 'Furious riding or driving' put the lieges in fear of their lives. The populace fell over wheelbarrows on the pavement or stepped into 'mud &c. collected from off the streets' to avoid 'persons with bulky and projecting burdens ... [and] boys selling pies'. Coopers were wont 'to heat or smoke their casks on or at the sides of the streets or lanes' and glass, bricks and timber collected on thoroughfares months before the commencement of building work. Burgesses might walk into a carelessly situated tub, basket, blind, shade, awning, ladder or pole — or be entangled in a rope, cord or washing line stretched across the vennel — or fall into an open sewer — or be struck by a flower pot or kitchen pan falling from an upper window sill or a crowded tenement.

There is indication that privies overflowed regularly — even those in unventilated inhabited cellars — and dung heaps on waste ground and in yards awaited 'the Horses and carts employed in the removal' of manure or insanitary matter well into the warm forenoon. Even then the nightsoilmen slopped 'offensive stenching matter' all along the roads. Inhabitants threw out their 'ashes filth' from 'doors, windows, or stairs' any time of the day or night, and cleaned tripe, offal, carrion, fish and vegetables at the public well. Pigsties fronted the streets and swine attacked passers-by in the centre of town. Dogs with 'canine madness', unmuzzled bears, vicious monkeys, wild cats, sheep with ticks, untended cattle and unhaltered horses shared the streets with nightwalkers loitering or importuning, wanton youths discharging firearms, boys throwing snowballs or making dangerous slides on ice, and kite fliers.

Unthoughtful shopkeepers sold gunpowder 'by gas, or candle, or other artificial light'. Dealers in rags or bones stored insanitary material in shops and cellars. Unlicensed chairmen or porters cheated clients and fly-by-night traders pushed trucks and barrels into the thoroughfare 'for the sale of vegetables, potatoes, fruit, fish, or other commodity'. Travellers set up 'shows, booths, caravans, tents, fly-boats, hobbie-horses, wagons and stages' without permission.

During the 1830s and 1840s towns appointed 'day and night patroles'. These men were supposed to be 'calm, civil, and obliging, but firm and steady ... attentive to sobriety and temperance'. Adequately remunerated and usually full-time, policemen were not permitted to 'keep a public house or sell liquor ... or deal in second hand goods ... '. Replacing part-time nightwatchmen, the constables promoted law and order by 'searching for, detecting, and apprehending, all persons being charged with having committed street-robberies, house-breakings, assaults, thefts, pocket-picking, swindling, breaches of the peace, breaking the public lamps ... '. They 'apprehended all vagrants, when found begging or prowling ... and all ballad singers ... causing a crowd of idle people to collect'. One of the patrol would 'attend at the arrival and departure of the stage-coaches, for the purpose of looking after any suspicious characters'.

The archives of police committees show that the new forces were concerned with improving town life, ensuring that regulations about water, sanitation, housing, smoke, cleansing, slaughter of animals and rights of way were obeyed. They pursued inconveniently situated, or dangerously rolling, sedan chairs, barrels, bakers' baskets, pails or chimney-sweepers' ladders. They frowned on 'foot ball, shinty, or other games' in the lanes and indecent words on walls. They investigated 'vagrants, common prostitutes, or disorderly persons, or reputed thieves' occupying staircases, closes and outhouses.

Canny councillors listed to the 'breeze's boding sound' but, when the whisperings were unclear from government or public opinion, steered away from dangerous waters. Indeed the proud but pragmatic burgesses of Forres in Moray studiously ignored an event as nationally significant, but as locally sensitive, as the 1745 uprising. A burgh in the path of the pretender's troops, such as Paisley, would be forced to take cognisance of events. The harassed provost and bailies of that burgh thus detained hostages and imposed a forced loan 'Which is required to be Implemented Against Six of the Clock this afternoon'.

Similarly the town council in Inverness organised the defence of the burgh during the uprising of April 1719 when the Spaniards actually landed in the west. A cry to Edinburgh in 'our extream necessitie' bore news that rebels 'from kintaill have entred glenelg & the mcdonalds Countrey, and wt the outmost expedition are gathering togither'. From one hundred miles to the south, the provost of Perth wrote immediately to Inverness 'heartily to Sympathize'. This followed local gossip 'publickly that betwixt three & four thousand of the Spanish Fleet were landed within 40 miles of your Town'. The provost of Perth, so close to the restless highlands yet so distant from reliable sources of information, trusted in the power of the British army, hoping that 'all attempts against His Majesty King George's Government shall prove abortive'. The sentiments of Perth were echoed time and again throughout the 18th century as many Scottish burgesses perceived that economic prosperity resulted from the union of the kingdoms under the Hanoverian dynasty.

Meanwhile there was talk in the north that the 'highland gentlemen who hade Children here [in Inverness] at Schools have call'd them all home which gives us ground to Believe they have Some bad Design agt this town'.

In the event the rebellion soon ended, as burgh records reported in May: 'Two of the Kings Ships came before Island Donan Closs to the Shoar and haisted Spanish Colours and Immediatly the Spainards and rebells flock'd to the Shoar Upon which there was a full broad Side Discharg'd at them which putt All their Camp . . . in such Confusion . . . The rebells being thus Surpriz'd The Kings Ships . . . took the Castle of Island Donan with thirty or fourty Spanish Soldiers and one Irish Captain who Commanded them . . .'.

Religious matters featured largely in the official business of Scottish burghs. In April 1708 the town council of Inverness heard from the moderator of the general assembly of the established church 'proposing the division of the Town & Parish into three equal parts'. Before the risings of 1715 and 1745, with the consequent destruction of Highland language, culture and society, it could be proposed as a matter of course to Gaelic Inverness that the bailies should arrange matters 'by continuing the Parishioners using the Irish language under the Charge of two of the Ministers & transferring all those speaking English if not exceeding 1500 to the 3d Minister'. Contained in this division is evidence of the linguistic structure of the population. The word Gaelic was seldom written, Irish being the usual term — though not necessarily implying a value judgment. Johnson and Boswell touring the Highlands in the 18th century preferred the word Erse for the language of Ossian and the Scots people.

Witches worried townsfolk and their councillors, perhaps because these people were regarded as nuisances, responsible for inexplicable deaths or famine, possibly because madness frightened the godfearing bourgeoisie. The bailies in Scotland normally obtained a form of commission for trying such as 'have confest the abominable cryme of witchcraft in entering into paction with the divell Renunceing their baptisme and many otherwayes'. The town could then 'cause iustice be administrat & execute vpon them conforme to the lawes of the Kingdome'. The proper authorities, informed of a conviction, would 'pronunce sentence of death . . . cause strangle hir and burne hir bodie and doe everie requisit in sic caices . . .'.

The Inverness burgh archive contains a document dated 1589 bracketing together the three apparently unconnected but antisocial crimes of witchcraft, pykerie and sorning. Piking is theft. Sorning is 'sturdy begging' or sponging, indicating a possible revulsion in the minds of Christian folk against all fit people not willing to undertake an honest day's labour.

Not a few borough councils grew moribund over the centuries by reason of human inertia, peculation or unbridled industrial and population growth. In such places, as well as in unincorporated towns such as Manchester, improvement commissioners were appointed by Act of Parliament to develop lighting, paving, police and sanitation. In 1833 parliament enabled Scottish burghs to establish 'a general System of Police' by resolution in order to supplement, regulate and extend the common law powers of the old town councils. The new police commissioners acquired powers of watching, lighting, cleansing, paving and sewage. They functioned alongside the provost, bailies and councillors. Populous places were to gain similar powers and become police burghs during the course of the century. In 1900 parliament reformed town councils, which could be served by a variety of paid officials including clerk, surveyor, medical officer of health, schoolmaster, librarian, parks superintendent, engineer, sanitary inspector and harbourmaster. These councils governed royal and police burghs from 1901 until 1975 when they were replaced by the new regional and district councils.

From early Norman times the economy of boroughs was influenced by the concerted decisions and actions of prosperous men through their guild merchant. Members of this commercial plutocracy became free of irksome local tolls, monopolised trading save in victuals, and distributed money to unfortunate brethren in times of sickness and adversity. Whether in cooperation with or in opposition to the town council, the bloated men of the medieval guild merchant made their weight felt in local affairs, as evidenced in surviving records in the guild hall. Indeed, as often as not, the brazen corporation councillors borrowed the guild's headquarters as their own meeting place. In Inverness in 1592 the

INVENTORY

OF THE

PRINCIPAL WRITINGS

AND

CHARTERS

BELONGING TO

THE TOWN OF ELGIN,

AS MADE UP BY

MR BURNET, TOWN CLERK, *suspended 19 Sept 1774*

IN 1755.

GENERAL CHARTERS.

No. 1. A Grant from Alexander the 2d, to the Burgh of Elgin, of the privilege of a Guildry as other Burghs had dated. 1234.

2. Ratification by David the 2d, of a grant given by his predecessors, "Recollendæ memoriæ religiosis viris, fratribus predicatoribus de Elgin, de decem, ( ) Sterlingorum annuatum, precipiend ex Thanageo de Aberkerdore, infra vice commetatum de Bauff." 1359.

3. Charter from King David, whereby he takes these "fratres predicatoribus" under his care and protection, and enjoins the Town of Elgin to do them justice, and to do them no harm or injury under pain of his highest displeasure. 1369.

4. John Dunbar, Earl of Murray, in consideration of the many hardships and devastations the Town of Elgin had sustained since the death of his two uncles, Thomas and John Randolphs, Earls of Murray, grants a Charter of exemption to the Town, of the Excise, or duty of ale brewed within the Town, payable "constabulario castri nostri de Elgin," and warrants the grant under the penalty of allowing the Burgh to retain "contra solidos de firma dicti Burgi nobis debitis," in case they were anyways troubled or molested thereanent thereafter. 1390.

5. Thomas Dunbar, Earl of Murray, grants to his Alderman, and Bailies of his Burgh of Elgin, and Burgesses thereof, "all the wool, cloth, and other things that goes by ship out of the haven of Spey uncustomed." 1393.

6. The same Thomas de Dunbar, Earl of Murray, ratifies Alexander the 2d's Charter to the Guildry, (No. 1, which is recited verbatim in the Charter.) 1390.

7. The same Earl takes the Town under his protection, and enjoins all his Judges to do them ready justice when they complain to them. 1396.

8. Robert the 3d directs a precept to enquire into a dispute betwixt the Town of Elgin and the Bishop of Murray, about the property of the fishing on Lossie. 1403.

9. James the 2d grants a Charter of confirmation to the Town, of all the lands, rents, revenues, and possessions, and all other privileges in general, with particulars mentioned. 1445.

10. Archibald de Douglas, Earl of Murray, confirms the Guildry Charter in the same terms it had been formerly confirmed by Thomas Dunbar, Earl of Murray. 1451.

THE AUGHTEEN PARTS.

1. CHARTER—King James the 2d (already mentioned under general charters) wherein he *inter alia* dispones "per expressum" the Greeshop Lands, &c. Dated 5th November, 1457.

2. Charter by the Magistrates of Elgin in favours of James Petrie, merchant, burgess of Elgin, upon an aughteen part. 19th September, 1600.

3. Charter—The said James Petrie, from the Magistrates of Elgin, of the aughteen part, &c., mentioned. 5th March, 1602.

4. Registrat Disposition—The Town of Elgin to James Petrie, of an aughteen part for upholding the Church. Dated 1600, registrat the 8th June, 1608.

5. Registrat Contract betwixt the Magistrates and James Petrie, whereby they sell him an aughteen part, and he to uphold the Kirk. 24th July, 1600.

Elgin, Moray, inventory of the principal writings and charters 1755 charter allowed burgesses to 'have any Gildrie viz merchand gildrie (Except walkers and weivaris) and ʒeirlie to chuse ane deakon'. The deacon, or dean, of guild remained until local government reorganisation in 1975 a most important town councillor especially in the area of building regulation.

A town's chest or cadjet guarded borough muniments, though neither solid oak nor metal hasps withstood sudden incursions of predatory barons, flash floods, mad mobs or melancholic lunatics. Much of the archival heritage of the Moray Firth coast probably perished at the hands of Alexander Stewart, Earl of Buchan and Ross, fourth son of Robert II, the dreaded Wolf of Badenoch, during his raids on Forres and Elgin in 1390.

One of the bailies of Elgin inventoried the parchments and other writings in the town's cadjet during 1835 and 1836. Mr. Miller, the magistrate, opened 'a Round Black Leather Box' and came upon 18 parchments concerning the burgh's privileges and properties from as early as the 'Charter of Alexander the Second to the Guildry of Elgin. Granted, 1234'. Actually this document has survived every mischance to this day. We can read that the parchment was drawn up in November during the twentieth year of the king's reign and that the grantor was named only as Alexander, by the grace of God, King of Scots. A 17th-century archivist, or possibly antiquarian, however had endorsed the charter with the date '1234', the twentieth year of Alexander II. But one of those testifying to the king's wish, Reginald le chen', described himself as chamberlain. Reginald served in that capacity only for the years 1267-9, during the reign of Alexander III. The charter thus dates from November 1268, during the twentieth year of that monarch's reign.

Mr. Miller also discovered 'In a Leather Bag' documents referring to the town's proper mortifications including the Beadmen's Close on the south side of the castle motte later known as Lady Hill. A beadhouse, originally a building in which men prayed for the soul of the founder or benefactor, was converted after the reformation into an almshouse. There were additionally 'Contracts with the Sang, and Grammar Schoolmasters, from 1566 to 1769' indicating the Scottish burgh's intimate connection with education and with maintenance of dignified worship in the parish kirk.

Charters, custumals, bylaws and ordinances specify the basis of the corporation's authority and the constitution by which the town organised its affairs. The town tended to seek additional charters from succeeding monarchs, confirming rights, privileges and lands, incidentally crossing the monarch's palms with silver, but all in the good cause of burghal independence. The Inverness charter of 1591/1592 confirmed previous royal grants of Kings William, Alexander, David and James. But whereas early medieval documents tended to assume that people knew the extent of burgh property — 'that land which is outside the burgh which is called Burchhalev, that is, what is between the hill and the water' — the 16th-century lawyer earnestly perambulated its bounds, 'Beginnand at the Burne callit aldinhemmere now callit ye burne of killodin entrand in the sey at the northeist Quhilk burne ascendis to a burne callit aldnacreich at ye south eist and fra that as wind and wedder scheiris To ane know callit knoknacreich, now callit carnemewarrane at the south wast and fra that as ye samyn passis to Glascarnacreich quhilk merchis the baronie of Dalcus at ye south, and ye saidis landis of Drakes at ye north and fra ye said Glascarnacreich, northwest to ane well or funtane callit Toberdonich . . .'.

This same charter confirmed to the burgesses the profitable right to organise 'tuo mercat days oulklie vpone Weddnesday and settirday in our said burgh of Inuernes, Togidder with auct frie fairies auchtymes in ye zeir . . . And ilk ane of the saidis frie fairies for ye space aucht dayis to continew, and to . . . collect The customes commoditeis tribute or toillis . . . with all and sindrie burrow maillis Toillis customis and pittie customis'. The profits of burgesses would be enhanced by the regulation of shipping in the firths of the north east coast, by controlling fishing in the Ness river and loch, and by forbidding forestalling, that is the pre-emption of goods outwith the town's mercat in order to monopolise supplies and enhance prices. In days when the administration of justice could be both lucrative and beneficial to those in charge of the court, burgesses thankfully accepted the 'proffeitis commodities and casualiteis' accruing out of the 'libertie and Iuris-dictioun in all veyages of Iusticiarie and Iustice airis and vther courtis quhat-sumevir'. The opportunity to be 'in all tyme cumming Coronellis' permitted local inquiry into murder, slaughter and similar disasters.

Bundles of title deeds including leases, plans, surveys, agreements and rentals refer to town lands within and outwith the walls. Titles to burgage plots or 'roods of burrow bigged land' not only carry the history of sites in the town centre back to medieval days but indicate the names and status of owners and the condition of the property market.

In boroughs, parishes and counties, from as early as the 14th century in some instances, specific rates or taxes on the annual value of property financed such services as bridges, poor relief, highways and drainage. An Act of 1744 allowed ratepayers to examine these financial records, probably encouraging officials to compile presentable lists in bound volumes rather than on scraps of paper. The householder's name and address are shown against the annual value of the pro-perty and rates due. Names of streets appear during the 17th century, house numbering in London after 1767, elsewhere usually after 1847. From 1855 Scottish valuations have been deposited annually with the public records in Edinburgh.

Ratebooks facilitate research on previous occupants of an assessed site. By locating the property in an up-to-date ratebook, the historian works back, year by year, recording changes of householder, address, rateable values and rates due. In order to avoid errors, the researcher must record details of three households on either side of the relevant site, that is, seven adjoining properties in all. The researcher requiring to identify the present address of the home of an historical character commences by finding an entry in an old ratebook for that person. He then traces the house forward to the present day, noting all changes of house numbering, rateable value and, again, three householders on either side of the relevant site. Ratebooks determine when a house was first built, rebuilt, altered, divided or demolished, recording old street, house or place names, factories, shops, markets, hospitals, estates or farms. Volumes occasionally distinguish householders, owners, lessees and tenants-at-will.

Town councils sought money from charities, gifts, rentals and tolls on local produce. In 1722 parliament granted an Act 'for laying a Duty of Two Pennies Scots, or One sixth part of a Penny Sterling, upon every Scots Pint of Ale or Beer that shall be brewd for Sale, vended, or tapped within the Town of Elgine, and Privileges thereof, for paying the Publick Debts of the said Town, and for other Purposes therein mentioned'.

Borough courts heard criminal cases involving assault, illegal trading, unruly alehouses, theft, traffic offences, drunkenness and refusal to pay rates. Magistrates also accepted civil and commercial cases as well as those affecting freemen or apprentices. Special courts administered markets, fairs, licensing of public houses, enrolment of deeds and admiralty jurisdiction. Although voluminous bundles of process papers support most cases, the order book remains the authentic final record of the case and sentence.

In April 1773 Thomas Mason, a hirer in Forres, addressed the 'Hon[ora]ble the Magistrates of the Burgh of Forres' in the hope of pulling the wool over their eyes concerning his theft of fodder from 'the Castell yard'. He averred that 'it was [my] misfortune when ... young to be pressed to enlist for a Soldier, and being in his majesties Service Sometime I was badly used and Suffering loss of blood and other hardships turned me Crazie in the head and being brought so weak I could never Since take any drink Sooner than it renders me Unconcerned for any thing I do Thus my Misfortune attends me that about two days agoe happening to get more than Ordinary drink and throwing off all fear of the Laws of God and man presumtously ventured to ... carry away corn and Straw as much as I could in my Arms in order to suport my horse ...'.

The hard-bitten bailies Dunbar, Grant and Forsyth listened but believed not a word. On the same day they 'ordain him to remain in the Prison of Forres till tomorrow at ten OClock in the forenoon when they appoint his hands to be tyed behind his back and a Label put on his Breast with these words in Capital Letters *A Notorious Thief* and then to be brought from the Prison to the market Cross of Forres where he is to be put in the Joggs till the hour of Eleven OClock in the forenoon and thereafter to be drummed thro' the Town of Forres with a Sheaf of Corn, & Straw upon his back, to which Burgh or Liberties he is never to return with Certification that if he does so return this Sentence will be again put in Execution & he will be whiped thro' the Streets of said Burgh by the hands of the common Hangman'.

The merchants and landowners who served as justices did not flinch from such stern summary measures to keep the peace. Just before Christmas 1719, William Lamb, a confessed thief, was condemned by the burgh magistrates to be taken to the mercat cross of Forres 'twixt the hours of two and three in the afternoon ... to be stigmatized and burn by the hand of the common executioner upon the cheek with the Touns marking iron And thereafter to be publickly whipt throw the Toun upon the back from the midle upward And to receave the following stryps ... viz Twentie at the shireffs gate and ten at Robert Harrelds house, ten at the Kirk vennall and twentie at the mercat cross ... fourtie at the east end of the Toun ... [and so on by tens] Makeing in all ane hundred and fiftie stryps And thereafter to be banished from the Toun ... And this the magistrats gives for doom'. That this punishment would seem to amount to a death sentence may be explained by the fact that Lamb had stolen from his master who at the time was serving as provost of the burgh, no man to trifle with.

The Scottish court of the dean of guild, a jurisdiction connected with the guild brethren or merchant company of a burgh, gradually assumed the duty of regulating the construction and alteration of buildings within burgh. As sole or principal judge, the dean maintained files of applications, plans and warrants to ensure there was 'neither encroaching on private property nor on the public streets or passages'. Dean of guild archives of even ancient royal burghs may not antedate reform of the law in 1892, though the court's activities are documented in certain burghs from the 16th century. Scotland forged ahead of England and Wales in regulating building but Victorian legislation south of the border required local government authorities there to insist on specified minimum standards, especially in urban areas.

In addition to plans deposited compulsorily by local or national regulations, officers of the borough drew or commissioned numerous plans of roads, bridges, sewers, public buildings, houses, parks and common land, from the 18th century onwards.

Cholera outbreaks in Britain late in 1831 engendered a general concern about public health. The provost, bailies and councillors of Elgin immediately issued instructions for combating the 'Cholera Morbus' by calling 'on the Inhabitants to continue their exertions in removing their Dunghills and other Nuisances'. The parish and burgh authorities of neighbouring Forres formed a board of health in November to inspect and report on cottages in the crowded insanitary closes or vennels adjoining the high street where disease lurked, whilst already a committee of public-spirited men had raised money to establish a cholera hospital. The volume of paperwork surviving in Forres from the years 1831–2 indicates the terror aroused in the public mind by cholera. But when the scare passed, the various organisations in the burgh ceased work and in 1836 the hospital even served as a temporary gaol. However, public opinion by that date would not permit a proud royal burgh to be without some medical provision for the sick and deserving poor. In 1837 a dispensary was established. The painstaking officers of that facility registered the names and illnesses of patients with details of the prescriptions and treatments recommended.

Town records also include minute and account books of the water, gas and electricity undertakings; registers of property transfers; photographs and paintings of the Victorian townscape and of memorable events such as riding the marches; and splendid medieval ecclesiastical parchments, perhaps employed as the bindings of 16th-century court or council books. Elgin's gas light company was established as early as 1830 and was taken over by the burgh in 1880. Its extensive archive includes stove ledgers, slot meter stove rent books, penny meter collection books, rentals showing the volume and price of gas consumed by each household, cash books and minutes. The same burgh's official correspondence, which runs from 1754 until 1975, contains tens of thousands of incoming letters addressed to three generations of the Duff family, successively town clerks, who served also in a variety of other official posts, maintained a private practice as writers in the town, and cultivated a wide circle of influential friends. These incoming letters obviously offer only one side of a correspondence exchange, but — like letter books — contain sufficient evidence to enable the diligent researcher to reconstruct the whole story. Town clerks' files — of letters in and out with all the enclosures accompanying the correspondence — are an undeservedly neglected source of history, referring to a wide range of local activity: A.R.P., council housing, evacuation, farming, fishing, graveyards, harbours, hospitals, industrial pollution, listed buildings, military tribunals, sewerage, sport, squatting, tramways, venereal disease, W.R.I., W.V.S., Y.H.A., youth clubs and zeppelin air-raids.

CHAPTER TEN

GOBBETS

Business strongroom

BUSINESS RECORDS include minutes of meetings of directors, shareholders or partners, annual reports, correspondence files, letter books, double-entry ledgers, vouchers, cash books and abstracts of accounts. Some documents conceal, gloss over or obscure certain aspects of business affairs and the finer detail of transactions — and financial acumen is required to extract significant information for a history. Craftsmen's specifications, submissions of tenders, bills of quantities and conditions of contract refer to goods manufactured by or on behalf of a firm. The commercial advertisement catalogue contains specifications and prices, perhaps even an engraving of the factory premises.

The earliest documents in the archive of an insurance company may consist of policies concerning fire risk. Each document is identified by a reference number entered in a register. This same number is embossed on a plaque, known as a firemark, for attaching to the wall of the relevant property as a sign to a private fire brigade. The Sun Fire Office, the first of such concerns adequately organised on business lines, was established in London in 1710. Its records are deposited in the Guildhall Library. Sun Fire insurance agents required the name, residence and occupation of the client; a description of each item of property insured, including relevant remarks such as 'thatched'; the amount insured and the rate; and the date the policy was to fall due. One drawback in searching registers, the lack of indexes by person or place, must be balanced against their value to the historian of houses, factories, furnishings or industrial products. The growth of a manufacturer's prosperity may be measured by the increasing stock in his warehouses, the acquisition of storage facilities along quaysides and the appearance of expensive comforts in his home.

Many businesses care for their own records, though few offer such splendid research facilities as the centre at St Helens created by Pilkingtons, the glass manufacturers. Business records may be located in the offices of solicitors who served as company secretaries. Since 1939 the business archives council has encouraged firms to preserve records and allow historians access to noncurrent documentation.

Newspaper office

Newspapermen in London and provincial towns from Charles II's reign onwards have reported events, advertised goods or commented on politics for the benefit of contemporaries, and unbeknown to the original reporters, for the greater joy of posterity. For historical studies of local and national happenings the newspaper is an essential primary source.

The London Daily Post and General Advertiser, for the period 1734–94, was the most popular of 18th-century papers. The proprietors dared to print the so-called letters of Junius which lampooned the royal prerogative in denying the politician, John Wilkes, his seat in parliament. A catholic collection of articles including science, geography, antiquarianism, genealogy and economics enlivened the *Gentleman's Magazine* from 1731 to 1883. The *Illustrated London News* from 1842 thrilled readers with visions of faraway countries, grim industries, 'orrible murders and rustic scenery.

Although local newspapers before about 1820 relied on national reports reproduced from the London prints as a means of filling their columns, the files of *Norwich Post* from 1707, *Bristol Post Boy*, 1709, Williamson's *Liverpool Advertiser*, 1756, and many others also exhibit enjoyable sources of local history. Numerous small-town newspapers sprang up following the abolition of government levies between 1855 and 1861, the 'hated taxes on knowledge'.

By consulting directories in the reference library, the researcher discovers the names of newspapers which now are, or formerly were, printed in each town. These reference sources include Willing's annual *Press Guide* and the *Handlist of English and Welsh Newspapers 1620–1920*. There are indexes by subject, person or place, compiled by newspapermen, libraries or enthusiastic historians. Palmer's index to *The Times* of London is arranged by subjects for the period 1790–1941. Newspaper files themselves may be read in newspapers offices, record offices or libraries. The British Library's newspaper repository at Colindale has copies of national and provincial papers.

News and advertisements concerning property transactions reveal forgotten place-names, long-dead occupiers, significant former uses of a site, acreage, furnishings, conditions of lease and land values. A typical advertisement of 1832 describes 'all those seven cottages in Lydiart Lane lately converted from one messuage then used as a farmhouse and barn'.

Reporters attended criminal trials for murder or robbery. They sensationalised cases of wife beating or arson in order to sell copy. The paper printed calendars of prisoners awaiting trial and noted their sentences: '*Prisoner* Henry Binham *Offence* on 8th of February charged with feloniously stealing at Newington one leg of pork *Age* 16 (can neither read nor write) *Sentence* 14 days solitary confinement & privately whipped'.

The historian of industry, agriculture and trade diligently analyses reports on cotton prices at Liverpool, the stock market, bank rate, cost of fruit, vegetables, coal, timber and corn, railway construction, bankruptcy, weather, harvest, farm sales, agricultural shows, wages, a colliery strike, iron production and so on. When I was studying the building of the Trent & Mersey canal in central Cheshire, the local newspaper of 1775 offered me my first reference to the construction of one of the long brick tunnels, among the earliest in Britain. In 1793 the *Gloucester Journal* mentioned a patent machine invented by Mr. Carne of St Austell, Cornwall, 'for expediting the formation of Canals'. However, the demand for human muscle survived Mr. Carne's engine, and the navvies were still in work four decades later, not digging canals, but bedding down the sleepers of the new railway lines.

Biographers and family historians discover births, marriages, deaths, obituaries, verbal profiles, speeches and reports concerning local people. Occasionally offering much fuller information than such other sources as parish registers, newspaper statements should however be taken in context and with a pinch of salt. A woman's 'good-humoured irascibility' may be interpreted from evidence in alternative sources as violent bad temper. A Georgian gentleman's passing away as 'a martyr to pain' might in truth represent the death from gout and obesity of a man more fond of his food and his port than of the principles of rational moderation preached by the poets and critics of the age.

Newspapermen report on the arts, theatre, travel, foxhunting, horseracing, boxing, cricket, fairs, bearbaiting and the circus. Their advertisements record naturalisation of aliens and changes of surname.

Illustrations require special care. Thousands of notices relate to shipping and harbours but the very common miniature representation of a vessel may purport one week to show the ship *Danzig* bound for the Baltic with salt and passengers, another week to be the *Maria* bound for Lisbon with cotton cloth. The identical gruesome evocation of a gibbeted body is employed time and again to illustrate execution stories. Even the 'true confession' from the condemned cell or speech from the gallows made by X differs hardly at all from those reported a week later of Y and Z. From around 1840, pictures of actual events, whether colliery explosion or royal visit, may be drawn from rough sketches, memory, imagination or someone else's description, perhaps because the artist was not skilled enough to capture animated scenes speedily. The journalist artist seems more reliable in his drawings of civil engineering feats, public buildings, machinery and scenery when he could take his time. Photographs superseded engravings between 1880 and 1905.

Solicitors' office

Solicitors' offices serve as repositories for estate, business, official, legal and parochial documents, accumulations as varied, and occasionally as voluminous, as the entire collections of the smaller county record offices. Because the solicitor served as legal strategist to the local laird, clerk to the canal company, clerk to the lieutenancy, coroner, insurance agent, building society representative, taxation expert, land valuer, political agent, president of the county agricultural show, militia officer, librarian of the law society, chairman of the debating club and chief shareholder in the mill, his accumulation of archives and papers may become truly enormous. Even if his firm was founded only in 1850, his clients may deposit documents dating back to the 12th century.

The archive of the law business itself, though rarely available for researchers, may consist of bound files of incoming and outgoing letters with volumes of legal drafts of wills, title deeds, law cases, leases and related plans. The organisation of such a business archive rarely dates from before 1830. Because most solicitors and archivists emphasise that documents must be 100 years old before access is permitted, the earliest volumes of such archives are only just now becoming available for research. Lawyers insist that documents referring to a client cannot properly be shown to a third party except with the client's permission or under a court order. The solicitor must therefore examine material before release to researchers, and this obviously demands more time than is normally available to a busy professional.

Almshouse

Through the piety and charity of generous benefactors, towns and villages have for centuries been blessed with charities for education, the aged, sick, poor, orphans, distressed mariners, bridges, chantries and similar public services. Numerous medieval benefactions disappeared in course of time and at the religious reformation of the 16th century.

The solicitors to the charity may nowadays preserve the foundation deed, minutes of trustees, financial ledgers, correspondence, applications for aid, registers of recipients, estate papers, plans and personal files. The archive is occasionally stored in the almshouse itself though more frequently in the solicitor's strongroom or at the record office. Local and national record societies have reported on and listed the papers of almshouses and medieval hospitals, including, for instance, Ewelme in Oxfordshire, whose statutes date from about 1450, and Bishop Bubwith's in Wells, another 15th-century foundation.

Charity commissioners

The board of charity commissioners was established in 1853 to inquire into the administration of charitable trusts. Although educational charities were removed to the education department's superintendence from 1899, other trusts continued to deposit annual accounts and conduct necessary correspondence with the commissioners. Their archive in London includes original documents accumulated by the former commissioners for inquiring into charities during the years 1817-50.

Church commissioners

Known as the ecclesiastical commissioners until 1948, the church commissioners have been entrusted, since 1836, with the administration of property belonging to the established Church of England. They preserve title deeds to ecclesiastical buildings and estates. During the years 1836-1948 the commissioners reformed church administration; shaped and endowed new parishes; and acquired estates of bishops, deans, chapters and other cathedral officers. Capitular records not normally required for current business may have been deposited in local record offices. Central archives also contain papers referring to sprawling Victorian suburbs built on ecclesiastical land.

The commissioners' strongroom contains minute books, files of requests for grants, legal papers and plans of new parsonages, an accumulation belonging to the governors of Queen Anne's bounty. Chartered in 1704, this fund was established to augment the incomes of impecunious clergymen. Another archive arose out of the activities of the church building commissioners of 1818–56. Their minute books, surveyors' reports and correspondence relate to the conveyance of sites for — and subsequent erection of — churches and parsonages.

Craft guild hall

Guilds to further the interests of craftsmen within towns flourished during medieval times. Hammermen, cutlers, fishmongers, bakers, glovers and other artisans drew up instruments of incorporation, a written constitution, bylaws, minutes and financial accounts. Surviving archives of these guilds may be located either at the guild's own archive centre or in the local record office. Much documentation of the London guilds is in the Guildhall Library, though several crafts have appointed their own archivist.

Among the most useful of records, especially for biographical information, are quarterage books, setting out the dues of court members, liverymen and yeomen. These registers occasionally mention members' addresses and the career of craftsmen. One of the earliest, dating from 1440, was compiled by the coopers of London. Registers of craftsmen admitted freemen of the guild as well as books recording details of those bound apprentice survive from the 17th century onwards. The inland revenue archive at the Public Record Office includes registers of stamp duty paid on indentures for the years 1710–1811. These specify the names of masters and apprentices, as well as some trades and places of residence. Boyd's index of apprentices compiled from the records up to 1772 may be consulted at the Guildhall Library and at the Society of Genealogists in London.

Quest and search books record the regulation of workmanship by craft members of long standing and good repute. Documents also contain investigations into the behaviour of members, occasionally on a countrywide basis. For instance, London's pewterers surveyed manufacturing throughout England between 1635 and 1723. Cutlers and coopers of the capital authenticated individual craftsmen's monograms and ciphers in mark books, now essential reference sources for the antique collector and museum curator.

Certain towns supported a guild of scriveners, incipient notaries public. The income of these writers depended on drawing up legal deeds and the arranging of loans. Their business developed in England into that of solicitor or attorney. In Scotland solicitors, until a generation or so ago, continued to be referred to as 'writers' and have always acted as notaries public.

Schoolmaster's study

Not a few schools proudly exhibit the founder's original deed, ancient statutes, minute books of governors, financial accounts and estate records. Under the will of William Lynche, his son in 1574 granted lands in Horsmonden to trustees for the raising of money to establish a grammar school at Cranbrook in Kent. Title deeds to school lands cover the period 1375–1851 and, with the remainder of the school archive, are deposited in the county record office. During the 16th century ancient schools were additionally endowed and reformed, numerous grammar or public schools founded.

In Scotland almost every parish supported a church school. Though comparatively few pre-Victorian school archives survive, town council or kirk session minutes refer to educational opportunities.

In 1801 Joseph Lancaster, a member of the Society of Friends, opened a school on the monitorial system where for economy's sake, older children were encouraged to instruct younger pupils. Lancasterian schools were often of nonconformist bias, despite the founder's dislike of denominationalism, and religious studies formed the kernel of such educational institutions. Lancaster inspired the formation of the British and Foreign School Society.

The National Society for Promoting the Education of the Poor in the principles of the established church financed parochial schools following the Reverend Andrew Bell's pioneering experiments since 1789 on monitorial teaching. Archives from as early as 1811, held at the society's London headquarters, relate to these church schools.

The government financially aided schools by grant from 1833. Minutes and reports of the committee of the privy council on education from 1839 to 1899, in printed annual volumes, refer to many parochial schools in England and Wales. Scotland is included with the formation of a separate committee in 1872.

The Newcastle Commission, appointed in 1858, inquired into the 'state of popular education in England'. Its successor, the Clarendon Commission of 1861, investigated public (that is, private) schools. The Taunton Commission of 1864 reported on endowed, grammar and secondary schools.

School records also include registers of admission, attendance and leaving, scrapbooks, correspondence, class photographs, teachers' lesson notes and pupils' exercise books. Details in the head teacher's log book, an official diary of events within the school, vary from writer to writer, but normally specify staff absences, inspectors' reports and abnormal bouts of illness among the scholars. There may be notes on reasons for leaving: 'Dead . . . gone to New Zealand'; or on the conduct or capacity of an individual pupil: 'J. Macdonald has passed well, but should attend to History' (1833). Older registers contain incisive summaries of character 'Intractable . . . Dilligent but a dull scholar . . . Trifling . . . Sly'.

Quaker meeting house

The religious Society of Friends, known as the Quakers, began to preserve its archives from the middle of the 17th century. The society is organised in local preparative or particular meetings; groups of preparative meetings, known as monthly meetings; quarterly meetings for whole shires; and yearly meetings on a national scale. Each Quaker meeting appoints its own clerk of records. Older documents are usually deposited in record offices, the Public Record Office and Scottish Record Office.

Archives include registers of births, marryings and deaths, minute books, records of the sufferings of members, correspondence, charity papers and title deeds to meeting houses. These documents illustrate the development of districts in which the Quakers became prosperous. The Darbys, iron manufacturers, the Cadburys and Frys, cocoa and chocolate manufacturers, the Gurneys and Barclays, bankers, were among Quakers who influenced the course of British history.

Methodist manse

Methodist records reflect the rise to respectability and influence of members of Wesley's religious sect during the middle years of the 18th century onwards. Particular societies appointed lay or 'local' preachers while groups of societies, organised in circuits, financed salaried and ordained ministers. Methodists engaged in education, charity and poor relief in addition to religious devotion, as recorded in minutes, financial accounts, Sunday and day school log books and correspondence files. The inception of organised groups may be traced through circuit or preaching plans. These name local preachers and society officials, noting their engagements to officiate at worship or preside at administrative meetings. Records of constituent societies and circuits may be located in the circuit safe, which itself is situated in the central church or hall of that circuit. Noncurrent documents may be deposited in local record offices or the Scottish Record Office. The John Rylands University Library of Manchester is a central archives and research centre of the Methodists.

Roman Catholic presbytery

The Roman Catholic presbytery may offer a home to registers of baptism, marriage and burial, financial ledgers, school log books and correspondence of former priests. The influential mission at Claughton in Lancashire possesses archives from 1685, papers of priests from 1757 to 1899, estate deeds covering the years 1662–1916 and charity documents for the 19th century. The archive has been deposited in the county record office.

Registries of deeds

The optional public registration of deeds, conveyances and wills 'whereby any Honors, Manors, Lands, Tenements, or Hereditaments . . . may be any way affected in Law or Equity' commenced in Middlesex and the three Ridings of Yorkshire following Acts of 1704, 1707, 1708 and 1735.

Centuries before this experiment, boroughs attempted to register transfers of property in order to duplicate copies of vulnerable charters, to publicise ownership of land and to ensure the honouring of obligations of feudal tenure. Scotland and Holland maintained efficient national registration systems during the 17th century. In 1663 the corporation administering the drained lands of Bedford Level provided for the compulsory enrolment of all deeds concerning property throughout the level. This corporation was abolished only in 1920, and its archive later came into the care of the Cambridgeshire Record Office.

Landowners, manufacturers and other people in need of capital recognised the advantages of registration, having 'frequent Occasions to borrow Money upon their Estates for managing their said Trade, but, for want of a Register, find it difficult to give Security to the Satisfaction of Money Lenders'. The Act of 1708 establishing the Middlesex registry clearly stated the problems: 'by the different and secret Ways of conveying Lands, Tenements and Hereditaments, such as are ill-disposed have it in their Power to commit Frauds, and frequently do so, by Means whereof several Persons (who through many Years Industry in their Trades and Employments, and by great Frugality, have been enabled to purchase Lands, or to lend Monies on Land Security) have been undone in their Purchases and Mortgages by prior and secret Conveyances, and fraudulent Incumbrances; and . . . utterly ruined'.

The new registries accepted bargains and sales, leases and releases, mortgages, leases of twenty-one years or more and various other conveyances, but not copyhold deeds or short leases. Unfortunately until 1885 Yorkshire registrars tended to mark all conveyances by the generic term 'indenture', which hinders the identification of the nature of each transaction. All conveyances and wills not registered — and registration remained voluntary — were 'adjudged fraudulent and void against any subsequent Purchaser or Mortgagee for valuable Consideration'. Such parties therefore, perhaps decades later, would insist on registration of the earlier deeds to assure their own title.

The registrar charged a fee for copying relevant information from a deed onto a parchment memorial before returning the original to the landowner. Details from the memorial subsequently transferred to bound registers include the names, styles and places of abode of the parties and witnesses; a description of the property; the date; a plan, especially after 1800; and in Middlesex, the type of document rather than merely the word 'indenture'. Memorials do not show the agreed price of the transaction, but from 1885 a reformed system of registration permitted parties the choice of having complete copies of deeds recorded.

The provision of alphabetical indexes of persons and places varied in value and completeness, Yorkshire being better served than Middlesex. A book of reference offered a chronological index to registered deeds from 1885, listing the parties involved and the type of document, but not the nature of the property. By 1914 nearly five million deeds had been registered by the four offices in England.

In 1862 parliament organised a voluntary national land registry. This proved ineffective, except in the metropolis when registration became compulsory. As a result the Middlesex office gradually lost business, until ceasing to function altogether in 1940. Its voluminous and invaluable archive, now in the Greater London Record Office, was scheduled for disposal but miraculously emerged from a depot of a London waste paper company through the action of an alert official. National registration extended to Yorkshire in 1962, necessitating the closure of the deeds registries between 1972 and 1976. Their archives, portions of which nearly perished following a decision to save space by microfilming in 1966, passed into the care of the county record offices of North Yorkshire, West Yorkshire and Humberside.

Archives of the various deeds registries facilitate the tracing of the history of an estate, dwellinghouse or other property; the activities of a builder, speculator, purchaser or money lender; trends in property prices and the growth or decline in demand for houses. The extent and quality of available land, the structure of the money market and the financing of trade through property mortgages also offer fruitful fields of study. The archive furnishes, especially in the absence of original bundles of title deeds, generations of personal names attached to family possessions.

Through registration of deeds in Ireland the authorities sought to obviate malpractices in land dealings and to supplement penal laws against Roman Catholics. An Irish Act of 1707 established one national registry for the whole island 'for securing purchasers, preventing forgeries and fraudulent gifts and conveyances of lands, tenements, and hereditaments, which have been frequently practised in this kingdom, especially by papists, to the great prejudice of the protestant interest thereof'.

The Irish registry accepted leases, mortgages, conveyances, settlements — the major varieties of deeds — and documents involving rights of way, commons, tithes, annuities, rents, game, waters, whether formally sealed in the presence of lawyers or not, by which interests in land were transferred, created or in any way affected. Thousands of wills were registered. The archive therefore ranges wider than deeds registries in England.

Legislation in Ireland excluded registration of leases for under twenty-one years, where the actual possession goes along with the said lease, the sole type of property which the law allowed Roman Catholics to hold. This provision ensured that papists lost security of tenure. Whenever conflict arose, registered deeds gained priority over unregistered documents which were regarded as fraudulent and void. Though always voluntary, registration necessarily became the normal practice and remains an essential part of the Irish legal scene.

Complete copies or very comprehensive abstracts of title deeds, known as memorials, in most instances furnish the nature of the transaction, whether mortgage, lease and release or marriage settlement; a precise description of the property, 'one full moiety of a messuage or house situated on the south side of Castle street in the city of Dublin, formerly known by the sign of the three squirrels ...'; and the financial consideration, mortgage principal, rate of interest and length of loan. Documents specify jointures, children's portions, conditions of settlement, terms of rent payments and family trees or relationships. Indeed these Irish memorials, readily accessible through alphabetical indexes of grantors and lands from 1708 onwards, serve as very acceptable substitutes for the now frequently mislaid original deeds and documents.

The comprehensive nature of Irish registration facilitates the study of changes in property ownership, land prices, rates of interest, conditions of jointures, the occupational structure of the population and sources of capital. The archive is useful for genealogical research. It shows how and to what extent Roman Catholic landowners were disabled during the 18th century. It documents urban development and the history of the land market.

Workhouse

The mounting cost of relieving parochial paupers, especially during the French War of 1793-1815, frightened ratepayers. The rapid increase of population, wretched harvests, falling agricultural profits, low wages, the booms and depressions of industry, even the debates of economists about birth control or emigration as a means of stemming the growth of pauperism, all contributed to the demand for a public inquiry into the working of the Poor Laws in England and Wales. Appointed in 1832, a royal commission laid the foundations of the 1834 Poor Law. This established central government control of unions of parishes of convenient size for financial and administrative efficiency. Parishioners assessed to the poor rate elected a representative to the board of guardians of the union. Each board, battered by a veritable deluge of directives, orders, regulations and memoranda from London, was charged with the erection of a workhouse for the reception of people incapable of earning a living and with the appointment of schoolteachers, doctors, relieving officers, cooks, workhouse master and overseers. Although the aged, infirm, unemployed or orphans were generally despatched into the workhouse, the guardians did offer outdoor work on the roads or pensions during sickness on appropriate occasions. The system survived until 1929.

Records of the unions include minutes of meetings of the guardians; reports on individual families by visiting relieving officers and medical officers of health; accounts for supply of food or clothing; school attendance registers; lists of inmates with dates of admission; and rate books. The Victorian minute books of Helmsley union in Yorkshire recount the drunkenness and incompetence of one workhouse master and the machinations attending the appointment of his successor. A local agriculturalist, John Wilson, persevered in struggling for the top job and his determination may have been inherited by his great-grandson, the prime minister, Harold Wilson.

The Scottish Poor Law, reformed in 1845, facilitated the union of parishes, especially those sparsely populated. Parishes in the rural county of Moray thus united in 1865. The ponderous register of Morayshire union poorhouse includes admissions, withdrawals and particulars of the poor during the period 1865-1947.

Union records are generally held in the county record office. The Public Record Office preserves minutes, correspondence, circulars and other administrative documents of the poor law commissioners and their successors. Much of this documentation refers to the general subjects of poor law, local government and public health, being arranged by counties and unions. Enemy action destroyed the more modern portion of the archive during the Second World War.

Turnpike trust office

From the reign of Charles II until well into the age of the canal and railway, local groups of landowners and merchants combined in trusts to obtain statutory authority for the purpose of improving highways. These roads were known as turnpikes from the bars or pikes that were turned open following payment of toll. The trusts raised the initial capital by subscription in order to finance the tedious and expensive parliamentary work; the subsequent construction of toll gates and houses; land purchase; road building; and appointment of salaried surveyor, clerk or treasurer. The public prints advertised the lucrative privilege of toll collecting for lease to the highest bidder, though the entrepreneur could not exceed charges and conditions laid down in the Turnpike Act. The statute even specified the location of gates along the road.

Not infrequently still in the possession of the solicitor whose predecessors served as clerks to the trust, turnpike records include minute and account books perhaps with correspondence, vouchers, agreements and road plans. After 1813 plans of proposed turnpikes were deposited with the clerk of the peace; after 1822 annual accounts of the trusts were also despatched for registration.

Commission of sewers

A Statute of Sewers in 1531 provided for the appointment of commissioners to administer specified marsh, meadow and bog subject to flooding. The legislation dealt with drainage, together with the building of sea-banks, but not with sewers in the modern sense. Each commission maintained a minute book, perhaps also ratebooks, accounts, correspondence and plans, to record the colonisation of low-lying or waterlogged lands, the existence of watermills and the construction of sluices. A local solicitor probably served as clerk to the commissioners, and on the abolition of the authorities in 1930 may have transferred archives to an appropriate river or drainage board.

Commercial directory

A commercial directory provides information concerning a town or parish. The compiler records the names of craftsmen, shopkeepers and professional men; details of railway and canal services; banks; post office; charities; churches; clubs and societies; schools; manorial descent; and parochial history. Dating from 1780 onwards these printed volumes facilitate the study of social composition and economic activity.

CHAPTER ELEVEN

RECORD OFFICE

COUNTY AND BOROUGH record offices were established during this present century to preserve the heritage of documentary material scattered through every shire. English and Welsh county offices developed out of the department of the clerk of the peace, the officer responsible for the creation and safeguarding of records of the court of quarter sessions. Although rarely in command of sufficient financial resources to equip an adequate strongroom at the shirehall, the clerk preserved large quantities of documents from destruction — even if merely by storing them in sacks 'mixed together'. Often records survived rather by chance than by the clerk's activities. For years records of Suffolk sessions lay promiscuously in a wooden press at the *Fountain Inn* in Bury St Edmunds at the mercy of intruders and predators.

Borough record offices originated in a town's muniment room for charters, deeds and minute books. There in Victorian times an aged clerk from the legal department, an enthusiastic master from the grammar school or some other well-meaning amateur might be given licence to attempt the arrangement of the archive — extracting the more eye-catching items from the files for exhibition or transcription. Occasionally during Edwardian times such archives became the province of the borough librarian, perhaps financed by a Carnegie grant and in urban areas have often remained in the care of the public librarian. The royal burghs of Scotland maintained archives in the town clerk's care, either in the town's tolbooth or at the clerk's private legal office.

The first county record office on modern archival principles was set up in 1924 by Bedfordshire County Council through the prescience and initiative of Dr. G. H. Fowler, chairman of the records committee. Fowler, the author of a seminal book on *The Care of County Muniments*, established classification codes for records and required the archivist's involvement in the management of modern records. Noncurrent administrative material, occasionally required by officials and councillors, and historical documents of interest to researchers, were entrusted to the care of Dr. Fowler, subsequently appointed county archivist.

During the ensuing 40 years almost all English counties established record offices under trained archivists, while certain boroughs also followed this example. Local government reorganisation in England and Wales in 1974 facilitated the opening of additional offices. Through the foresight of some — though by no means all — of the new district and regional councils following local government reorganisation in 1975, archival services were established in Scotland. The Orkneys, Shetland, Grampian, Central, Strathclyde, Moray, Edinburgh, Dundee,

Argyll & Bute and Perth & Kinross by 1981 provided services for the local administration and for all interested in local studies.

In addition to caring for administrative and historical documents traditionally deposited with local government authorities, the archivist offers expert advice to owners of documentary collections. He advises on storage, repairing, listing, access and appraisal, visiting waterlogged cellars under commercial offices and pestilential attics above genteel drawing rooms, collecting a small bundle here from the widow's welsh dresser, dozens of tea chests there from the lord lieutenant's stables. The archivist comes upon manuscripts which are stained and congealed by damp, nibbled by mice, scorched by fire, wormeaten, faded, brittle, musty, grimy and generally nasty. With the owner's consent everything is piled into containers for removal to the record office. There, the collection is officially memorialised in the accessions book with date and conditions of deposit, name and address of the depositor, and a short description of the material.

Conservation

The archivist's *primary* duty entails immediate conservation of documents entrusted to official care. Damp documents are dried in a current of clean air; silverfish and other insect pests destroyed by fumigation with paradichlorbenzene. Thymol vapours provide an effective fungistat while patient staff dust and clean the documents with an artist's gum eraser. During these early stages, researchers may glimpse recent accessions spread out in the sorting room or piled to the ceiling near the strongroom door.

Documents may need skilled repair in the conservation workshop. The old and tested method of conserving paper documents requires flour paste, silk gauze and handmade paper as its three basic ingredients. Canadian red wheat plain flour, with thymol added, is boiled up into a paste in a double saucepan. The conservationist then pastes handmade paper to the dorse of the damaged document in such a way that the new material forms a strong backing and a frame two inches wide all around the edges. The repairer may horrify first-time spectators by sponging document and repair paper with deacidified water until both are soaking wet. But this is an essential part of the process — to neutralise the atmospheric acids which the paper has absorbed through the centuries as well as to facilitate adhesion and to remove creases. Ancient inks, unlike the products of modern chemistry, rarely run or drastically fade. When the fragile document has writing on both sides, sufficient of the backing of handmade paper may be scored with a bodkin and torn away to reveal the original text. Occasionally a damaged document requires an additional covering of silk gauze across the text, with repair paper serving as a frame, though this proves expensive and dulls the appearance. As a further safeguard the repairer employs a soft camel-hair brush to add a coating of size which strengthens the paper. This size is produced from simmering parchment scraps. The document is then pressed and dried.

Parchment must be repaired with pieces of fresh buffed parchment, pasted as before. When appropriate, 'windows' are cut into the additional strengthening material in order to reveal any text which would otherwise be hidden.

The conservationist's basic principle requires leaving 'the nature and extent of his repair unmistakably evident'. He repairs but does not restore. He does not fill in missing words or details on documents or seals, does not colour his paper and parchment exactly to resemble the old. His repaired documents do not disguise the fact that they have been conserved.

Official custody

The archivist continues the line of responsible custodians, requisite for the legal acceptability of local and national government records. In order to prove the unblemished nature of this custody, the archivist secures documents in the strongroom and monitors their use in the searchroom. This invigilation may irk certain readers but removes the suspicion of dastardly deeds practised on not a few occasions in the past by researchers against documents. The apposite case of *Lydeyard* v. *Seyntcler* in 1432 is told by L. C. Hector in *Palaeography and forgery*. John Lydeyard bribed a government clerk to search inquisitions *post mortem* in the Tower of London. Left alone by the official in charge of chancery records, the bribed clerk scratched out with his fingernail the given age, 40 years, of the deceased's nearest heir, one Peter St John. The roman numerals *xl* written in 1353 were replaced by *xl* written in 1432. This change, carelessly blotted, showed plainly to the court, implying that the original document stated *ix*, *xv* or some other age under *xxi*, and that the nearest heir had, in 1353, been under age, a minor, and thus incompetent to offer evidence. Moreover the court suspected Lydeyard's opponent rather than Lydeyard himself of having falsified the record. However Lydeyard's opponent turned the tables by forging letters, supposedly from Lydeyard, and won the day.

Archive strongroom

A windowless, reinforced-concrete strongroom, equipped with a steel vault door, affords protection from the ravages of fire, weather, vandals, terrorists, aerial bombardment and the myriad other threats to our documentary heritage. Temperature and humidity control, the filtration of incoming air to remove dust and chemical pollutants, and *automatic* fire alarm and extinction systems, are the normal features of an archival storage area. The installation of metal shelving reduces the risk of damage to documents by insect pests and fire within the repository. And the archivist commissions kraftlined chipboard boxes, acid and lignin free, as a further protection for fragile volumes and bundles of loose papers in the presses.

Appraisal and disposal

Surprising though it may seem, the archivist often disposes of more documentation than he retains! A vital part of the modern archivist's task is to ensure that neither the record office strongrooms nor the filing cabinets of the employing authority become choked with a mass of administratively or historically useless paperwork. The archivist prepares schedules to govern the destination of records created in the departments. Certain categories may be marked for disposal after a period of years, other items must be individually appraised for retention. Everyone has his own opinion as to the merits of retaining archival material at all. John Booker, archivist of Lloyds Bank, discovered in *Le Figaro* newspaper of December 1980 one layman's suggestion for handling archival material: 'Pour classer ses archives vite et bien, une corbeille à papiers en métal laqué noir, bleu ou rouge'. A wastepaper basket assuredly offers one possible solution to the problems of appraisal and storage with the single determined remedy 'disposal'.

Arranging archives

The entire accumulation of a record office may be divided into two general categories: those documents emanating from local authorities and those deposited from elsewhere, including private individuals, businesses, estates, churches and corporations. The archivist's *secondary* duty — following attention to adequate storage and conservation of the documents — entails arranging and listing the collections to facilitate access for research purposes. Accumulations of documents tend to lie neglected and under-used if owners and researchers alike experience difficulty in readily locating specific items and information. Indeed time and again in the past — perhaps nowadays also — archives were opened only when the enquirer could quote a definite date, preferably a recent one, or an exact entry in the roll or minute book. The archivist's retrieval system is the key which unlocks the door to the enjoyment of archives.

In sorting out an accession of documents, the archivist arranges the collection in such a manner as to bring out the interrelationship and archival significance of each item as clearly as possible. A town clerk's minute book remains in sequence with its companions rather than elsewhere. The arrangement reflects the administrative objects and relationships of each item and of the collection as a whole. These objects and relationships cannot be discovered in arrangements by chronology, subject, Dewey decimal library classification, provenance etc., or by ordering the collection according to size, format, colour, binding, style etc.

The archivist takes account of provenance, the office from which the archive originated. But provenance is not normally regarded as justification for the division of a collection into convenient geographical or subject order.

Some visitors to the record office are surprised that the archivist's catalogues are labelled with the names of local authorities, legal firms, estate owners or ancient administrative units rather than arranged parish by parish, century by century or subject by subject. The archivist explains that the unit of prime significance is known as the archive group; the most basic of all principles of archive administration respects the sanctity of the archive group. This has been defined by Sir Hilary Jenkinson as the 'Archives resulting from the work of an Administration which was an organic whole, complete in itself, capable of dealing independently, without any added or external authority, with every side of any business which could normally be presented to it.' The administration referred to in Jenkinson's definition could equally well be a multinational company or a one-man business, an ancient royal burgh or a newly formed quango.

Before arranging his material, the archivist asks three practical questions. Who created the documents? For what purpose were the items written? Why were the documents found in such and such a location? Let us say that a Colonel Smith of Edinburgh wishes to deposit six letters addressed to the clerk of a parish vestry in Devon. The documents, dated 1826, concern poor relief and were discovered among the papers of the colonel's mother-in-law. The letters were written by a solicitor on behalf of a pauper family wishing to claim poor relief from the vestry meeting. They were addressed to the vestry clerk, who became the owner of the physical objects, though not of the copyright. The papers passed into private ownership because the clerk was a direct ancestor of the colonel's mother-in-law. The letters are part of the *archive group* of vestry records and should be reunited with that archive in Devon, though not without a note of their provenance, Colonel Smith.

Record office catalogues therefore are arranged according to administrations. Each catalogue is divided internally to reflect the departmental organisation: town clerk, chamberlain, treasurer, burgh surveyor, dean of guild, transport officer, gas works manager, burgh court, architect, cemetery supervisor. The arrangement of each department's records reflects the work of the office.

The archivist arranges estate and family collections to mirror the various activities of the household and estate office: manorial, title deeds, estate leases, rentals, financial accounts, business correspondence, legal papers, tithe claims, enclosure, charities, ecclesiastical dues, family settlements, correspondence, papers of public office, building plans, wine-cellar inventories, game books. The muniments of private persons complement the record office holdings of official records. Moray District Record Office in Scotland possesses the papers of Hugh Falconer, one of the leading palaeontologists of the 19th century. This collection incidentally furnishes some lines of verse in the hand of Alfred Lord Tennyson. The office also secured the deposit of the scientific and family collection of Dr. George Gordon, minister of Birnie, who corresponded with T. H. Huxley, Cosmo Innes, Charles Darwin and other eminent Victorians.

Finding aids

The archivist's preliminary listing may refer to hundreds of documents in a single line: 'burgh records of Forres, 1496–1975 . . . architectural plans of J. & W. Wittet, Elgin, 1826–1939'.

A record office calendar offers a description of each document. The following is an example of an archivist's calendar entry for a document consisting of two pages:

Instrument of Sasine

in favour of Elspet Dunbar, spouse to Francis Forbes of Thornehill, following a disposition by the said Francis Forbes tuo ackers of Common Land Called the Sickmens housses . . . lyand within . . . the burghe of Forres betuixt the Landes of master John Dunbar present provest of the said burghe of Forres at the west and the Landes of Calsafoord at the eist the Kinges hie way that goes to elgin at the South and the Comon mearin nearest the Landes of Calsafoord at the northe

Registered 1 October 1660

1 Oct 1660

Each subject, personal name and place-name in the catalogues should be card indexed, though the full accomplishment of this task may remain beyond the means of an office. Because much research is subject based, requiring information on agriculture, education, farmhouse building, river improvement, etc., the carefully designed subject cards become a most essential finding aid.

The archivist provides each document with a unique reference number. This indicates provenance and facilitates retrieval. Although some offices continue to deface each item with an obtrusive stamp in indian ink, modern practice favours a pencilled reference only. Vigilance in the searchroom deters a thief as successfully as a glaring official stamp. It used to be the policy of records keepers from as early as the 14th century to fold each document two or three times, before endorsing with a note of the contents and a reference number. A royal confirmation to Hexham Abbey of the whole of Whitfield in Northumberland, dated 1166, was endorsed in the 12th century 'Willelmi Reg Scotie de Whitefeld' and in the 15th century 'ne videatur quia nihil prodest', probably implying that the document by that time yielded no significant information for legal purposes. Fortunately the medieval archivist did not destroy the charter merely on the grounds of its ceasing to have administrative usefulness.

An archival classification normally combines numerals and letters. The archivist marks by *letter* code the various categories of deposit, for instance, local (Z) or national government records (N), private loans (D), ecclesiastical documents (X). Within the general category of local government archives, there are subdivisions: parish (P), county (C), region (A), district (D), burgh (B), sheriff court (E). Departmental officials include town clerk (A), chamberlain or treasurer (C), dean of guild or building controller (D), planning officer (DE), police commissioner (F), harbourmaster (H), cemetery superintendent (X). A *numeral* system distinguishes types of documents: charters (1), minutes (2), title deeds (4), registers (5), financial records (6), correspondence files (7), court processes (32). This permits further subdivision within the main groups in the manner of the library's Dewey decimal classification. The archivist requires that the code should indicate the archive group, provenance and departmental organisation. A resulting example of an archival reference might be:

ZBFo
C72/969/101

This is made up of:

Z	local government archive
B	burgh
Fo	Forres
C	town chamberlain
7	correspondence
2	out
969	1969
101	item number 101

Readers in the searchroom locate their documents by seeking the archivist's guidance about relevant catalogues and index cards. The printing of an office guide, as in Kent or Lancashire, facilitates the choice of appropriate material for study before any visit. Requisitioning the documents in advance by telephone or letter saves time on the day. The record office library contains standard dictionaries, local and national histories, works on palaeography, archives, diplomatic, chronology and law.

Copying and publishing

The record office offers facilities for photocopying or photographing documents. For more extensive copying, a microfilm may be suggested.

Launching into the publication of manuscripts should be approached with a weather eye open for sirens in the tempestuous seas of copyright law. The owner of a manuscript does not normally possess the copyright. This vests in the writer rather than the receiver of a document. The copyright of a letter written by a famous personage therefore belongs to the author or his representatives, even though the document itself has always been in the hands of the recipient, or of someone who paid good money for the missive. The copyright of a house plan remains with the architect despite the fact that the client commissioned and paid for the drawing. Copyright in unpublished manuscripts is perpetual under present law. When material appears in published form the general period of copyright subsists for the author's lifetime and for 50 years following his death, or for 50 years following publication, if posthumous. The researcher treads warily in quoting from, editing, transcribing or otherwise handling manuscript material.

Research subjects

The archivist is normally delighted to help in the choice of subjects for research, in deciphering difficult handwriting, in translating from Latin, Welsh, French or Scots, and in recommending books for study. The officer cannot be expected to lecture to each researcher on the background of a chosen topic, transcribe extensive documents or interpret legal problems on behalf of litigants.

There is an onus on the researcher also to come equipped for the task in hand, and not to expect too much of the archivist. One young man intent on examining the entire quarter sessions archive with a view to writing a history of county administration before 1889 could not even interpret the meaning of the words 'quarter sessions' and 'justice of the peace'.

Because the record office offers thousands of documents on a multitude of subjects, the researcher should not request 'everything available'. Once upon a time an over-ambitious and somewhat overbearing visitor demanded 'everything available' on farming in the county from beginning to end. There happened to be at hand seven or eight archival boxes, holding several thousand farm leases of the 19th century. The leases provided names of tenants, rental, acreage, conditions of tenancy, notes on drainage, outbuildings and fencing, sufficient for three weeks of intensive statistical and historical investigation. But the enquirer seemed dissatisfied, demanding, with some asperity, material of a more general nature. It seemed evident that the impatient person really needed one document which on one page set out the history of farming in the county, and in plain English. Indeed the researcher had by now little time, the office shutting in half an hour, and he on his way to the pictures. The man went off soon afterwards happily clutching a photocopy of the article on agriculture in *Chambers's Encyclopaedia*.

Quarter sessions

Medieval guardians or keepers of the peace were appointed by the monarch to maintain internal peace in the shires. Documents begin to refer to these law-enforcement officers as justices of the peace during the 14th century. Any land-owner or merchant of independent means might be required to work unpaid in handling minor offences summarily in his own home, to conduct petty sessions for more serious cases, and to assemble from 1362 with fellow justices four times a year in certain towns for formal administrative and judicial sessions. A senior magistrate served as guardian of the records or *custos rotulorum* until the task became honorific during the 17th century and was taken over by the lord lieutenant of the shire. The actual work of writing, preserving and producing documentation fell to a lawyer, known as the clerk of the peace. At each court of quarter session this officer attended to advise on points of law and to write down court proceedings. Various county, manorial or parochial officers and the county grand jury also joined the throng in shirehall or fashionable hostelry. Quarter sessions was organised in England and Wales by the close of the 16th century. The system, planted in Scotland in 1609 by James VI, did not thrive north of the border, not acquiring extensive statutory authority and unable to compete with the prestige of the sheriff. Abolished in the 1970s, courts of quarter sessions bequeathed their records to county record offices in England and Wales and to the Scottish Record Office whence they may be transferred to local archives.

Magistrates were empowered to 'ouersie, trye and prevent all sic occasionis as may breid truble'. At a petty sessions in Scotland during 1771 two justices listened to various reports of a carousal at the house of Robert Gordon, vintner in Elgin. People 'were dancing & merry and were a long time there' before an army captain named Brodie entered and offered Thomas Nicol, 'being next the Door', one guinea 'to drink the King's health'. Nicol threw the coin to the floor or so some said, and it 'rolled to the other side of the Room'. However, others asseverated that Brodie 'addressed himself to the Company and said you know Lads I am a recruiting officer & pulled out his purse & gave Thos Nicol the Guinea as above deponed . . . That next morning the Deponent at the desire of Lieut Brodie called Thomas Nicol into the Room where the Lieut was & wished him Joy of being a Soldier and Nicol answered he did not think he was'. The magistrates therefore faced the tricky question of whether or not Nicol accepted the coin, even for a moment, or had immediately rejected the recruiting officer's stratagem. Wisely the justices 'Refer the Consideration thereof to the quarter Sessions'.

Magistrates in court assembled were charged to uphold the king's peace by taking cognisance of theft, trespass, riot, debt, nonpayment of rates, witchcraft, drunkenness and similar matters. The most serious offences, such as murder, treason or bigamy, were normally reserved to other authorities, though justices might take part in initial investigation or apprehension.

Petitions, recognisances, indictments, presentments and similar legal documents were offered to the clerk of the peace at the commencement of each quarter session to facilitate the completion of a schedule of proceedings for the attention of the justices. During the court's sittings the clerk or his deputy would write memoranda of proceedings and decisions for eventual fair copying into a minute book or session roll. The final record of the magistrates in each case appeared in formal order books which additionally contained precedents and recommendations for future action.

The village constable's presentments are preserved in the sessions bundle. This officer was expected to report in the following manner: 'Richard Miller and Mary Lee recusants do absent themselves from the church . . . one vagrant put in Stocks and whippt till his body be bloodied . . . William Hadfield a slaunderer & incloser of commouns . . . keeping a nunrulie tippling-house . . . moving boundary stones . . . beinge the sabaothe day did play an vnlawfull game called the fote bale whereon grew bludshedd'.

People were subsequently indicted for such offences as 'stealing four loaves . . . for erecting a cottage on the waste without layinge foure acres thereto . . . for assault . . . being a commoun scold . . . a contentious man . . . misbehaveing her tongue'. During the early part of the 17th century, witchcraft bedeviled the peace of many a peaceful village when those defamed were dragged to court for casting spells, giving the evil eye, poisoning sheep, and communing with satanic forces.

The justices examined suspects, witnessed statements and heard opposing deponents. In 1750 certain magistrates listened to the pleas of John Murdoch in Tomcock against his neighbour John Grant for allowing cattle to stray on land tacked to Murdoch by the Laird of Altyre. 'And whenever I Challenge him for his Cattle Then he gives me this most provokeing Language . . . by frequently Calling me a Damned Lyar and a Damned Develish Dog, and Severall other Scandalising Terms . . .'. Although straying cattle could not be disregarded, quarrels among neighbours left the magistrates uninterested, and often alienated. They prevaricated and permitted cases to lapse with the excuse of continuing investigations.

A decade later magistrates found themselves judging a clash of personalities on board the ship *Charming Jannet*, 'ordered to proceed from Leith to Findhorn where She now ly's with a Cargo of Salt from Lisbon'. The mate, George Provand, deserted in the Moray port and 'absolutely refuses to go to London w[i] t[h] a Loading of Corn he has now on board'. John Brown, as master, was 'put to great Straits for such a necessary hand to Navigate the Said Ship'. He must indeed have been desperate in demanding Provand's continuing service, despite the fact that the mate 'not only gave him bad Language on Shoar and aboard the Ship but gave him a blow on the face'. Naturally Provand claimed that the master 'had used him ill on board . . . he Considered himself in danger of his life'. The justices, facing an immediately difficult decision, especially in view of the perishable nature of the cargo, consigned the mate to gaol until he agreed to serve out his voyage, during which the master should treat his employee 'Civilly & Discreetly'. The case exemplifies the sensible pragmatic approach of many justices of the peace in not panicking, not punishing vindictively or unreasonably – and in knowing how to compromise.

In 1777 one bench considered cases involving a labourer's refusal to honour a half year's contract of service and his subsequent 'insolence in Court . . . in Speaking in Such an unbecomeing way' but he was allowed to plead mitigating circumstances '. . . Seeing I am in a bad State of health'; a miller 'not having wrought at the roads on Saturday last . . . he refused to part with his Ax' when confronted by the constable; a tenant 'for not paying and delivering . . . the Victual and money rent and the number of Wedders, Kidds hens and Eggs or the converted prices thereof and for not implementing and fulfilling the whole other Obligations . . .'. These men were incarcerated in the burgh tolbooth until agreeable to paying the fine or debts.

Magistrates meted out sentences of varying severity, perhaps depending more on the state of their livers or digestions, or on the smooth-tongued eloquence of a defendant, than on a strict regard to the facts or justice of the case. Summary punishments, including fines or duckings, were not uncommon, possibly because inexpensive to county ratepayers. Certainly the magistrates hesitated to lock a person in prison, the cost of food and gaoler's attention being so high. At the Bedford sessions of April 1658 a village butcher, then serving as town constable, paid a fine of one shilling following indictment for insulting magisterial authority by asseverating: 'I care not a fart for any Justice of the peace in England'. In certain cases the justices ordered a few hours in the stocks, whipping, branding, or banishment from the district.

From the 16th century onwards, government and parliament expected justices of the peace to accept burdensome administrative duties such as relief of the poor; supervision of religious conventicles and recusants; control of markets and fairs; maintenance of roads and bridges; answering of requests for information by the privy council; upkeep of shirehall, gaol and house of correction; supervision of asylum and courthouse; supervision of regulations on disease of animals; licensing of public houses; provision of militia stores; superintendence of village constables and later of the county constabulary. For such purposes the magistracy raised and administered the county rate.

Justices appointed appropriate 'persons of Skill' to investigate commercial or agricultural claims such as damage to goods belonging to merchants in their locality. In 1780 one group of businessmen 'commissioned from different Merchants in Rotterdam for the Petitioners account and Risque certain quantities of Flax and Flax-seed Clover seed and Mader a board the Brigantine called the Friendship of Findhorn bound for . . . Inverness . . . [but] the said Ship on her homeward Voyage . . . met with such extraordinary and tempestuous Weather that she shiped large quantities of Sea Water, and the same getting into the Hold part of the Cargo received much Damage'. The petitioners obviously traded as a temporary partnership to spread the cost and risk of chartering a vessel because each man's purchases bore an identifying mark: 'Alex^r Forsyth Six Hogsheads Flax seed and two Casks Clover seed under his Mark A.F.'. The invoices and bills of loading were examined 'for the behoof of the Insurermasters' by qualified flaxdressers appointed by the justices.

The office of the clerk of the peace additionally accepted the deposit, enrolment and registration of records. In England as early as 1536 deeds of bargain and sale were to be enrolled with the county clerk, wherever the property lay, or with one of the Westminster courts. For legal and financial reasons most people avoided this provision, though a number of deeds passed through for enrolment. Under an Act of 1717 wills and deeds of Roman Catholics were enrolled as a means of identifying possibly disaffected families whose names and properties had already been registered following the 1715 uprising.

Local Acts of Parliament required the deposit of awards of corn rents accompanied by plans of parishes during the 19th century.

The enclosure of open fields or common lands under Local and General Acts of Parliament necessitated an agreement, award and plan of the relevant property or parish. The Enclosure Act specified where the documentation should be deposited and, from the 17th century onwards, frequently nominated the clerk of the peace, but perhaps also one of the courts at Westminster, the parish chest or registry of deeds. Sessional papers of the House of Commons contain a list or return of enclosure awards, compiled in the session 1904 (50) lxxviii, and a similar register of Enclosure Acts of Parliament up to the session 1914 (399) lxvii.

Enclosure documents indicate the ancient landscape and distribution of land ownership in the village, occasionally the only such source before the production of tithe plans. The plans delineate the recently enclosed fields and farms while the awards serve as basic title deeds for all affected property. In areas of the country where, hitherto, open unfenced arable dominated the scenery new straight roads with grassy verges gave access to fashionable farmhouses, scattered in an untraditional pattern of walled square fields. The nucleated village, once residence of most families engaged in farming, tended to become the home merely of agricultural labourers and craftsmen. The town moor, formerly an economic asset shared by many townsfolk, was pegged out for suburban development, for the endowment of schools or charities, and for public quarrying. The awards provide the ultimate authority for the course and extent of highways, footpaths, drainage ditches, hedges and boundaries of farms.

Under an Act of 1786 returns of parochial charities were demanded by parliament through the registry of the clerk of the peace. That officer accepted the opportunity of preserving copies of these statements. From 1812 he also began to register memorials concerning the property of every charity within his county and, from 1853, to receive annual statements of account. His files from 1793 embraced the constitutions of friendly, sick, burial and building societies. Annual membership lists of lodges of freemasons were deposited under the Unlawful Societies Act of 1799. These extensive rolls indicate the migration of craftsmen and professional men during the industrial expansion of the early 19th century — mainly to the cities. The St John's operative lodge of masons, Rothes, Moray, in 1829 records the membership of a mason gone to Glasgow, a shoe-maker to Aberdeen and a writer — a solicitor — to Edinburgh. Rules of savings banks and annuity societies were deposited from 1817.

Under an Act of 1824 the clerk of the peace served as clerk of the court of insolvent debtors for his county. Following investigation, he memorialised details of their estates, collecting financial journals and inventories belonging to the businessmen. A complementary archive of the court of bankruptcy, dating from 1710, held at the Public Record Office contains registers, orders and depositions about persons, estates and goods. Bankruptcy papers are especially useful for writing a history of manufacturing industry during periods of commercial depression.

During the early years of the French revolutionary war parliament required justices of the peace to demand lists, from every parish, of men for various branches of the armed forces. This duty had for centuries been imposed upon local landowners, a most unpopular task involving tact, firmness and the qualities of 'a Daniel come to judgment'.

Between 1696 and 1832 village constables prepared lists of men qualified to serve on juries. The documents, indicating the name, abode, age and occupation, were returned to the clerk of the peace for safe keeping.

For the purpose of preserving game, the lord of each manor registered the name of his gamekeeper with the clerk of the peace. Numerous Acts protected the landowner's privileges, and this legislation was consolidated by an Act of 1831.

Magistrates licensed victuallers from 1552 and itinerant sellers of corn, fish, cheese or butter, known as badgers, from 1563. Each appellant entered into a recognisance of good behaviour. These bonds form an annual register of names of alehouses, sureties and victuallers. From 1780 until 1828 original bonds were preserved, setting out all the conditions specified by the licensing justices. Scots licensing magistrates ensured that the excise duty on retailing ale, beer and other liquors was not avoided. They required each publican to pay for a licence, costing 20s. 0d. annually in 1775, 'to keep an Ale-house, Tippling-house, or Victualing-house there, and no where else . . . to utter, sell and dispose of all kinds of Victuals, Beer, Ale or other exciseable Liquors by Retail'. In 1797 one James Gow or Smith was granted a licence to retail ale, beer or other British liquors free of duty at Bridgend of Dullnan, 'a Decent regular Victualing house usefull for accomodating all foot Travellers as well as Military'. The inn lay near the river crossing on the strategic 'publick or Millitary Roadside' between Fort

George and Stirling. The landlord may have anglicised his surname from Gow (a Gaelic word meaning 'smith') to Smith to please his English customers.

In 1692 a tax was imposed on real estate, tithes, public offices, shops, carriages and other items to raise money for the French War. Commissioners surveyed and valued property, relying mainly on the annual value of land. From this valuation the government required a varying rate from year to year. Commissioners, being influential landowners and magistrates, not infrequently filed parish assessments in their own estate records between 1692 and 1780, whence many have journeyed to the 'private deposit' section of the record office. The information in land taxes during these early decades might be as informally arranged as in this 1715 assessment: 'John Hobson for new house at Shaw-heath 2s. 3½d.'.

An Act of 1780 required that no man should vote at a county parliamentary election unless assessed to the land tax. This rule necessitated the deposit of a copy of the assessment for each parish annually with the clerk of the peace, setting out names of proprietor and occupier, description of the property, and sum assessed. The land tax became a perpetual charge in 1798, subject to redemption for a lump sum, and that year's assessment was carefully preserved as a standard. Deposit with the clerk of the peace ceased when electoral lists were introduced in 1832.

Land tax assessments enable the diligent researcher to build up a record of the parish's proprietors and occupiers; documentation on the division or amalgamation of properties; the appearance of new houses, canals or factories; the comparative extent of each holding; and of properties owner-occupied or of estates held by absentee landlords.

An electoral list of people qualified to vote in parliamentary elections specifies each person's name, place of abode, nature of qualification and location of the property. An example might be 'Thomas Cross, Church Hulme, owner of freehold houses at Tunnel Road, Barnton'. These registers date from 1832 onwards.

An Act of Parliament passed in 1696 required returning officers to deliver a copy of the poll to electors or contestants in order to establish claims. Such poll-books were deposited for public inspection from 1711. Pollbooks facilitate an analysis of local voting patterns and pressure groups; the influence of employers or priests; the impact of Irish immigration or industrial depression. In volumes providing occupations or addresses, the commercial or geographical distribution of votes may prove a significant study.

Annual window tax returns between 1696 and 1851 show names and residences of taxpayers with the number of windows in the premises. Tyburn tickets — certificates of exemption from offices for bringing a felon to justice — were enrolled from 1699. Certificates were issued to the owners of sporting dogs and guns from 1784-5 and to those paying one guinea for use of hairpowder from 1795.

Acts of 1744 and 1819 regulated the despatch of vagrants home to their legal settlements, perhaps to counties in faraway Scotland and Ireland. Justices registered the names of vagrants, their wives, children and other dependants, adding memoranda on the previous activities of these problem families. The magistrates filed details about convictions of recusants, tanners not paying the required duty, beggars, swearers of profane oaths, pawnbrokers and juvenile offenders. Documentation on the transportation of convicts dates mainly from the period 1790–1867 though from as early as the 17th century criminals, political subversives and religious nonconformists were sent to the plantations as indentured servants.

The clerk of the peace received a plan or map of each intended cut, canal, aqueduct or navigation within the county in accordance with standing orders of the House of Commons first issued in 1792. A deposited plan of a waterway, suitably referenced, relates to a book of reference showing the names of owners and occupiers of parcels of land along the route of the navigation. The clerk subsequently received documentation relating to docks, gasworks, railways, piers, roads, town improvements, tramways and other public undertakings.

From 1795 to 1871 all boats and barges exceeding thirteen tons on inland navigations required registration. The clerk of the peace recorded the name of each master and owner, delineating the boat's usual trade route. From 1822 he also received annual accounts of turnpike trusts.

From 1697 a landowner desiring to divert or close a highway was bound to approach quarter sessions. Documentation, including plans from 1773, may explain the course of a modern road as it meanders around the wall of an ancient estate or the existence of what is now but a footpath following the line of a former highway through a nobleman's park.

Men holding military or civil office were supposed to inform the sessions of their oaths and declarations concerning the sacraments of the established church, transubstantiation, the act of settlement, abjuration of the Stuart dynasty and allegiance to the Hanoverians. Such documents date variously from 1673 into the 19th century.

Protestant dissenters registered their meeting houses with the clerk of the peace after 1689. Papists registered from 1791. In 1829 the commons sought from each parish 'the number of places of worship, not of the Church of England, distinguishing as far as possible of what sect or persuasion, and the total number of each sect'. Original returns from each parish were lodged with the clerk of the peace.

Commissioners of supply

In the Scottish shires landowners and merchants, wearing their hats as commissioners of supply, undertook administrative duties concerning education, highways, gaols, poor relief and public health. Minute books from as early as the 18th century show that the commissioners made decisions of significance to the community — rather as the justices of the peace did in England. In Elginshire the Duffs acted as clerks to the commissioners, preserving correspondence in their own office files, together with records of other authorities for which the family worked as early as 1754. Much of this material was at some date tied up in hessian sacks labelled 'destroy', and dumped in a grimy basement. From this limbo, the district archivist rescued 130 linear feet of records in 1975. Among the commission documents are claims by militiamen, particularly during the period 1811–13, for payment of allowances to their families, including certificates by the commanding officer, minister and members of the kirk session, and the order by a justice of the peace to the treasurer of the kirk session for payment. These record the name of the county militia in which the man was serving, the maiden name of his wife, the date of their marriage, the names and ages of their children, place of residence, amount of weekly allowance, and the man's signature or mark.

Minute books of the Elginshire commissioners indicate the state of people cast into prison for theft, assault, debt or other causes. In 1822 the commissioners received a report on gaols at Elgin and Forres from a committee appointed under an Act of 1617 requiring 'where thair ar anye Gaillis and prisoun housses within anye burgh that þe same may be keipt vp and not suffered to decay'. Forres tolbooth gaol stood in the middle of the principal street. The bartizan was 'so much off from the Plummet that it threatens to Tumble down, and demolish some of the adjoining Houses, at no very distant period . . . The Black Hole or ground Floor of the Tower, is so great a nuisance, and so much filled with filth of every kind and human Excrement that it was found impossible to Inspect it. The smell was strong evidence of the impurity contained within, and as the entrance to it was immediately adjoining to the room where debtors are confined . . . the Effect on their Health and Spirits may readily be inferred . . . certainly not suitable to the improved state of society in which we have the happiness to live . . . The Cells damp, cold and nasty No places appropriated for easing nature. No regular attendants . . . paid to sweep . . . or to remove the filth and nastiness . . . Criminals Cell . . . has one window without glass, and a fire place, it is floored with Turf and ceiled with wood which is very rotten without Plaster, there are iron Fetters attached to the Wall'.

The records indicate that in such conditions prisoners were driven to somewhat desperate straits to render their distressing circumstances more bearable, or to secure some temporary oblivion from their squalid environment. A certain lieutenant, confined for debt in that same burgh tolbooth, bribed boys of the town to fetch him spirits, not a glass or mug but a full pail, and this during the hours of divine service. It seems to have been the timing of the escapade rather than the quantity of liquid that upset the worthy magistrates when they later heard the story. The local historical significance of the 1822 report lies in its date, a period of general dissatisfaction with insanitary towns and living conditions, hardly conducive to human progress in the most powerful kingdom on earth.

County council headquarters

Almost all the administrative burdens settled on the shoulders of justices of the peace and commissioners of supply over several generations were removed when an Act in 1888 created county and county borough councils.

County archives consist of minute books of the council and its committees, correspondence files, title deeds, motor vehicle registration and licensing registers under the 1903 Act, valuations, abstracts of accounts, building control and planning files, public health papers, waterworks plans and social work registers, reflecting the scope of the county council's activities from local government reform of 1889 until a similar reorganisation during the 1970s in England, Wales and Scotland.

CHAPTER TWELVE

PALAEOGRAPHY AND DIPLOMATIC

PALAEOGRAPHY, a branch of the science of documentary criticism, concerns the reading and interpreting of old documents, the influence of handwriting and illumination schools, the distribution of writing styles, various rules of calligraphy and scribal conventions, and the dating or origin of literary and ecclesiastical texts. The word itself means 'old writing'.

Until the 13th century cloistered monks in their scriptorium inscribed *annals*, which may be defined as summaries of events in local and national life, and *chronicles* or narratives of world history from creation onwards. The medieval chronicler, lacking documentary or authentic sources for research into past centuries, accomplished his task by reworking, adapting and improving the earlier histories and annals including legends, apocryphal tales and fables. He even deliberately composed or concocted stories. But in writing of events within living memory and in his own locality, he preserved much significant and genuine information. The classic compilation, the Anglo–Saxon Chronicle, was commenced in 892 probably at the instigation of that most learned of early English kings, Alfred. The text varied from monastery to monastery because the monks at each house desired to mingle their own local history within a national context. Additionally, certain houses aimed to protect the traditions of the English people against Norman conquerors. Peterborough monks boldly continued their account until 1156, nearly a century after the battle of Hastings.

The biography of ancient British kings and of Britain's national hero, Arthur, supposedly discovered in Brittany and allegedly imported from France by an Oxford cleric, was in fact the literary invention of Geoffrey of Monmouth. Contemporaries were not deceived regarding Geoffrey's candid and incredible romance, a classic of medieval literature rather than a work of history. But the Arthurian epic influenced politicians and poets for centuries. The first Tudor king, Henry VII, named his eldest son Arthur. The poet Spenser based his *Faerie Queene*, written in homage to Elizabeth I, firmly on the Arthurian legend, in tribute to the enduring vigour of Geoffrey's ageless myth and much vaunted masterpiece.

Monks who invented or elaborated stories for monastic annals were tempted to extend their forgeries to the drawing up of fictitious charters and other documents granting privileges to their own religious houses. Doubtless such forgers had no moral qualms. They believed they acted for the glorification of God and all his saints by emphasising the temporal power of the holy catholic church. By the exercise of such religious diligence, cathedrals, abbeys and charitable institutions gained title deeds to lands and privileges, which undoubtedly rightfully belonged to the church, but whose ownership had not previously been authenticated in writing. Forgers carefully and religiously completed the written evidence which previous generations had neglected. The transfer of property and privileges occurred in a public solemnisation before being recorded in such words as 'know that I *have* given, granted . . . and by this my present charter confirm'. The actual document could be written a week or month after the ceremony. A religious man might argue: if a month, why not a year, if a year, why not a century, following the investiture, provided that the charter honoured the donor's true wish and offered the donee his just deserts?

Some charters of Edward the Confessor and William the Conqueror, circulating during the 13th century, appear to have been forged 100 years earlier. Even William I's own religious foundation at Battle Abbey felt obliged to organise the production of deeds when written land titles were considered essential about the middle of the 12th century. In previous centuries people held property by dint of conquest, custom, word of mouth or jury inquisition. English lawyers eventually accepted this absence of written evidence in allowing the year 1189 as the practical limit of legal memory. Statements of individuals, juries or groups, such as the view of frankpledge, were still heard in the reign of Richard I but courts increasingly sought the production of written evidence of charters, diplomas, letters patent or inquisitions. This is emphasised by the creation and survival of charters in family collections, mainly from 1170 onwards.

But respectable, or more correctly not unrespectable, forgery was inspired by loyalty to the church rather than desire for monetary gain, though scribes themselves doubtless received some remuneration for work done. Owners of muniments would require to answer in the afterlife for neglecting any exertion for the prestige of holy church. Copying of charters may be regarded as akin to the praiseworthy beautification of the fabric and embellishment of shrines of religious buildings. Very different to the medieval mind was the reprehensible duplication of holy relics such as the pillow case asserted to be the veil of the Blessed Virgin Mary or 'the glass of pigges bones', supposedly from the bodies of saints, with which Chaucer's gentle pardoner 'made the person and the peple his apes'. Such forgery for profit, with the intention of deceiving the innocent and faithful, could not but be condemned. The educated or worldly-wise were not taken in for a moment by hypocrites 'Bret-ful of pardon, comen from Rome'. But a charter was a muniment of rightful title, not a means of deception. One example, from Scotland, illustrates the problem facing dedicated, saintly scholars. The church of Aberdeen almost certainly received royal charters from Malcolm IV, King of Scots from 1153 to 1165, granting lands, churches, rents, cain (tribute in kind) and other privileges. The originals in course of time strayed. However, they were recreated during the 14th century for insertion in ecclesiastical chartularies. The copies, far from depriving other people of their property, memorialised the wishes of a king of Scots for the well-being of one of his bishoprics. It was probably not uncommon for charters damaged by damp, mice or age to be rewritten onto new parchment or into chartularies to turn away criticism of careless storage levelled against embarrassed muniment keepers. Human errors in copying, and uncontemporary handwriting styles, would indicate to the expert an unskilled forgery. Little obvious harm was done, and no one deprived of land or privileges, by the decision of the archivist or scribe to rewrite — and then destroy the decaying original.

Almost all the older monastic communities based their claims to prized privileges, such as exemption from the control of the local bishop, on spurious documents, forged perhaps before about 1160, but forged possibly to honour the nuncupative will of a founder.

The priory of St Botolph, Colchester, prided itself on being the earliest community of Augustinian canons in England, founded about the year 1095, and rightful primate over all Augustinian houses in the country. The canons regarded themselves as exempt from the jurisdiction of the diocesan bishop and directly responsible to the pope. To reinforce their claims, St Botolph's priory produced a papal bull to support the allegations, supposedly written in 1116, but actually composed at some date between 1391 and 1527.

The monks of Westminster Abbey, an ancient foundation, rebuilt by the saintly Edward the Confessor, found themselves bereft of their patron by his death in 1066 and, more disquieting, without written muniments for the privileges and lands enjoyed hitherto. Regarding the task as a religious duty, the skilled diplomatists of the abbey scriptorium set about fabricating whatever charters and diplomas seemed requisite to aid their beloved foundation. By this means the abbey firmly established its privilege of crowning the monarchs of England. Edward the Confessor intended thus to honour his royal abbey and William the Conqueror respected the wish by accepting the crown in the abbey on Christmas Day 1066. The monks also fostered, or at the very least did nothing to deride, the legend of St Peter's miraculous visit to their marshy island during the early seventh century. This legend helped Westminster to overawe and compete with the Bishop of London's own cathedral, St Paul's, across the river, itself in truth founded during the seventh century. St Paul's Cathedral, though the bishop's seat, did not establish its position as royalty's premier place of worship.

Among the expert forgers at Westminster was one man, whose name has come down to us, the prior Osbert of Clare, a dedicated holy man whose devotion to his abbey and its saintly patron surpassed his loyalty to his king and abbot. Twice Osbert went into exile for quarrelling with the abbots, for his intolerant attitude to the rights of his abbey, and his disdain for royal authority.

A much quoted example of forgery related to the primacy which Canterbury claimed over York as a religious centre. Primacy entailed considerable legal, ecclesiastical and financial privileges. The Canterbury authorities would argue that their church, founded in 597 by St Augustine, envoy of the pope, and dedicated to Christ himself, deserved the primacy of all England, indeed had been recognised as such for centuries, and must at one time have possessed the relevant legal documentation. To recreate the documents seemed no crime, directing attention to the dereliction of religious duty by monks of past centuries in losing ancient charters. Eadmer the chronicler in 1120, for instance, reported: 'in these days there arose a fervour of research into the authorities and ancient privileges of the primacy which the church of Canterbury claims over the church of York'. The 'archivists' of Canterbury hunted high and low for charters, chartularies or bulls, praying to the saints for guidance in their search. Monks 'inspected the secret corners of ancient chests and holy gospel books hitherto serving solely as adornments' until divine relevation drew the gullible, or crafty, holy men to the place where some privileges miraculously materialised 'firm in all points and supported by papal authority'.

The York antagonists looked with suspicion on the parchments which their southern colleagues had recently 'found or thought up'. The ecclesiastics in Rome eventually threw out this evidence. The privileges proved undoubted forgeries, which the archivists at both centres must have realised, on account of the fortuitous presence of at least one professional 'improver' of muniments at Canterbury. Indeed one culprit on his deathbed years afterwards 'declared, with tears of repentance, that he had defended . . . the church of St Augustine at Canterbury with spurious papal privileges; and that he had received some precious ornaments as the price of his wickedness . . .'.

By no means all medieval forgery can be blamed on ecclesiastical fervour, because laymen too required written muniments confirming lands or privileges, evidencing financial claims, or establishing rights of patronage. Commissioning a forger to conjure out of thin air the relevant documentation occurred to the lay mind as readily as to the monkish. Incompetent forgers were occasionally caught when they wrote incorrect Latin, applied the wrong seal, neglected the normal form of address, carelessly doctored the ink to reinforce the illusion of age, or washed the parchment to disguise mistakes and erasures. Some unfortunate forgers even referred to witnesses as present at a certain time or place when on that day, and for some years previously, they had lain at rest with their ancestors and all the saints. Late in Edward III's reign one falsifier of evidence with access to the public records concocted a title deed to land in Northumberland supposedly dated 1293. Unfortunately the foolish knave dropped the forged document into the wrong file, one for the year 1303-4, and thus suffered immediate detection. And there were people in the land who undertook for a fee to refurbish the physical appearance of genuine muniments. Such improvers expected a free hand of illiterate or innocent owners to add to or subtract from the contents of the documentation. In depriving other people of their possessions, this work proved much more immoral, certainly a nuisance for contemporaries, and indeed for historical researchers endeavouring to sort out the true from the false.

Medieval documents need not all be judged as either entirely genuine or totally forged, because not a few — and especially those copied into chartularies — may appear as more or less careless copies of original drafts made in good faith or to preserve the content of irretrievably decayed, damaged originals before the latter's disintegration. Other material may indeed be 'improved' in one way or another through selective précising or tendentious copying, by adding a phrase here, erasing a place-name there, by altering acreage here, or omitting a condition there, in order to support the patron's case. As an example, a donor might grant his favourite monastery a valued estate by word of mouth. While he lived the monks could always expect his vouching for the gift. But eventually the monks would have to produce one or two charters, allegedly written by the original donor, in order to protect their interests. Such documentation might indeed bring the situation up to date, for example by recognising that a certain mill had already been sold, an additional village purchased, one manor exchanged for another. In certain cases unscrupulous lawyers copied documents in such a way that their fraudulent texts read differently from, or even opposite to, the spirit or letter of the originals.

Moreover an ancient, perhaps Anglo–Saxon, diploma was frequently issued in the king's name by scribes at a religious house. The names of witnesses were added by the scribe himself because few people could conveniently present themselves in person on the day of signing. A diploma bore no seal. If the king demanded the production of a diploma, which could not be found, the archivists might reasonably claim that a new document should legitimately be written, even in the name of a monarch dead these hundred years.

A high proportion of allegedly royal charters before 1189 do not therefore emanate from chancery clerks. Hundreds may be forged but the majority, probably, were written, at the request of the king, by the grantees themselves. It was not unusual when giving land to an abbey to persuade the monastic authorities to compose and inscribe their own charter. This was sealed by the king's seal rather than personally signed by the king. Thus the authentication of the charter could be completed at any distance from the royal court provided that a seal matrix was despatched to the appropriate scriptorium. It was possible for an entirely genuine document to be written by anyone in the kingdom. The copying of a particular chancery scribe's handwriting was not therefore one of the accomplishments required of the would-be forger.

Malcolm IV, King of Scots, died on 9 December 1165. A grant of lands to Melrose Abbey was confirmed shortly before that, while the monarch still lived. But this same document refers to Waltheof of Dunbar as an earl, though Waltheof's father, Gospatrick, remained earl until 1166. The charter may seem therefore a careless forgery. However, it was doubtless drafted in 1165 but completed for sealing only one year later when Waltheof had succeeded his father as earl. Malcolm's name would not be deleted because it had been *his* wish to bring the deed to fruition, a desire honoured by his successor.

Diplomatic

Medieval scholars practised the science of diplomatic, studying the authenticity and form of records, as one means of investigating monastic forgeries. Documents carelessly transcribed, tendentiously or criminally altered, or deliberately thought up to answer a rich man's request, all posed practical problems to the medieval lawyer. Scholars renewed their interest during the 17th century when investigating medieval documents, especially those of Benedictine houses, in order to comment on, or detect, forgery or authenticity.

A Benedictine monk of the congregation of St Maur, the Frenchman Jean Mabillon, 1632-1707, served in turn as poultry attendant, cellarer, custodian of abbey treasures at St Denis and annotator of the complete works of St Bernard.

Mabillon's mucking out the henhouse may serve as a salutary reminder to the modern local historian that he must also venture out of the cloistered archives, to don trenchcoat and wellingtons, and to explore the possibly miry terrain of the real world. The *Opera omnia Bernardi* permitted Mabillon to ponder and develop the science of textual criticism. This he used to advantage in the Maurists' chronological *Acta sanctorum*, lives of the monastic saints. Mabillon travelled, notably to Italy as buyer of items for the royal library. At the Abbey of St Germain-des-Prés in Paris where he lived from 1664, Mabillon communicated with some of the leading scholars of his day, including the learned Charles du Fresne, Seigneur Du Cange, author of glossaries on post-classical Latin and Greek languages. These conferences frequently concerned the authenticity of charters, especially those employed by noble families to prove title to property and ancient lineage. The precedence and prestige of not a few ecclesiastical authorities was discussed. This study of documents was termed diplomatic, from the classical word for an official letter of recommendation conferring favour, privilege or licence.

An early attempt to publish rules of diplomatic by the Bollandist Daniel van Papenbroeck resulted in Mabillon's masterly riposte, *De re diplomatica* of 1681. The Jesuit van Papenbroeck criticised the authenticity of Merovingian records including certain charters of Mabillon's former home, St Denis Abbey. Mabillon insisted that judgment on a document required expert examination of every element and criterion possible, of the parchment or paper, the seal, the testators' names, signatures, grammar, orthography, dating, the titles and style of the grantor, the consistency of the form and order of the sentences or phrases. He compared by means of facsimiles documents of doubtful date or provenance with those whose authenticity and history could not be faulted. *De re diplomatica* spread Mabillon's fame throughout Europe. He was summoned to the presence of Louis XIV as 'the most learned man in your kingdom'.

Mabillon turned his critical attention to human bones in Rome's catacombs, supposedly those of Christian martyrs and undoubtedly purveyed as such to the faithful of the Roman Catholic world. The diplomatist's doubts about the authenticity of the relics were however not publicised until long after his death.

In Britain two decades after the publication of *De re diplomatica*, George Hickes, nonjuring bishop and philologist, critically examined Anglo–Saxon charters for long regarded as sacrosanct. To Hickes's pioneering efforts the preface to the catalogue of the Harleian manuscripts in the British Museum, written in 1762, paid tribute. The 'famous Charter of King *Edgar*, wherein he is stiled MARIUM BRIT. DOMINUS [7513], on which great Stress has been laid, by several Writers, in Support of *England*'s Superiority over the *four Seas*; but which Charter Dr Hicks . . . hath evidently demonstrated to be spurious; and to have been (as many others in the same Language likewise were), forged after the *Norman* Conquest'.

Despite ill health and harassment by the mob for his religious and political principles. Hickes's learned and monumental treatise on old northern languages, entitled *Linguarum veterum septentrionalium thesaurus*, appeared in 1703-5. To this volume Humfrey Wanley, the librarian at the Bodleian, Oxford, contributed a catalogue of Anglo–Saxon manuscripts. Subsequently, Wanley undertook the sorting, arranging and listing of the Harleian manuscripts, a treasury of national and local history. His catalogue is arranged in the order bundles were placed in Harley's library. He also began a *'greater Catalogue'* but, as the preface to the Harleian manuscripts of 1762 put it, 'Death deprived us of him on the 6th Day of *July* 1726, when he had proceeded no further than Number 2407 of the present printed Catalogue'. The catalogue continues in use by researchers to this day.

Thomas Madox's *Formulare anglicanum* of 1702, the earliest diplomatic introduction to the forms employed by clerks in writing out royal or private charters, established the independence of diplomatic from palaeography.

In Scotland the lawyer James Anderson's opposition to the loss of the crown's imperial and independent status at the union of 1707 inspired his critical commentary on ancient charters of that northern land. After Anderson's decease in 1728, Thomas Ruddiman completed the task with his *Selectus diplomatum et numismatum Scotiæ thesaurus* in 1739. Ruddiman, a librarian, published facsimiles of charters dated from 1094 to 1412, transcribing each; engraving royal seals and coinage; extensively guiding on abbreviations, contractions and characteristic letters; and stressing the significance of diplomatic criticism of original evidence.

The study of diplomatic and palaeography advanced during the 19th and 20th centuries. Examples include publications of the record commissioners; of the palaeographical society, 1873–95; *Facsimiles of national manuscripts of Scotland*, 1867–72; texts issued by the Scottish history society; the series of *Regesta regum Scottorum*; Johnson and Jenkinson's *English court hand*, 1915; volumes of the Cymmrodorion record series; and works commencing in 1844 of the Chetham Society, 'remains historical and literary connected with the palatine counties of Lancaster and Chester'.

Handwriting in Britain

Charles Trice Martin, author of the standard archival textbook *The Record Interpreter*, regarded the ability to read and interpret documents as 'the foundation of all history . . . for to attempt to get information from old writings without thoroughly knowing the forms of the letters, and the different systems of abbreviations and contractions, would be like trying to keep accounts without knowing how to add up a column of figures'.

Derived from early Mediterranean examples, the Roman alphabet utilised capital letters of more or less equal height for inscriptions on stone or for other formal purposes. This type of clearcut square lettering is known as majuscule or 'two-line', with no tops or tails above or below the main line of the text. For writing on parchment or paper, Roman scribes developed rustic capitals, informal, curved, tall and slim, most with a serif as stylistic device, especially at the foot. Meanwhile other writers, possibly in northern Africa, adopted the uncial or inch-high alphabet, simplified, open and rounded, more swiftly penned than square capitals, but yet majuscule, and exemplified in the letters A, D, E, H and M.

ꟁ ꟶ Є ꟺ

Uncial a d e m

In southern Europe around the end of the fifth century appeared the half-uncial script, a 'four-line' or miniscule form permitting letters where appropriate to ascend as *d* or *l* and descend as *p* or *q* from the main line of the text. These letters were not necessarily joined together in either formal scripts or routine correspondence, each symbol being carefully and independently inscribed, save in the case of certain common ligatures.

depru

English half-uncial c750 d e p r n

Handwriting in Saxon Britain owed its form and beauty to the half-uncial round book hand of Irish scribes including missionaries at Iona and Lindisfarne. These clerics evolved for memoranda a neat, upright and compact script. The one influenced the other to form an 'insular' hand remarkable for its wedged serifs. During the period 650–850 this pointed half-uncial was used for such calligraphic masterpieces as the Lindisfarne gospels of about 700. The most characteristic hands were written and illuminated during the years 860–920. Anglo-Saxon scripts of religious homilies or gospels, even mundane perambulations in the vernacular in land charters, are shapely, comely and pleasing. The characteristic letters of Anglo–Saxon script are long *r* with shoulder dropping to the line of writing, *s*, *g*, crossed *d*, thorn for *th* and wen for *w*. Insular script survived in England after the Norman Conquest only for documents in the vernacular but in Wales even for Latin manuscripts, certainly until the early 12th century. And old-fashioned styles influenced northern English and Scottish handwriting during the Middle Ages in very much the same fashion.

ꞃ ꞃ ꟑ ꟶ

Pointed minuscule r s g d

But at an early date busy men adopted a cursive or current hand, scripted, scrawled, even scribbled 'at a running pace' to meet pressing needs of government and commerce. Cursive script influenced the development of uncials and of national fashions in writing in western Europe, except Ireland and England. From Merovingian cursive and scripts taught in the north of France during the eighth century, monastic scribes developed the Carolingian minuscule. Monks at Tours, under their English abbot Alcuin, and at Luxeuil and Corbie devised clear, upright, rounded but noncursive letters, ancestors of modern roman printing. The script interested, and received the blessing of, the emperor, Charlemagne, hence the term Carolingian.

The battering of Saxon England by Norse invaders delayed the introduction of reformed handwriting to the schools of these islands. Carolingian minuscule therefore crossed to Britain only about 960, reaching Wales about 1100. Such insular letter forms as long *r* and flat-topped *g* survived, but, in general, continental fashion was preferred.

Carolingian minuscule in England 1058 r s g d

Scribes of medieval books turned the curves of Carolingian script into angles, emphasising uprightness and solidity. They differentiated between light and heavy pen strokes as a point of style. Using broad pens, monkish calligraphers tended to shorten ascenders and descenders and to run together curvaceous letters such as *d* and *o*. This gothic, text or book hand was considered most appropriate for gospels, psalters, books of hours, chronicles and chartularies. Additionally, the local historian encounters examples in seals, monumental inscriptions and headings of manuscripts. Book hand influenced 15th-century pioneer printers, though renaissance scholars considered it gothic or barbarous. But even to this day compositors generally set roman letters unjoined and introduce gothic lettering for special commissions.

Carolingian 1058   Book hand 1340

Clerks of the royal court in England wrote in Carolingian minuscule virtually indistinguishable from book or literary hand before developing their charter, business or court hand during the 12th century for conducting the business of state. The court of exchequer adopted a cursive hand by 1125, chancery by 1200. In course of time the hands of several departments, readily distinguishable, became 'set' or fixed for decade after decade. Exchequer's pipe roll was written in a distinct set hand that varied comparatively little from the 12th century onwards.

In the process of shaping letters during the genesis of court hand, clerical officials preferred rounded forms such as uncial *d*, exaggerated ascenders and descenders, added an almost imperceptible notch to ascenders of *b*, *h* and *l*, bent the ascender of *d* backwards, but slightly bent forwards certain other ascenders. Roman capitals tended to be rounded but somewhat obscured with a vertical line through the centre of the letter, a mannerism which survived for centuries (245). The serifs of minuscule letters developed very gradually into the connecting strokes between letters to assist currency.

ꝺote

Court hand 1280

Thirteenth-century handwriting appears compact, small, backward-sloping and current, with thickened horizontals and marked distinction between thick and thin strokes, especially during the period 1250–1320. From 1220 ascenders and descenders luxuriate in loops, notches and floreation. The hook on the right-hand side of the ascenders of *b*, *h*, *k* and *l* developed into a defined loop as the century wore on. About the middle of the century, on the left-hand side of the ascender, a curved notch developed. This climbed higher up the ascender before entirely disappearing about 1300–20.

By about 1300 court hand reached a peak of excellence — upright, clear, no longer horizontally thickened, unornamented yet graceful. Letter forms, far from being crabbed, tended to enlarge. The left-hand notch of *b*, *h*, *k* and *l* was no longer used. After 1320 floreation and loops succumbed to undistinguished hooks, but loops on the left-hand side of descenders of *f*, *p* and long *s* proliferated. By 1330 the cursive *e* turned over (63–64). In the course of the century writing declined into an ill-disciplined, very cursive and not always readily legible matter of business, rather than an art, and by the end of the century a spiky angular script dominated the calligraphic schools of government administrators. Forms of capitals *C*, *E*, and *O*, may appear similar, offering reading difficulties especially in surnames or place-names.

Fifteenth-century hands appear vertical and angular, with fine connecting strokes from letter to letter. Even round letter forms gained angular backs while the *e* was reversed and *b* differed hardly at all from *v*. Towards the closing decades, 'free' hands of businessmen coarsened into cursive and occasionally almost indecipherable scrawls as the weight of paperwork burdened harassed clerks in counting houses and estate offices.

From about 1370 scribes mixed court and book hands in a 'bastard' script for administrative and business convenience. Bastard is regarded as a business set hand, generally angular, upright, laterally compressed and legible, with its own calligraphic rules, widely employed in due course by departments of state. Scriveners eschewed connecting strokes, serifs and long descenders or ascenders. By about the year 1400 the writing masters were compromising on clarity by accepting cursive looped *d*, reversed *e*, long-stemmed *r* and double-storeyed *a*. The bastard script facilitated the writing of vernacular texts such as Chaucer and *The Vision of William concerning Piers the Plowman*. Thorn and yogh survived, round *r* after *b*, *h*, *o*, and *p*, hooked ascenders, *s* resembling *b* (220), but comparatively few abbreviations apart from such useful ones as *qd* for quoð, that is 'quoth'.

English vernacular 1450

By 1460 a form of bastard, apparently vertically compressed but splaying out sideways, foreshadowed the typical script of 16th-century secretaries. Minims sloped backwards, connecting strokes forwards, giving a saw-toothed look to the writing, as in the numeral iiij on page 170. Characteristic letters are *e* (68), *g* (98), *p* and *x* (168) written in one stroke, *r* (197) and *t* (239).

From 15th-century 'splayed bastard' under the influence of free hand styles, scriveners developed a current script known as 'secretary'. Clerks used the hand from about 1525 to 1680 for entries in parish registers, wills, diocesan act books, petitions to quarter sessions and correspondence, taught by writing masters such as John Baildon, who, with Jean de Beauchesne, published in 1571 *A booke containing divers sortes of hands*.

Tudor secretary hand seems flamboyant, with bold, looped, tall letters; stout descenders sweeping into the line below; a *t* theatrically leaning forwards; and somewhat dashing sloping letter-forms for mundane business documents. The influence of italic after 1590 tended to clarify and reduce the size of many letters of the alphabet. Characteristics of secretary hand include a diagonal stroke rising to the right for *a, c* and *i*; *h* sinking well below the line; *p* resembling *x* written in one stroke; *r* with two stems but not the long shoulderless form of court hand; reversed *e*; final round *s* but long *s* as medial or initial. The punctuation and capitalisation of secretary writers was somewhat idiosyncratic.

Secretary hand: preaches   1580

Initially employed in Italy about the year 1400, humanist writing looked back to Carolingian minuscule with its graceful, legible, upright and noncursive letters. The upright roman version profoundly influenced printers in the 15th century, and to this day. When written cursively the script could be adopted for official documents and everyday correspondence especially items despatched to continental courts. Roman or italic entered Britain by about 1500 and was taught to Mary, Queen of Scots, and to Henry VIII's children alongside secretary. Thus a letter in secretary might display quotations, marginalia or headings in italic, possibly for emphasis. Indeed cursive italic was first used as a means of indicating emphasis by an English printer in 1545.

Inspired by the example of the royal family, writing masters taught the children of 16th-century gentlefolk the elements of secretary and italic. One such teacher, Peter Bales, a much respected calligrapher, was persuaded to copy, accurately, love letters written by the recently executed Robert Devereux, Earl of Essex, to his wife, Sir Philip Sidney's widow, before and after their clandestine marriage. The correspondence must have been regarded as politically embarrassing because of Elizabeth I's passion for the earl, and the countess paid an enormous sum in blackmail for Bales's copies. That particular case, however, was not kept secret, being called to the Court of Star Chamber in 1601.

Between about 1600 and 1620 the mating of italic and secretary engendered a mixed hand, which, influenced by Dutch and other continental styles, evolved into a cursive round hand, usually known as copperplate from its employment by copperplate engravers. This soon dominated the calligraphy of the English-speaking world, remaining in fashion into the 20th century. Letters generally sloped rightwards, ascenders and descenders looped, up-strokes grew fine and down-strokes thickened. No one on the up and up dared neglect to cultivate his copperplate. As junior clerk to an attorney's firm, the young Joseph Porter in *H.M.S. Pinafore* 'copied all the letters in a big round hand' and, with that start in life, rose to become 'Ruler of the Queen's Navee'.

Developed from late 14th-century bastard, departmental set hands can be distinguished from the late 15th century. Chancery set hand from 1470, exhibited in letters patent and trust deeds, spread sideways with short ascenders or descenders, enabling lines of writing to approach closely. Upright and rounded, letters were rarely connected. An undistinguished horizontal mark above the words sufficed to indicate the majority of Latin abbreviations.

In such documents as recusant rolls and pipe rolls, exchequer from before 1500 emphasised ascenders, descenders, angles and connecting strokes between letters which sprawled slightly to left or right.

Clerks of the law courts adopted a distinctive legal style of handwriting during the 15th century for such documents as fines, recoveries, commonplace books and title deeds. Letters stood rigidly upright, though later examples sloped backwards, with long descenders or ascenders, and wide sweeping angular bows. The gothic capital letters especially *C, E, G* and *Q* retained the confusing internal strokes which make deciphering personal or place-names difficult. Legal hand, scathingly referred to by a contemporary as resembling the ribs of a pig in its monotony of letter forms, became known as *the* court hand to gothic revivalists of the 18th century.

1620   chancery   1590   exchequer   1664   legal

By the middle of the 17th century departmental set hands were regarded critically by most people — apart from the relevant clerks with a livelihood at stake. Indeed the hands were but rarely employed in everyday life. Abolished with Latin in 1650, restored with Charles II, the departmental scripts were finally abandoned in 1733, to be replaced by 'a common legible Hand and Character, as the Acts of Parliament are usually ingrossed in . . . and not in any Hand commonly called *Court Hand* . . .'.

In preference to the set hands, clerks in certain government departments and legal offices began to write in an expansive vertical engrossing hand from around 1580, profitable to those remunerated by the page rather than number of words. The style, influenced by secretary, italic and round hands, appeared about 1640 and continued in use until about 1900 for marriage settlements, title deeds and enclosure agreements. The typewriter with its roman letter forms ousted the engrosser after about 1900. The unchanging letter forms of the common-law engrossers permitted the introduction of forgeries into the files. A document written in 1840 could be falsely dated 1740 with reasonable hope of escaping detection, provided that the parchment and ink were suitably aged by exposure to damp, dust or sunlight.

1670

It is often difficult to date a document closely by the handwriting, on account of stereotyping of styles. Moreover, a sheriff clerk writing in 1450 may have attended lessons in 1380 offered by a calligrapher himself born in the year 1320. A priest in Cullen, Caernarfon, Cork or Combe Martin would not necessarily be familiar with the fashionable calligraphy of Oxford or Flanders. A manorial steward with grubby parchment, roughcut pen, thickened ink or suffering from draughts through the arras could not but be deleteriously affected in his handwriting by one or all of those conditions, falsely swaying the judgment of the modern researcher as to the dating of the document.

Deciphering handwriting

Deciphering handwriting in English, Scots, Welsh or Latin requires practice. Textbooks chronologically describe the characteristics of various scripts and of individual letters, but the printed word impresses on the mind only slowly what the eye notices relatively swiftly. By dint of continual practice and a degree of tuition, 17th-century secretary hand may be learned as well as vernacular scripts of the 15th century. Indeed the researcher probably deciphers Domesday more readily than the handwriting of not a few eminent Victorian scholars.

I taught myself to read old handwriting by obtaining a clear photocopy of a document in secretary script dated 1590. Arming myself with a model 'secretarie alphabete' of 1571, printed in a palaeographical textbook, I tentatively identified the very first letter of the document. Then followed the second, third and subsequent letters, with spaces unfilled where the letters seemed indecipherable. I abandoned the normal custom of reading entire words or phrases at a glance.

Before long I recognised the more usual letters, notably *e, a, r, h*, and examined with a magnifier the loops, curlicues, hairlines, bows, serifs and other strokes employed by that particular scribe. By understanding the formation of a letter, I more confidently identified even the scribe's more wretchedly scribbled versions.

Both *A* and *a* offer few difficulties (1–14), though capital *A* may resemble *D* in the early 14th century. Carolingian headless *a* acquires a downwards stroke about 1200 to resemble *q* but tends to gain an upper bow after about 1270 (2). Secretary *a*, drawn with two strokes of the pen, may appear with an open top resembling a *u* (6) or frequently with an attaching line (8).

1: 1210 2: 1285 3: 1380 4: 1440

5: 1450 6: 1570 7: 1610 8: 1611 9: 1700

10: 1235 11: 1400 12: 1430 13: 1590 14: 1625

B and *b* alter little (15–30), though certain forms with loops, notches or floreations confuse the uninitiated (17, 25–27). Fifteenth-century B (27) can be written in one stroke beginning at the head.

15: 1170 16: 1200 17: 1240 18: 1380 19: 1470

20: 1570 21: 1610 22: 1695 23: 1180 24: 1215

25: 1230 26: 1240 27: 1420 28: 1510 29: 1580 30: 1625

The reading of lower case *c* (31–37) ought to offer no problem but the letter often deceives, because of its resemblance to *t* (31). When combined as *ct*, as in 'action', the resulting ligature can be taken for an *a* (32–33). Indeed the scribe may have written double *c*, as in 'accion', rather than *ct*. Secretary *c* with attaching stroke (35) and capital *C* recumbent (42) might mislead. *C* (38-44) is sometimes confused with *D* or *E*.

The head of early 13th-century *d* loops completely (47). If *D* and *d* (45-59) are very dashingly written in business hands, the letters may be read as *e* (49-50), *B* or *E* (55-57). In court hand the ascender of *d* bends backwards (47, 49) in contrast to the perpendicular text *d* (45).

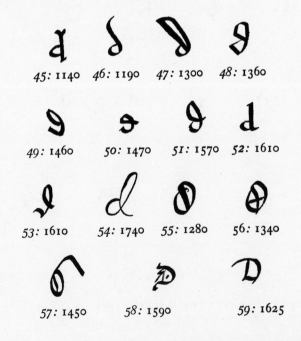

The form of *e* alters considerably from century to century, providing a ready method of dating handwriting. During the 13th century *e* seems to fall over backwards and recline peacefully by 1330 (60–63). After this date the letter, now recumbent, can be written with one pen-stroke (64–65). During the three succeeding centuries the *e*, produced from bottom left in an anticlockwise direction, gradually becomes the reversed *e* characteristic of secretary hand (66–68, 70, 74). Carolingian or italic *e* reappears during the renaissance (69, 71–73, 75). Capital *E* by about the year 1200 gains an uncial form of curved back, two vertical lines and one horizontal stroke (76). *E* as a circle and cross resembles *D* (77). The letter is angular after 1400 (78) and very current from 1450 (79). Secretary *E* may resemble a *k* (80) but the beautifully rounded italic *E* cannot be mistaken (81).

60: 1190   61: 1260   62: 1290   63: 1330

64: 1330   65: 1390   66: 1430   67: 1446

68: 1500   69: 1506   70: 1570   71: 1610   72: 1610

73: 1610   74: 1616   75: 1700

76: 1200   77: 1310   78: 1410   79: 1480   80: 1610   81: 1625

The development of *f* is straightforward (82–91), though the letter usually resembles one form of *s* (85, 90–91). Capital *F* is shown, with few exceptions, by double small *f* (87–88), writ large, until the 18th century.

82: 1150   83: 1180   84: 1280   85: 1300

86: 1380   87: 1380   88: 1495
                   ff   ff

89: 1590 90: 1612 91: 1740

Saxon or insular flat-topped *g* continued in use in English until about 1450, to serve for the guttural sound *gh*. This developed into the Middle English letter yogh. Its form differs markedly from medieval three-stroke *g* (92–100) and from italic *g* (101–102). Capital *G* seems a bewildering letter but fortunately comparatively rarely occurs (103–105).

92: 1210   93: 1212   94: 1215   95: 1315   96: 1320

97: 1430   98: 1470   99: 1500   100: 1570 101: 1615

102: 1720   103: 1210   104: 1440   105: 1590

Like *b* and *l, h* tends to be notched (106) and, about 1250–1280, floreated (107). These excrescences retreat before loops from about 1310 (108) and straight hooks on the right-hand side of the stem later in the 14th century (109–110). The triangular hook (110) disappears as scribes write more swiftly or carelessly (111). Indeed the letter loses its hooks and shapeliness by secretary-hand times (112–115), the descender sweeping down into the text on the line below. Italic (116) and round hand (117) *h* contrast startlingly with the secretary form. Small *h*, perhaps writ large and bold, normally serves as capital letter also, but occasionally *H*, of uncial rather than square capital form, must be expected (118-120).

106: 1180   107: 1270   108: 1330   109: 1380

110: 1410   111: 1450   112: 1450   113: 1508

114: 1570   115: 1610   116: 1610   117: 1710

118: 1220   119: 1300   120: 1600

The *i* and *j* are two forms of one letter until about 1700 (121-122) and capital versions remain very rare (123-124). Successive *i*'s frequently appear as *ij*, in, for instance, *iunij* 'of June'. The *j* becomes only a consonant, rather than a vowel, from the 18th century.

121   122   123: 1350   124: 1610

To some extent *k* and *K* (125-132) and *l* and *L* (133-140) follow the development of *b*. The minuscule *k* usually resembles an *R*.

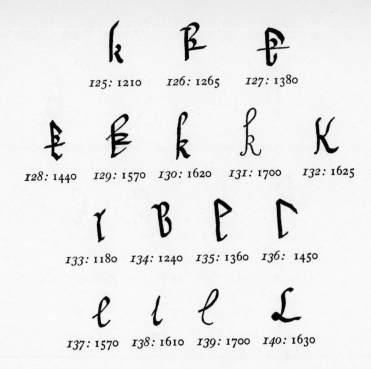

125: 1210   126: 1265   127: 1380

128: 1440   129: 1570   130: 1620   131: 1700   132: 1625

133: 1180   134: 1240   135: 1360   136: 1450

137: 1570   138: 1610   139: 1700   140: 1630

Composed of minims, *m* and *n* develop together, often indistinguishable from other forms such as *ui, ij, ju* and *in* (141–146). Medieval *M* (147–149) follows uncial rather than square capital models. Old *N* (150–154) seems always one of the most perplexing letters encountered in documents, on account of its resemblance to other letters such as long *s* (153) or *H* (150) and its non-resemblance to its modern self (155). The adapted roman capital N with distinctive cross strokes (151) of the period 1190–1260 can readily be distinguished from the large *N* of the years 1300–1350 (153).

141: 1220   142: 1250   143: 1460

144: 1570   145: 1610   146: 1755

147: 1195   148: 1250   149: 1590

150: 1150　*151:* 1190　*152:* 1200　*153:* 1310

154: 1590　*155:* 1600

Scribes cannot vary *o* (156-158) much, though after about 1600 numerous clerks scribbling at speed leave the top open like a *u*. Capital *O* may offer more scope for mischievous misreadings (159-160).

156: 1190　　*157:* 1380　　*158:* 1610

159: 1470　*160:* 1590

P and *p* present few problems (161-176), save when *p* is combined with another *p* or an *o* (165-167). Its swiftly drawn form resembles *x* (168, 171, 173, 281-282).

161: 1140　*162:* 1200　*163:* 1250　*164:* 1340

165: 1250　　*166:* 1295　　*167:* 1340

168: 1460　　　*169:* 1470　*170:* 1570
xp

171: 1620   172: 1620   173: 1620   174: 1725

175: 1220   176: 1570

While some versions of *q* (177–183) resemble *g*, *Q* (184–188) occasionally looks like *O*. The origin of the modern question mark may be discerned in forms such as the 1590 *Q* (187).

177: 1150   178: 1270   179: 1370   180: 1500

181: 1610   182: 1610   183: 1710

184: 1120   185: 1170   186: 1390

187: 1590   188: 1625

The *r* offers an important means of dating a document. One early form gains an unmistakable shoulder and, until about 1190, a slightly curving stem falling below the line of writing (189–191). By the 13th century this *r* could be written without raising the pen and, by about 1225, the point from which the shoulder sprang was lowered considerably (193). Writers abandon the shoulder altogether by about 1260 (194). A second early form of *r*, employed originally mainly in the ligature of *or* (192), appears subsequently with any rounded letter such as *w*, *h*, *y*, *p*, *b*, *o*, *d* (195). Both forms of *r* persist, the long *r* without shoulder predominating (196), the round *r* positioning itself elsewhere (195, 197). Secretary *r* develops from a combination of bastard shouldered *r* (196) and round *r* (192) to offer several distinct shapes (198–199, 201). There is a common open *r*, written in one stroke (199) and a curious *r* following *o* or *a* (198, 202). Italic (200) and round hand (203–204) forms return to the shouldered Carolingian letter.

Scribes write capital *R* currently until about 1600 (205–210). The letter may be difficult to distinguish at first glance from *B*, *D* or *E*. The final stroke, which in modern forms (211–212) crosses diagonally downwards from left to right, usually in medieval times dashes horizontally (205–210).

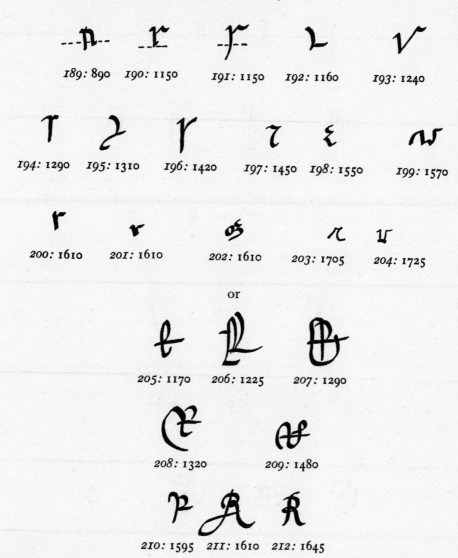

189: 890   190: 1150   191: 1150   192: 1160   193: 1240

194: 1290   195: 1310   196: 1420   197: 1450   198: 1550   199: 1570

200: 1610   201: 1610   202: 1610   203: 1705   204: 1725

or

205: 1170   206: 1225   207: 1290

208: 1320   209: 1480

210: 1595   211: 1610   212: 1645

There are two versions of *s*, one a short form employed as early as 1160 (215-216), the other a long *s*, with serif or hook, especially reserved for initial or medial position by 1280 (213-214, 217-219). Later forms develop from these versions (220-229), the distinctive diamond shape frequently occurring in late medieval documents (221). Early *S* is Carolingian (230) but by about 1140 its tail curves and its stem doubles up (231). Its belly swells to the beaver-tailed *S* of the period 1240-1320 resembling *M* (232). From 1300 to about 1520 *S* follows the form seen in the example of 1340 (233). Later examples, though normally clearly decipherable, may be confused with *G* (234) or unidentifiable (235). Italic *S* predominates by the 17th century (236).

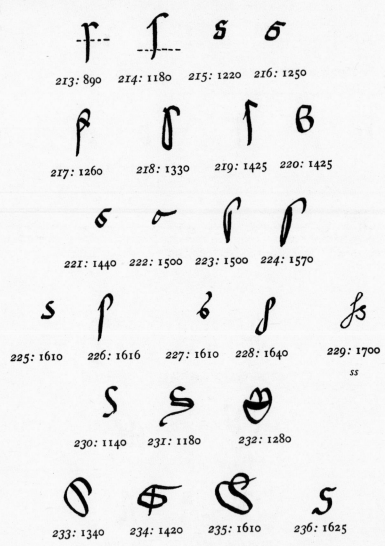

213: 890   214: 1180   215: 1220   216: 1250

217: 1260   218: 1330   219: 1425   220: 1425

221: 1440   222: 1500   223: 1500   224: 1570

225: 1610   226: 1616   227: 1610   228: 1640   229: 1700

ss

230: 1140   231: 1180   232: 1280

233: 1340   234: 1420   235: 1610   236: 1625

T and t (237–247) need offer no reading problems, except in so far as t resembles c and the ligature st savours of A (237–240). Court hand scribes probably introduced the rounded T (245).

| 237: 1220 | 238: 1390 | 239: 1480 | 240: 1600 |
| st | st | st | st |

| 241: 1570 | 242: 1610 | 243: 1705 | 244: 1740 |

| 245: 1450 | 246: 1610 | 247: 1625 |

In writing documents, scribes did not normally distinguish between the letters u and v (or U and V), though by about 1270 v was used initially and at the end of a word, u medially, and in due course u was adopted as a vowel, v as a consonant (248–264). A horizontal convex mark over u is often used to distinguish the vowel from an n.

| 248: 1160 | 249: 1210 | 250: 1475 |

| 251: 1570 | 252: 1640 | 253: 1700 |

| 254: 1190 | 255: 1235 | 256: 1280 |

| 257: 1395 | 258: 1395 | 259: 1450 |

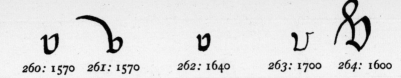

260: 1570   261: 1570   262: 1640   263: 1700   264: 1600

W and *w*, establishing in place of Saxon wen *þ* by the beginning of the 11th century, resemble in shape two *v*'s (265). During the 13th century the shape radically alters (266–270) and the old form returns only after about 1490 (271–275).

265: 1180   266: 1270   267: 1315

268: 1420   269: 1430   270: 1470

271: 1500   272: 1610

273: 1610   274: 1615   275: 1700

On account of its employment as the figure ten in numerals, *x* is important. The letter unfortunately frequently resembles *p* or *y* (276–283).

276: 1190   277: 1235   278: 1280

279: 1375   280: 1450   281: 1510

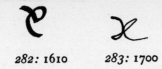

282: 1610   283: 1700

The tail of *y* curves to the right (284–288) before the victory of italic forms around 1600 (289–290).

284: 1215   285: 1285   286: 1390

287: 1460   288: 1570   289: 1610

290: 1700

Scribes rarely require to write *z* (291–294). The letter may resemble a tailed round *r* (292).

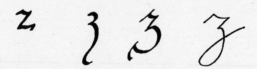

291: 1230   292: 1350   293: 1600   294: 1740

In origin a Scandinavian rune, the old English letter thorn, equivalent to hard *th*, occurs in Anglo-Saxon and early medieval manuscripts. In documents written in English or Scots after about 1420 the thorn reappears, especially as the first

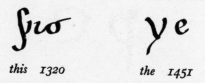

this 1320   the 1451

letter of a word. It may resemble a *y*, and scribes, entirely ignorant of the existence of thorn, write *y* from about 1500 in such words as 'the', 'they', 'this', 'that', especially in abbreviated forms such as *yt* for 'that' and *oyr* for 'other'. For this reason 'the' appears as 'ye' in, for instance, *Ye* Red Lion Inn. The researcher may reasonably transcribe this as *The* Red Lion Inn, though the late medieval scribe did indeed write a *y* rather than a thorn.

Until as late as the sixteenth century, Middle English yogh, a descendant of insular flat-topped Saxon *g*, represented certain values now shown by *g* in again, *gh* in knight, *w* in law and *y* in ye. Abandoned by some writers as early as 1250, the yogh stubbornly persisted in documents written in Scots and northern English

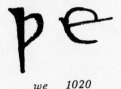

lawe *1340*   myght *1380*

beyonde *1420*

your *1451*

where the guttural sound on the roof of the mouth fell easily from boreal lips. Yogh resembled a *z* or *y*. This caused confusion, still indicated nowadays in the surname Menzies, whose *z*, really a yogh, requires the surname's pronunciation as *Mingies*. The occupation and surname tailor may be written as tailzour in early modern documents.

Saxon wen or wyn, *p*, the equivalent of *w*, rarely appears in documents after the Conquest. It resembles both thorn and *y*.

we 1020

The use of abbreviation marks, symbols or shortened forms of words persists in the modern instances a/c for 'account', & for 'and', Mr for 'mister', Ltd for 'Limited'. Scribes dauntlessly scatter such shorthand from well before the 11th century until forbidden specifically to do so in court records under the Act of 1731, though permitted by an Act two years later to employ 'such abbreviations as are now commonly used in the English language'.

The most common medieval mark, a straight line over or through an abbreviitiated word, indicates the omission of various letters, usually *m* or *n*. The line through *L* (abbreviation of *libri*, 'pounds') remains to this day in the £ sign.

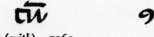

cum (with) *1263*

This formerly straight line curls up and, by the 15th century, resembles the modern apostrophe. Elizabethans employ the sign to indicate the change from *-cion* to *-con* as in 'commendations'. Writers frequently abbreviate but omit the

commendacions

apostrophe, as in 'theyll' meaning 'they will', 'tis', for 'it is' or 'thourt' for 'thou art'. The modern possessive apostrophe shows the omission of an *e* in the genitive, 'the manes house' becoming 'the man's house'.

Clerks were permitted to suspend words so that only a few letters were actually written before a full stop, an appropriate flourish or a curved line over or through the final letter. Among other advantages suspension saved the face of a cleric with not unfaulty knowledge of Latin terminations. The researcher now recognises *s* for *solidi*, 'shillings'; *d*, *denarii*, 'pence'; *li*, *libri*, 'pounds'; *T*, *testibus*, 'with

solidi *1410*   *manerium* *1420*

witnesses'; *m*, *manerium*, 'manor'; *anno rr*, *anno regni regis*, 'in the year of the reign of king . . .'; *par.*, 'parish'; *pet.*, 'petitioner'; *bap.*, 'baptised'; *memo.*, *memorandum*, 'it is to be remembered'.

Alternatively scribes were wont to contract words, such as *do* for *ditto* meaning 'the same'; *lb*, *libra*, 'pound weight'; *Xps*, *Christus* 'Christ'; *no*, *numero*, 'number', *.n.*, *enim* 'for, because', *.i.*, *id est*, 'that is'.

Superscript letters facilitate the omission of certain letters in w^t 'with'; ma^{tie}, 'majestie'; y^{or} 'your'; y^t 'that', g^a *erga* 'against', g^i, *igitur*, 'therefore'.

Special signs include the flourish, attached to a word's final letter, standing for *-es* or *-is* especially in nouns denoting possession such as *kinges house* for 'king's house'. A similar flourish near the foot of the letter also abbreviates *R*, *rex*, 'king';

kinges 1509   recipe   penny 1460

R, recipe, 'doctor's prescription'; *d, denarius,* 'penny'. The mark through small *r* as in *bonorum* or *suorum* produces an unusual *y* or double *2* effect, as in *Sarum*. This sign for *-rum* at the end of a word occurs in certain place-names when written in their Latin forms. Thus Saresberia and Blandford Forinseca shortened

Sarum

to Sar' and Blandford For', were then carelessly extended with only a *-um* to produce Sarum and Blandford Forum, the modern forms.

The symbol, resembling an elongated *s*, exemplified in the 1420 form of the word 'every', represents *er*. Following *p* however this identical flourish means *-re*,

every 1420   present 1450

party 1420

as in 'present' of 1450. Clerks replace the *-er* or *-ar*, in such words as 'parish' or 'party', by a line through the descender of *p*, noticed in the two forms of 'party'

provided

in 1420. On the other hand they write the *-ro* in 'provided' by extending the bow of *p* backwards into a second bow.

A sign hardly distinguishable from a modern semicolon denotes *-us, -ue* or *-et*, though in course of time scribes write the mark as a *z*. This sign may do duty for various omitted letters as in *oz* for 'ounce' and *viz* for *videlicet,* 'that is to say'.

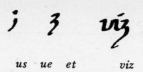

us   ue   et   viz

Clerks use a sign for *con* as part of such longer words as *conventio* 'agreement'; *ur* as in *vocatur* 'is known as' and *quod* meaning 'because'. The *ser* sign replaced *sieur* or *seigneur* in documents written in French.

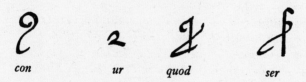

con   ur   quod   ser

Tiro, freedman of Cicero, invented a type of shorthand known as Tironian notes to facilitate speedy dictation. Tiro's sign for *et* 'and' resembles a *z* or 7.

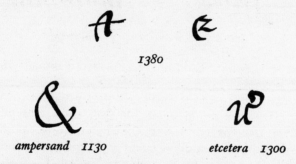

1380

ampersand *1130*   etcetera *1300*

Writers frequently employ Tironian *et* plus *c* for *etcetera*. However, the ampersand derives from the ligature *e* and *t* rather than from Tiro. Another symbol, resembling the schoolboy's long division sign ÷, stands for *est* 'is' until about 1240.

est

Until as late as 1800 when a form of long *s* prevailed, an *s* and *f* look very much alike. However, the *s* is correctly written with a crosspiece only to the left

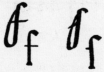

of the stem, the *f* crossed right through the stem. A double small *f* stands for capital *F* until the 17th century.

Similarly, medieval *c* and *t* can hardly be distinguished, but secretary hand accents the *c* from about 1520.

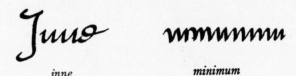

There is no regularity in the use of *i* and *j*, *u*, *w*, and *v* as in 'iunior', 'neuer', *iij* (roman numeral 3), 'vther', 'ws'.

The reading of minims in *m*, *n*, *u*, *v*, *w*, *i* and *j* presents obstacles when several adjoin as in the word 'minim' itself, *sine* or *sive*, *minor* or *junior*, *imitare* or *mutare*, or *unum*, *minimum*, *annum*. The example from a Tudor document of the word 'Inne' could be deciphered as the month 'June'. Similarly, the name of the

inne   *minimum*

Scottish island of Ioua, where Columba established a monastery in the year 563, was later misread as Iona.

Writers add, substitute or omit vowels seemingly without rhyme or reason to produce such forms as 'kinge, bargayne, howse, abowt, mynde, verie, yt, sive, cold (for could), gode (for good), newe, quenes, com, mak'. The most usual changes include *o* and *ou*, *w* and *u*, *i* and *y*, *e* and *ea*, *c* and *t* (as in 'accion' instead of 'action'), *c*, *k* and *ck* (as in 'publicke' or 'sik').

Numerals

When counting-house clerks braved the rigours of roman numerals for calculation, the wise ones counted on an abacus. Even the royal accountants in London spread a chequered cloth, physically moving tokens from one square to another. Numerals were merely letters of the alphabet: i (1), ij (2), v (5), x (10), l (50),

1–6

C (100), D (500), M (1,000). The final *i* in *ij*, *iij*, *iiij* (2, 3, 4) was normally downturned as *j*. The accountant wrote *xx*, *C* and *M* above numerals to indicate scores, hundreds and thousands, as in iii^{xx} for three score, vij^c for seven hundred.

9–10

Some clerks in Britain adopted arabic numerals as early as the 13th century, but conservatives clung to inconvenient roman methods for another 300 years.

1–9, 0   c1380

Documentary languages

I recall my initial attempt at transcription from the Latin, confounded by three adjacent minims (?*iu, ui, ni, in, m*) and confused by the resemblance of *c* and *t* in the one word which was proving the stumbling block. I considered *cincia*, 'a little bag for gems', *tuitio*, 'protection', *tincar* 'borax', *tinctio*, 'baptism', or possibly 'staining', *cinctio* 'girding of armour', even *tinea* 'ringworm'. The context rather than the handwriting eventually provided the answer.

Fortunately for me, despite the resemblance of certain medieval letters, scribes adapted uncomplicated grammatical constructions and Latinised numerous vernacular words. Clerks in holy orders, government servants and counting-house agents wrote in Latin during medieval centuries. Indeed conservative legal men and administrators continued to employ the language until an Act of 1731 required the adoption of English in courts of justice in England and the court of exchequer in Scotland from 1733. The provision was extended to Wales also in 1733.

Latin forms of proper names occur in documents of all centuries, even nowadays occasionally puzzling the unwary. William Ebor may thus refer to William Temple, Archbishop of York from 1929 to 1942, *Eboracum* being the Latin name for the Scandinavian place-name Iorvík, and *Ebor* its abbreviation. The degree MA (Cantab) derives not from Canterbury, whose Latin name appears as *Cantuaria*, but from Cambridge, *Cantabrigia*.

Christian names have been latinised as, for instance, *Willelmus*, William, *Johanna*, Joan or Jane, *Radulfus*, Ralph or Randulf. Even surnames may be similarly treated, *filius Johannis* for Johnson, *De Ponte* for Bridge, *De Fontibus* for Wells, *Molendinarius* for Miller, *Rotarius* for Wheeler or Rutter. Researchers usually refer to C. T. Martin's *The Record Interpreter* for guidance on Latin forms of proper names.

In 1381 Sir John Cavendish composed his final will, shortly before his murder by the mob in the Peasants' Revolt. He commenced in Latin but 'quia lingua gallica amicis meis et eciam michi plus est cognita et magis communis et nota quam lingua latina, totum residuum testamenti mei predicti in linguam gallicam scribere feci ut a dictis amicis meis facilius inteligatur'. Cavendish closed the document in the more popular French tongue.

Spoken by polite society in Britain from the 11th century, Norman–French dominated conversation at court, in court and by courtly folk until Chaucer's time. Even legal documents less ceremonious than charters appeared in French. The language ceased to be employed for parliamentary statutes in 1487, surviving however in the monarch's traditional assent to an act 'le roi le veult'. Educated people persevered in writing modern French, especially in their correspondence, until the 19th century, and Prime Minister Walpole happily conversed with German King George in that tongue. Records in the Channel Islands, the portion of the Duchy of Normandy remaining to the crown, were normally written in French until 1948.

Frankish influence reached the Lowlands of Scotland by the early 12th century. The renowned William I, The Lion, who ruled from 1165 to 1214, was son of Ada of Warenne and grandson of Maud of Senlis. An anonymous 13th-century scribe described him and his brother as 'Frenchmen in race, manners, language and culture; they keep only Frenchmen in their household and following and have reduced the Scots to utter servitude'.

Though English people continued to speak English despite the Norman Conquest, writers increasingly employed the vernacular from the 15th century onwards. Local and national government clerks preferred English to Latin from the 16th century. In October 1438 Anne, Countess of Stafford 'of hool and avisid mynde' decided to write her testament 'in Englisshe tonge for my most profit redyng and undirstandyng in þis wise'. This will, proved before Archbishop Henry Chichele of Canterbury in 1441, was immediately preceded and followed in the register by documents in Latin.

Informal documents in Scots commence from the late 14th century. At that date John Barbour, the father of Scottish poetry, was employing the 'Inglis', a form of northern English eventually known as Scots. The language adopted the distinctive English letters thorn and yogh, for instance in *yt* for 'that', *ye* for 'the', *ʒeir* for 'year'. Writers tended to replace the English ending *-ing* with *-and*, that is *passand* for 'passing', *entrand* for 'entering'. The past tense in *-ed* as in 'ascended' became *ascendit*. Modern English *wh* was written as *qu* creating forms such as *quhatsumevir* for 'whatsoever', *quheit* for 'wheat', *quhit* for 'white'. Early and middle Scots was written by lawyers and administrators until about 1620, when replaced by English forms. The northern tongue then developed into various regional, usually unwritten, dialects.

Welsh people continued to speak their own language from Roman times, evidenced in a handful of inscriptions on stone in Ogam writing, a few parchments and religious texts in Welsh, and the chronicles of folk-lorists. By the 11th century, cathedrals and monasteries were influenced by Norman incomers and Latin learning, though the bards at princely courts doggedly spoke and wrote the native tongue. The monastic house of Strata Florida strenuously preserved Welsh traditions, including the version of the Brut legend in the red book of Hergest, setting out the origin and history of the ancient British race and kings. Welsh was later written in medieval court and book hands, secretary and italic, generally differing little from English forms.

Scribal materials

Priests, lay brothers belonging to monastic scriptoria, manorial stewards, sheriff and town clerks, notaries public, scriveners and court officials dipped their pens into inkwells during the Middle Ages to write for business or devotional purposes. Goose, swan or crow quills, cut obliquely and constantly resharpened, if held at an unchanging angle to the surface, produced the up and down thick and thin strokes typical of gothic handwriting. When the pen was cut straight or the hold varied, thickening appeared diagonal or horizontal. Later round hands depended on the quill cut to a straight fine point. The introduction of steel nibs, dating from 1830, may be recognised by thick downstrokes and thin upstrokes produced by deliberate alteration in pressure as a stylistic device.

Medieval ink contained acidic galls or oakapples; gum; and copperas (vitriol) or protosulphate of iron. The mixture of acidic galls and iron salts endures for centuries, strengthened with blood, urine, even beer. A 15th-century recipe for ink stated, 'to make hynke Take galles & coporos or vitrial quod idem est & gumme of everyche a quartryn oþer helf quartryn & a halfe quartryn of galles more & breke þe galles a ij oþer a iij & put ham to gedere everyche on in a pot & stere hyt ofte & Wythinne ij Wykys after ze mow Wryte þerWyþ'. Such medieval ink, which blackens with age, bites into parchment or paper and is difficult to remove even by damping. Ink appears reddish brown until about 1380, greenish black until about 1520. From the 16th century a suspension of carbon, usually lampblack, in gum water produced very black ink which may not bite into the material and is not waterproof. When the constituent gum rots in the course of time or through careless storage, the ink may be scraped off. This vintage of ink also fades, though the ultra-violet lamp facilitates reading of the words without causing damage to the document. Sad to say, in the bad old days, zealous researchers treated faded ink with chemical reagents such as solutions of gallic acid. These caused the ink temporarily to appear very black and easy to decipher. But eventually the applied chemical itself darkened, obscuring perhaps the text of an entire page with an ineradicable stain.

Medieval calligraphers from the 12th century employed lead for ruling lines on which to write their text. The modern pencil, though known as black lead, consists of graphite, worked in Britain from the 16th century and occasionally used by writers from that date.

Scribes wrote on parchment, a material supposedly perfected at, and deriving its name from, the town of Pergamum but probably known since Egyptian and Babylonian times. This supplanted papyrus during the third century. Skins of goats, sheep or calves, scraped free of hair, reduced in thickness, soaked, stretched, smoothed, pumiced, chalked and dried, formed the writing surface of European scribes until the 16th century, and later. The most expensive material, vellum or veal-parchment, appears thin and smooth, the flesh side seeming whiter and shinier than the hair side or dorse.

For charters and similar significant documents, scribes wrote only on the flesh side, known as the recto, though endorsements might well occupy the hair side, verso or dorse. Each piece or membrane of parchment may be separately referenced by modern archivists, as, when dealing with rolled parchment, m2r for membrane 2 recto or m2d for membrane 2 dorse. The reverse of the leaf of a foliated manuscript is known as the verso.

Certain clerks sewed membranes together head to tail, to form a strip of parchment perhaps dozens of feet long, which could then be rolled, as in chancery style. Clerks in law courts and exchequer piled membranes one on top of another, flesh side uppermost, and secured the pile with cord at the head. This stout bundle would also then be rolled, but individual parchments could be consulted conveniently without unfolding an entire roll.

People could purchase supplies of paper in Britain during the 14th century, though its successful manufacture in these islands dated from no earlier than the 17th century. Until the early 19th century paper was made by hand from mechanically pulped vegetable fibre such as linen rag. A wire screen was dipped into the mash and sufficient pulp lifted out to form one sheet of paper. The wires of this screen left marks in the paper known as chain and laid lines. The sheets were then pressed, dried, sized and hand finished. Rag-based handmade paper is a far more enduring material than much of the mechanically produced wood-pulp paper which began to appear in the mid-nineteenth century. A papermaker usually introduced into each sheet his trademark, and these watermarks facilitate the dating or authentication of documents. For excise purposes 19th-century paper may contain a mark indicating the name of the maker and year of manufacture, essential for cataloguing such documents as undated architectural drawings. Obviously the paper may have been held in the legal or draughtsman's office for some years after the date of manufacture, but presumably for no more than three or four years.

Seals

The popes employed a seal during the early seventh century as a means of authenticating their documents in any age of general illiteracy, instability and forgery. Monarchs, clergy, nobles and corporations imitated. The seal conferred legitimacy on a medieval document: the parties neither composed the text nor signed their names. The stamp or matrix which produced the clearest impression consisted of latten, silver or lead. The seal itself was normally of wax of various colours ranging from white through green to red, though the popes traditionally employed a leaden bulla or seal. The seals applied to the surface of documents from the 16th century onwards are usually of shellac, a resinous substance purified and formed into thin red sheets. The 18th- and 19th-century wafer seal, of a flour mixture, was impressed on paper documents. The seal could be applied directly to the document's surface or appended by parchment tag, leathern thong, silken yarn or hempen cord from the base. Occasionally the foot of the parchment itself was cut from the right-hand side to within a short distance of the left-hand side. On this tongue — or, as the diplomatists stated *sur simple queue* —

the wax seal was fixed. More frequently, the foot of the parchment was folded over and a cord, tag, lace, or ribbon passed through slits for supporting the pendent seal. A double parchment tag was often employed for this purpose in an arrangement known as *sur double queue*.

Seals were not proof against the careful forger because a genuine royal, papal or private seal could be removed from its charter and re-attached to a forged document. This involved cunning manipulation of the parchment tag and silk cord as well as the splitting and reheating of the wax or lead. An original seal matrix was not immune to theft and subsequent surreptitious reintroduction to the treasure chest. However a pendent seal with impressions on both sides foiled all but the most diligent forgers because of the superlative skill required to attach a genuine seal to an unauthentic document without damaging the impression itself.

As early as the pontificate of Innocent III, 1198-1216, the popes established principles for the criticism of seals adjudged suspect, and chanceries throughout Christendom were alerted to the devious minds of fabricators and tamperers. The falsification of seals in the days before written signatures might result in damnation because, as it was said, by attaching an unauthentic bulla 'the mouths of all the pontiffs may be opened or closed'.

The majority of families requiring a seal, following royal examples, decided on a circular version, though clergymen and noblewomen preferred the pointed oval. The English and Scottish royal seals depicted the king enthroned in majesty on one side, his equestrian figure on the other. Ecclesiastics chose a conventional picture of a church or a stylised representation of a patron saint or a Madonna and Child. Towns adopted the outline of their city gate, harbour or guildhall. Educational institutions displayed the chancellor and masters in convocation. Knights naturally preferred armed equestrian figures often in battle array. The seals of the gentry tend to be less formal, bearing images of beasts, flowers or trees.

The legend around the seal, usually stated the name and style of the owner: SIGILLUM ILBERTI DE LACEO meaning 'Ilbert of Lacy's seal; +IOhANNES DEI GRACIA REX SCOTTORVM, 'John by god's grace, king of Scots'; SIGILLUM COMMUNE BURGI DE SANQUHAR, 'common seal of the burgh of Sanquhar'. The script may be distinguished as roman capitals before the 12th century and after about 1500; Lombardic about 1150-1370; and black letter about 1370-1500.

ERA   ERA   era

Roman   *Lombardic*   *Black letter*

Chronology

During the Saxon and Norman period churchmen celebrated the new year on 25 December, the traditional day of Christ's birth. The church in Europe moved the anniversary, from as early as the ninth century, to 25 March, the day of the child's conception, known as Lady Day. This practice, though common on the continent, initially found little favour in Britain. In some European cities men reckoned the commencement of the year from the 25th March following Christmas. This emerged as early as the 11th century in England and seems to reflect the influence of the reforming abbey of Fleury with its devotion to the Virgin Mary. The choice of a date for the beginning of the year may also stem from the rivalry among towns and communities, some choosing the Lady Day before Christmas, their opponents deciding on the Lady Day after the feast. Indeed the first method, as preferred in Pisa, is usually termed the *calculus pisanus*, the second method, from Florence, the *calculus florentinus*.

There was yet another reckoning for the start of the year, a non-religious day, known in Scotland as ne'er day, new year's day. Scotland adopted 1 January from the year 1600, England, Wales and British dominions only from 1752.

A document dated between 1 January and 24 March in old style calendar years should therefore be treated cautiously. The day of Charles I's execution, for treason, was for English contemporaries 30 January 1648. For Scots and modern researchers it is 30 January 1649. Historians write such old style/new style dates as 30 January 1648/9 or 1648/1649.

The adoption of the Julian calendar throughout Christendom facilitated the reckoning of time, though the number of hours in Julius Caesar's year corresponded inexactly with the solar year. In fact over the centuries it became evident that communities working on this ancient system were falling behind the sun by a matter of some days. As a result much of Catholic Europe adopted the reformed calendar of Pope Gregory XIII.

By 1752 Britain had fallen 11 days behind the calendars of European countries using the Gregorian reckoning. James VII & II departed from London shortly before Christmas 1688 but because France was already one and a half weeks ahead of Britain the exiled monarch reached the continent to discover the festivities attending Christ's birth already completed. Contemporary writers familiar with both practices might employ two dates: 28 July/7 August 1588.

In 1752 parliament decided to bring Britain into line with the remainder of Europe and removed eleven days out of that year. The day following Wednesday 2 September became Thursday 14 September. People rioted to recover the 11 days lost from their lives. Taxpayers gained compensation. The start of the financial year, traditionally commencing on Lady Day, 25 March, was altered 11 days, to 6 April, evidenced on annual tax returns.

Charters before the 12th century may not be dated at all. In Scotland the beginnings of a dating system were built on the 'date of place', that is, the royal charter being witnessed at a certain manor or town, such as *apud Rochesburgum*. A knowledge of the monarch's itinerary offers a means of discovering the probable year. At the very end of the 12th century scribes inserted the month and day in royal charters, but only from the 1220s does the year of the king's reign occur. Private documents began to be dated from the end of the 13th century.

A regnal year commences with the day of the monarch's accession. The second regnal year begins one year later and bears no relationship to the year of grace.

The tenth year of Henry VI of England runs from 1 September 1431 until 31 August 1432. The regnal years of David II, King of Scots, began on 7 June 1329. Although David spent the years 1346-57 as a prisoner of the English, his chancery continued issuing charters in his name — except seemingly during the regnal year 24 (7 June 1352-6 June 1352). Is it perhaps significant that this hiatus coincides with David's parole during the spring of 1352? But when, by 10 October 1353, charters were again issued, they were dated (perhaps owing to a clerical error) *annon regai ostri vicesimoquarto* — as though year 23 had been 24 months long!

Medieval scribes and chroniclers dated documents by significant events. In the same way villagers must have recalled events in their lives. It is possible that a couple remembered the day of their marriage 'following the great storm when the church steeple fell', or spoke of their entry into service at the manor house on the weekend 'the young lord was slain in the hunting field'. One charter of Glasgow cathedral church was written on the day of the fencing of a boundary at Ashkirk in Selkirkshire. Villagers could pinpoint this momentous event to the Sunday next before the feast of Saints Simon and Jude next after the French King Louis VII first went into England to visit the shrine of St Thomas at Canterbury. The charter must have been written on Sunday 21 October 1179.

Because feasts and services of the church dominated people's lives, writers frequently alluded to saints' days, collects or introits as a convenient means of chronology. When about 1440 Agnes Paston wrote a 'lettere' to her 'worshepefull housbond' William Paston, a justice of the court of common pleas, she ended with the place and date: 'Wretyn at Paston in hast the Wednesday next after Deus qui errantibus, for defaute of a good secretarye'. Now, the collect for the third Sunday after Easter commences with the words *deus qui errantibus*, 'almighty god, who shewest to them that be in error the light of thy truth', as the book of common prayer translates the Latin phrases. In 1440 the Wednesday following Easter 3 fell on 20 April.

In the year 1183 the Archbishop of Canterbury commanded certain people to meet him at Caen in Normandy *ad viri Galilei*. The Primate of all England referred not to a French hostelry known by the sign of the Man of Galilee but to the introit or epistle for Ascension Day 'viri Galilei . . . ye men of Galilee, why stand ye gazing up into heaven?' Richard of Dover may indeed have had notions of relaxing with a wench in a comfortable tavern but in his letter was merely confirming an appointment for 26 May, Ascension Day 1183.

Postscript

Researchers, whether local historians or genealogists, postgraduate students writing a thesis or schoolchildren studying a project, are seekers after historical truth. But ambiguities or enigmas may emerge from even the most complete series of records — and many records series are frustratingly incomplete. Charles Trice Martin, for 45 years an archivist at the Public Record Office, did not underestimate 'the difficulties and dangers' encountered in studying 'the various kinds of documents which are likely to be found among the title-deeds of an estate, or among the archives of a parish or a corporation'. He knew the frustration of researching collections of documents lacking certain significant items, records censored or damaged, muniments posing insurmountable diplomatic or palaeographical problems, and archives susceptible to various interpretations.

On the occasion of the marriage of his daughter Lizzie, on 8 June 1872, the wealthy Cheshire salt manufacture, H. E. Falk, inaugurated Meadow Bank schools. He designed the premises; his men did the building; brick and clinker from his waste tips provided the materials; and he paid the salaries of the teachers. He asserted that 'the advantage of a liberal education... attracting the masses to music and to the contemplation of the arts' must 'ameliorate the desperate state of gross materialism' of the age.

But how should the historian interpret Falk's actions? The documents permit the reader to make at least two different assessments. Perhaps Falk was indeed an enlightened employer and generous benefactor, a philanthropist who — had his circumstances been otherwise — would have gone into teaching or the arts. But it is equally possible that his sponsored education service might gradually break 'the rebellious spirit' of his people. Perhaps when Falk complained of the 'gross materialism' of the age he had in mind the presumptuous wage demands of the workers rather than the luxurious lives of the bourgeoisie. Falk's motives cannot be certainly known from the surviving sources, though he was notorious for breaking a strike in 1868 by employing migrant German labourers, replaced afterwards with the more 'docile' Poles and Hungarians.

At 3.30 in the morning of the feast day of Bertelinus of Stafford 1889, Frank Willis, a merchant seaman on board the ship *Langdale* in San Francisco Bay, awoke to cries of 'fire! fire!'.

'The whole wharehouse to which we were laying had taken fire & the wind was blowing directly down on to us.'

One ship, *Armenia*, was enveloped in flames and 'as she drifted down passed us we could hear the dying entreaties of people aboard for help, but ...'.

Fire spread to neighbouring ships. The *Honauwar* constructed entirely of wood drifted helplessly. Willis's *Langdale* 'tried to avoid a collision, but we could not & she came right on to us, all hands took to the boats, the captain of the "Kenilworth's" wife & baby being with us, the "Langdale" then took fire forward... & all hands rushed aboard to extinguish the fire which with the help of a reel & a steam pump we did ...'.

Willis hastened to record that morning's events for his sweetheart, Emily Woosnam, in England. His letter ends with the subscription 'Yours ever till death'.

But shortly afterwards the romance ended. Whether Willis was untrue to my grandmother or whether she spurned him in favour of another cannot be known. A well-meaning descendant destroyed most of the letters written later than 1889 as 'unimportant or repetitive' — but retained the envelopes with postmarks and postage stamps as 'interesting and valuable'.

The reader, having read this far, fully appreciates that archives are important, valuable, informative and interesting. To be enjoyed archives must first be preserved. The letters, diaries, photographs and ephemera which clutter our cupboards are the source material for recording our own lives and times. The reader would never contemplate disposing of his own archive; but the thoughtful historian should also be active in saving his neighbours' archives — rescuing an album from next door's dustbin or a ledger from the bonfire at the corner — gaining personal satisfaction in this life and the thanks of posterity.

Charles Trice Martin wrote: 'all persons who interest themselves in the documents to which they may have access . . . are helping in the grand work of making clear the laws and customs and mode of living of our ancestors' — even if we cannot certainly interpret Falk's motives or document the shipwreck of Frank and Emily's love affair.

BIBLIOGRAPHY

x Books discussing Palaeography.

† Books discussing Chronology.

* Dictionaries.

The following books may be available on loan through your public library or on sale through your bookshop.

Anderson, J., *Selectus Diplomatum et Numismatum Scotiæ Thesaurus*, 1739.[x]

Andrews, J. H., *A Paper Landscape: the Ordnance Survey in Nineteenth-Century Ireland*, 1975.

Appleby, J. T. (ed.), *Chronicon Richardi Devisensis de Tempore Regis Richardi Primi. The Chronicle of Richard of Devizes of the time of King Richard the First*, 1963.

Ashton, T. S., *An Eighteenth-Century Industrialist, Peter Stubs of Warrington, 1756–1806*, 1939.

Bagley, J. J., *Historical Interpretation*, 1972.

Baker, J. H., *Manual of Law French*, 1979.

Baker, W. P., *Parish Registers and Illiteracy in East Yorkshire*, 1961.

Ballard, A. (ed.), *British Borough Charters, 1042–1216*, 1913.

— and Tait, J. (eds.), *British Borough Charters, 1216–1307*, 1923.

Bardsley, C. W., *Dictionary of English and Welsh Surnames*, 1901.*

Barker, T. C. and Harris, J. R., *A Merseyside Town in the Industrial Revolution: St Helens 1750–1900*, 1954.

Barley, M. W., *The English Farmhouse and Cottage*, 1961.

— *A Guide to British Topographical Collections*, 1974.

Begley, D. F., *Irish Genealogy: a Record Finder*, 1981.

Bell, W., *A Dictionary and Digest of the Law of Scotland*, 1838.

Beresford, M. W., *History on the Ground: Six Studies in Maps and Landscapes*, 1957.

— *Lay Subsidies and Poll Taxes*, 1963.

Beveridge, W., *Prices and Wages in England from the Twelfth to the Nineteenth Century*, 1939.

Birch, W. de G. (ed.), *Cartularium Saxonicum*, 1885–99.

— *History of Scottish Seals*, 1905–7.

Bloch, M., *The Historian's Craft*, 1954.

Bond, M. F., *Guide to the Records of Parliament*, 1971.

Bracegirdle, B., *Photography for Books and Reports*, 1970.

Briquet, C. M., *Les Filigranes: Dictionnaire Historique des Marques du Papier dès leur Apparition vers 1282 jusqu'en 1600*, 1907.*

British Standards Institution, *Recommendations for the Storage and Exhibition of Archival Documents*, 1977.

Brooks, P. C., *Research in Archives: the Use of Unpublished Primary Sources*, 1969.

Buck, W. S. B., *Examples of Handwriting 1550–1650*, 1973.[x]

Buckinghamshire County Council and Buckinghamshire Quarter Sessions Joint Committee, *Calendar of Quarter Sessions Records*, ed. by W. Le Hardy, in progress, 1933–

Bullough, D. A. and Storey, R. L., *The Study of Medieval Records*, 1971.

Burke, A. M., *Key to the Ancient Parish Registers of England and Wales*, 1908.

Burnett, J., *A History of the Cost of Living*, 1969.

181

Cam, H. *The Hundred and the Hundred Rolls: An Outline of Local Government in Medieval England*, 1930.

Camp, A. J., *Wills and Their Whereabouts*, 4th edn., 1974.

Cappelli, A., *Dizionario di Abbreviature Latine ed Italiane*, 2nd revised edn., Milan, 1912.*

Celoria, F., *Teach Yourself Local History*, 1958.

Chaplais, P., *English Royal Documents: King John–Henry VI, 1199–1461*, 1971.

Cheney, C. R., *Handbook of Dates for Students of English History*, 1961.†

Clanchy, M. T., *From Memory to Written Record; England 1066–1307*, 1979.

Cockerell, S. (ed.), *The Gorleston Psalter: a Manuscript of the Beginning of the Fourteenth Century in the Library of C. W. D. Perrins, Described in Relation to other East Anglian Books of the Period*, 1907.

Coleman, D. C., *Courtaulds; An Economic and Social History*, 1969.

Colwell, S., *The Family History Book*, 1980.

Cook, M., *Archives Administration*, 1977.

—   *The Management of Information from Archives*, 1985.

Cope, A. D. Baynes-, *Caring for Books and Documents*, 1981.

Cornwall, J., *How to Read Old Title Deeds XVI–XIX Centuries*, 1964.

Cox, J. and Padfield T., *Tracing your Ancestors in the Public Record Office*, 1981.

Crafts Advisory Committee, *Conservation Sourcebook for Conservators, Craftsmen and those who have Historic Objects in their Care* , 1979.

Cranfield, G. A., *A Handlist of English Provincial Newspapers and Periodicals 1700–1760*, 1952.

Crombie, J., *Her Majesty's Customs and Excise*, 1962.

Davies, J. C. and Lewis, E. A., *Records of the Court of Augmentations Relating to Wales and Monmouthshire*, 1954.

Dawson, G. E. and Kennedy-Skipton, L., *Elizabethan Handwriting 1500–1650: a Guide to the Reading of Documents and Manuscripts*, 1968.[X]

Dickson, P. G. M., *The Sun Insurance Office, 1710–1960*, 1960.

Douch, R., *Local History and the Teacher*, 1967.

Dowell, S., *A History of Taxation and Taxes in England*, 3rd edn., 1965.

Duchein, M., *Archive Buildings and Equipment*, 1977.

Duckett, K. W., *Modern Manuscripts; a Practical Manual for their Management, Care, and Use*, 1975.

Dunbar, A. H., *Scottish Kings; a Revised Chronology of Scottish History 1005–1625 with Notices of the Principal Events, Tables of Regnal Years, Pedigrees, Calendars, &c.*, 1899.†

Dunning, R., *Local History for Beginners*, 1980 (first published as *Local Sources for the Young Historian*, 1973).

Dymond, D., *Writing Local History, a Practical Guide*, 1981.

Dyos, H. J., *Victorian Suburb: a Study of the Growth of Camberwell*, 1961.

Edwards, G. Hamilton-, *In Search of Ancestry*, 1966.

—   *In Search of Welsh Ancestry*, 1985.

Ekwall, E., *Concise Oxford Dictionary of Place-Names*, 4th edn., 1960.

Emmison, F. G., *Archives and Local History*, 1966.[X]

—   *Guide to the Essex Record Office*, 2nd edn., 1969.

—   *How to Read Local Archives 1550–1700*, 1967.[X]

—   *Introduction to Archives*, 1964.

— and Gray, I., *County Records*, revised edn., 1973. ·1834' in *Bedfordshire Historical Record*

Ernle, *Lord* (Prothero, R. E.), *English Farming Past and Present*, 6th edn., with introduction by G. E. Fussell and O. R. McGregor, 1961.

Everitt, A., *New Avenues in English Local History*, 1970.

—   *Ways and Means in Local History*, 1971.

Eversley, D. E. C. and Glass, D. V. (eds.), *Population in History*, 1965.

Finberg, H. P. R., *Early Charters of Wessex*, 1964 (Calendar with Introduction).

—   *The Local Historian and his Theme*, 1952.

—   *West Country Historical Studies*, 1969.

Finberg, H. P. R. and Skipp, V. H. T., *Local History: Objective and Pursuit*, 1967.

Fleury, M. and Henry, L., *Nouveau Manuel de Dépouillement et d'Exploitation de l'État Civil Ancien*, 1965 (Demography).

Ford, P. and G., *A Guide to Parliamentary Papers: What They Are: How to Find Them: How to Use Them*, 1955.

— *Select List of British Parliamentary Papers 1833–1899*, 1953.

Foster, J. and Shepherd, J., *British Archives: a Guide to Archive Resources in the United Kingdom*, 1982.

Fowler, G. H., *The Care of County Muniments*, 1923.

France, R. S., *Guide to the Lancashire Record Office*, 2nd edn., 1962.

Galbraith, V. H., *The Historian at Work*, 1962.

— *An Introduction to the Use of Public Records*, 1934.

— *Studies in the Public Records*, 1948.

Gardner, D. E. and Smith, F., *Genealogical Research in England and Wales*, 1956–64.

Gibson, J. S. W. (comp.), *Census Returns, 1841, 1851, 1861, 1871, on Microfilm: a Directory to Local Holdings*, 1979.

— *A Simplified Guide to Probate Jurisdictions*, 2nd ed. 1981.

— *Wills & Where to Find Them*, 1974.

— and Peskett, P., *Record Offices: How to Find Them*, 1981.

Glover, R. F. and Harris, R. W., *Latin for Historians*, 3rd edn., 1963.*

Gooder, E. A., *Latin for Local History*, 1961 (with useful formulary of some common documents).*

Goss, C. W. F., *The London Directories 1677–1855*, 1932.

Gough, R., *The History of Myddle*, 1979.

Grieve, H. E. P., *Examples of English Handwriting 1150–1750*, 1954.[X]

Griffith, M., *A Short Guide to the Public Record Office of Ireland*, 1964.

Grigg, P. J., chairman, *Report of the Committee on Departmental Records*, Cmd. 9163, 1954.

Gross, C., *A Bibliography of British Municipal History*, 2nd edn., 1966.

Guildhall Library, *London Rate Assessments and Inhabitants Lists in Guildhall Library and the Corporation of London Records Office*, 2nd edn., 1968.

Hall, H., *Formula Book of English Official Historical Documents*, 1908–9.

Hansard, J. and L. G., *Hansard's Catalogue and Breviate of Parliamentary Papers 1696–1834*, 1953.

Harley, J. B., *Maps for the Local Historian*, 1972.

— *Ordnance Survey Maps; a Descriptive Manual*, 1975.

— and Phillips, C. W., *The Historian's Guide to Ordnance Survey Maps*, 1965.

Harvey, J., *Sources for the History of Houses*, 1974.

Hatfield Workers' Educational Association, *Hatfield and Its People*, 12 pamphlet volumes, 1961–4.

Hector, L. C., *The Handwriting of English Documents*, 1958.[X]

— *Palaeography and Forgery*, 1959.[X]

Hodgkiss, A. G., *Maps for Books and Theses*, 1970.

Hodson, J. H., *The Administration of Archives*, 1972.

Hollaender, A. E. J., (ed.), *Essays in Memory of Sir Hilary Jenkinson*, 1962 (seals, palaeography, archives, Public Record Office).[X]

Hollingsworth, T. H., *Historical Demography*, 1969.

Hooper, M. et al., *Hedges and Local History*, 1971.

Hoskins, W. G., *English Landscapes*, 1973.

— *English Local History; the Past and the Future*, 1966.

— *Local History in England*, 1959.

— and Stamp, L. D., *The Common Lands of England and Wales*, 1963.

Hunnisett, R. F., *Editing Records for Publication*, 1977.

— *Indexing for Editors*, 1972.

Iredale, D. A., *Local History Research and Writing*, 1974.

Irish Record Commissioners, *Chartæ, privilegia et immunitates; being transcripts of charters and privileges to cities, towns, abbeys, and other bodies corporate [in Ireland], 18 Henry II to 18 Richard II, 1171 to 1395*, 1829-30.

Jackson, D., *The Story of Writing*, 1981.[x]

Jenkinson, C. H., *The Later Court Hands in England from the Fifteenth to the Seventeenth Century*, 1927.[x]

— *A Manual of Archive Administration*, 2nd revised edn. with Introduction and Bibliography by R. H. Ellis, reissued 1965.

— *Selected Writings of Sir Hilary Jenkinson*, 1980.[x]

— and Johnson, C., *English Court Hand, A.D. 1066 to 1500*, 1915 (volume 1 is a treatise on the handwriting of medieval administrative documents and contains the text of documents reproduced in facsimile in volume 2).[x]

Jones, V. L. Eakle, A. H. and Christensen, M. H., *Family History for Fun and Profit*, revised edn., 1972 (originally appeared as *Genealogical Research: a Jurisdictional Approach*).

Judge, C. B., *Specimens of Sixteenth Century English Handwriting; Taken from Contemporary Public and Private Records*, 1935.[x]

Juridical Society of Edinburgh, *A Collection of Styles; or a Complete System of Conveyancing, adapted to the Present Practice of Scotland*, 1787-94.

Kelham, R., *A Dictionary of the Norman or Old French Language*, 1779, republished 1978.*

Kemble, J. M., *Codex Diplomaticus aevi Saxonici*, 1839-48.

Klingender, F. D., *Art and the Industrial Revolution*, 1947, revised by Sir A. Elton, 1968.

Knight, R. J. B. (ed.), *Guide to the Manuscripts in the National Maritime Museum: Volume I, the Personal Collections*, 1977.

Ladurie, E. Le Roy, *Montaillou; Cathars and Catholics in a French Village 1294-1324*, 1978.

Laslett, Peter, *The World We Have Lost*, 1965.

Latham, R. E., *Revised Medieval Latin Word-List*, 1965.*

Leadam, I. S. (ed.), *The Domesday of Inclosures 1517-1518*, 1897.

Leeson, F., *A Guide to the Records of the British State Tontines and Life Annuities of the Seventeenth and Eighteenth Centuries*, 1968.

Le Hardy, W. (ed.), *Guide to the Hertfordshire Record Office*, 1961.

Library Association County Libraries Group (Readers' Guides), *Sources of Local History*, 4th edn., 1971.

Livingstone, M., *A Guide to the Public Records of Scotland*, 1905.

Loyd, L. C. and Stenton, D. M. (eds.), *Sir Christopher Hatton's Book of Seals*, 1950.

MacFarlane, A., *A Guide to English Historical Records*, 1983.

— *Reconstructing Historical Communities*, 1977.

Maitland, F. W., *Domesday Book and Beyond*, 1897.

— (ed.), *Select Pleas in Manorial and Other Seignorial Courts, Volume 1: Reigns of Henry III and Edward I*, 1889.

Major, K., *A Handlist of the Records of the Bishop of Lincoln and of the Archdeacons of Lincoln and Stow*, 1953.

Martin, C. T., *The Record Interpreter: a Collection of Abbreviations, Latin Words and Names Used in English Historical Manuscripts and Records*, 2nd edn., 1910.*

Martin, G. H. (ed.), *The Royal Charters of Grantham, 1463-1688*, 1963.

Millar, E. G., *The Luttrell Psalter*, 1932.

Ministère des Affaires Culturelles, Direction des Archives de France, *Manuel d'Archivistique*, 1970.

Mullins, E. L. C., *Texts and Calendars: an Analytical Guide to Serial Publications*, 1958.

Munby, L. M. (ed.), *Short Guides to Records*, (series reprinted from the journal *History*), 1961-71.

National Library of Wales, *Handlist of Manuscripts in the National Library of Wales*, in progress, 1940-

Newton, K. C., *Medieval Local Records; a Reading Aid*, 1971.

Nickson, M. A. E., *The British Library: Guide to the Catalogues and Indexes of the Department of Manuscripts*, 1978.

Norton, J. E., *Guide to the National and Provincial Directories of England and Wales, excluding London, published before 1856*, 1950.

Ordnance Survey, *Facsimiles of National Manuscripts of Scotland*, 1867–71.

Owen, D. M., *The Records of the Established Church in England Excluding Parochial Records*, 1970.

Parker, R., *The Common Stream*, 1975.

Parkes, M. B., *English Cursive Book Hands, 1250–1500*, 1969.[x]

Petti, A. G. R., *English Literary Hands from Chaucer to Dryden*, 1977.[x]

Poole, R. L., *Medieval Reckonings of Time*, 1918.[†]

Powell, W. R., *Local History from Blue Books: a Select List of the Sessional Papers of the House of Commons*, 1962.

Powicke, F. M. and Fryde, E. B., *Handbook of British Chronology*, 2nd ed., 1961.[†]

Pryde, G. S., *The Burghs of Scotland: a Critical List*, 1965.

Public Record Office, *A Guide to Seals in the Public Record Office*, ed. by C. H. Jenkinson, 1954.

— *Guide to the Contents of the Public Record Office*, 1963–8.

— *Maps and Plans in the Public Record Office, 1. British Isles c. 1410–1860*, 1967.

Pugh, R. B. (ed.), *Calendar of Antrobus Deeds before 1625*, 1947.

— *How to Write a Parish History*, 1954. (6th ed. of J. C. Cox's standard work).

Purvis, J. S., *Introduction to Ecclesiastical Records*, 1953.

Ranger, F. (ed.), *Prisca Munimenta: Studies in Archival and Administrative History*, 1973.

Ravensdale, J. R., *History on Your Doorstep*, 1982.

Reade, A. L., *The Reades of Blackwood Hill*, 1906.

Reaney, P. H., *A Dictionary of British Surnames*, 2nd edn., 1976.*

Record Commissioners, *The Acts of the Parliaments of Scotland*, 1814–75.

— *Calendars of the Proceedings in Chancery in the Reign of Queen Elizabeth*, 1827–32.

— *Rotuli Hundredorum*, 1812–18.

— *Rotuli Scotiæ in turri Londinensi et in domo capitulari Westmonasteriensi asservati*, 1814–19.

— *Taxatio ecclesiastica Angliæ et Walliæ auctoritate P. Nicholai IV, circa A.D. 1291*, 1802.

— *Valor ecclesiasticus temp. Henr. VIII*, 1810–34.

Redstone, L. and Steer, F. W., *Local Records: Their Nature and Care*, 1953.

Reed, R., *Ancient Skins, Parchments and Leathers*, 1972.

Richardson, J., *The Local Historian's Encyclopaedia*, 1974.

Riden, P., *Local History: a Practical Handbook for Beginners*, 1983.

Rogers, A., *This Was Their World*, 1972 (2nd edn. entitled *Approaches to Local History*, 1977).

Ross, C. D. (ed.), *The Cartulary of Cirencester Abbey, Gloucestershire*, 1964.

Rowe, M. M. (ed.), *Tudor Exeter: Tax Assessments 1489–1595, including the military survey 1522*, 1977.

Royal Commission on Historical Manuscripts, *Record Repositories in Great Britain*, 7th edn., 1982.

Rycraft, A. (ed.), *English Mediaeval Handwriting*, 1972.

Salter, H. E. (ed.), *Facsimiles of Early Charters in Oxford Muniment Rooms*, 1929 (sometimes known as *Oxford Charters*, contains charters dated before 1170).[x]

Sawyer, P. H. (ed.), *Anglo-Saxon Charters: an Annotated List and Bibliography*, 1968.

Schellenberg, T. R., *Modern Archives: Principles and Techniques*, 1956.

Scott, H., *Fasti ecclesiæ Scoticanæ*, 1915–61.

Seymour, W. A. (ed.), *A History of the Ordnance Survey*, 1980.

Simpson, G. G., *Scottish Handwriting 1150–1650, an Introduction to the Reading of Documents*, 1973.[x]

Smith, C. R. Humphery-, *The Phillimore Atlas and Index of Parish Registers*, 1984.

Spufford, M., *Contrasting Communities: English Villagers in the Sixteenth and Seventeenth Centuries*, 1974.

Steel, D., *Discovering your Family History*, 1980.

Steel, D. J. and A. E. F. *et. al.* (comps.), *National Index of Parish Registers*, in progress 1966– (published by Society of Genealogists; volumes 1–2 contain introductory matter).

Steer, F. W. (ed.), *Farm and Cottage Inventories of Mid-Essex 1635–1749*, 1950.

Stenton, F. M., *Facsimiles of Early Charters from Northamptonshire Collections*, 1930.[x]

Stephens, W. B., *Sources for English Local History*, 1973.

Stephenson, M., *A List of Monumental Brasses in the British Isles*, 1926.

Storey, R. L., *A Short Introduction to Wills*, 1966.

— and Bullough, D. A., *The Study of Medieval Records*, 1971.

— and Madden, L., *Primary Sources for Victorian Studies*, 1977.

Tate, W. E., *The English Village Community and the Enclosure Movements*, 1967.

—   *The Parish Chest*, 3rd edn., 1969.

Taylor, H. A., *The Arrangement and Description of Archival Materials*, 1980.

Thomas, D. St J., *Non-Fiction: a Guide to Writing and Publishing*, 1970.

Thompson, F., *Lark Rise to Candleford*, 1945.

Thomson, J. M., *The Public Records of Scotland*, 1922.

Thoyts, E. E., *How to Decipher and Study Old Documents*, 1893.[x]

Tyacke, S. and Huddy, J., *Christopher Saxton and Tudor Map-Making*, 1980.

Vincent, J. R., *Pollbooks: How Victorians Voted*, 1967.

Wagner, A. R., *The Records and Collections of the College of Arms*, 1952.

Wake, J., *How to Compile a History and Present-Day Record of Village Life*, 1925.

Walne, P., *English Wills; Probate Records of England and Wales, with a Brief Note on Scottish and Irish Wills*, 1964.

Ward, W. R., *The Administration of the Window and Assessed Taxes (1696–1798)*, 1963.

—   *The English Land Tax in the Eighteenth Century*, 1953.

Wardle, D. B., *Document Repair*, 1971.

Watt, D. E. R., *Fasti ecclesiæ Scoticanæ medii aevi ad annum 1638*, 1969.

Webb, S. and B., *History of English Local Government*, 1903–29 (1 *The Parish and the County*; 2–3 *The Manor and the Borough*; 4 *Statutory Authorities for Special Purposes*; 5 *The Story of the King's Highway*; 6 *English Prisons under Local Government*; 7–9 *English Poor Law History*; 10 *English Poor Law Policy*; 11 *The History of Liquor Licensing in England*).

Weinbaum, M. (ed.), *British Borough Charters, 1307–1660*, 1943.

West, J., *Town Records*, 1983.

—   *Village Records*, 1962.

Whalley, J. I., *English Handwriting 1540–1853*, 1969.

Wood, H., *Guide to the Public Records of Ireland*, 1919.

Wright, A., *Court Hand Restored*, 1776.[x]

Wright, C. E., *English Vernacular Hands from the Twelfth to the Fifteenth Centuries*, 1960.[x]

Wright, J., *The English Dialect Dictionary; the English Dialect Grammar*, 1898–1905.[*]

Wrigley, E. A. (ed.), *An Introduction to English Historical Demography*, 1966.

Wyon, A. B., *The Great Seals of England*, 1887.

Young, N. Denholm-, *Handwriting in England and Wales*, 2nd edn., 1964.[*]

Youngs, F. A., *Guide to the Local Administrative Units of England; Volume I: Southern England*, 1979.

PERIODICALS

Agricultural History Review
Archives
Business Archives
Business History
Economic History Review
The Genealogists' Magazine
Geography
History
History Today
Industrial Archaeology
Journal of Economic History
Journal of the Society of Archivists
Journal of Tranport History
Local Historian (Amateur Historian)
Local History
Local Population Studies
Population Studies
Textile History
Transactions of the Ancient Monuments Society
Transactions of the Newcomen Society
Transport History
Urban History Yearbook

SELECT LIST OF
RECORD REPOSITORIES AND USEFUL ADDRESSES
IN BRITAIN AND IRELAND

Aberdeen — University Library, Manuscripts and Archives Section, King's College, Aberdeen AB9 2UB.
— City of Aberdeen District Archives, Town House, Aberdeen AB9 1AQ.
Aberystwyth — *see* Dyfed.
Anglesey — *see* Gwynedd.
Angus — District Council, Director of Administration, County Buildings, Forfar, Angus DD8 3LG
Argyll and Bute — District Archives, The Court House, Inverary, Argyll PA32 8TX.
Avon — Bath City Record Office, Guildhall, Bath BA1 5AW.
— Bristol Record Office, Council House, College Green, Bristol BS1 5TR.
Bedfordshire — Record Office, County Hall, Bedford MK42 9AP.
Belfast — *see* Ireland, Northern.
Berkshire — Record Office, Shire Hall, Shinfield Park, Reading RG2 9XD.
— British Broadcasting Corporation, Written Archives Centre, Caversham Park, Reading RG4 8TZ.
— Institute of Agricultural History *and* Museum of English Rural Life, University of Reading, Whiteknights, Reading RG6 2AG.
Birmingham — Public Libraries, Archives Department, Chamberlain Square, Birmingham B3 3HQ.
— Birmingham University Library, Special Collections Department, Main Library, PO Box 363, Birmingham B15 2TT.
Bolton — Metropolitan Borough Archives, Civic Centre, Le Mans Crescent, Bolton BL1 1SA.
Borders — Regional Library, St Mary's Mill, Selkirk, Borders TD7 5EU.
Bradford — West Yorkshire Archive Service, Bradford, Central Library, Prince's Way, Bradford BD1 1NN.
Buckinghamshire — Record Office, County Hall, Aylesbury HP20 1 UA.
— Buckinghamshire Archaeological Society, County Museum, Church Street, Aylesbury HP20 2 QP.
Caernarfonshire — *see* Gwynedd.
Calderdale — West Yorkshire Archive Service, Calderdale, Central Library, Northgate House, Northgate, Halifax HX1 1UN.
Cambridgeshire — Record Office, Shire Hall, Castle Hill, Cambridge CB3 0AP, *and* Grammar School Walk, Huntingdon PE18 6LF.
— Cambridge University Archives *and* University Library Department of Manuscripts, University Library, West Road, Cambridge CB3 9DR.
— Churchill College Archives Centre, Churchill College, Cambridge CB3 0DS.
— Peterborough Museum and Art Gallery, Priestgate, Peterborough PE1 1LF.
Cardiff — *see* Glamorgan.
Cardiganshire — *see* Dyfed.
Carmarthenshire — *see* Dyfed.
Central — Regional Council Archives Department, Old High School, Spittal Street, Stirling FK8 1DG.
Ceredigion — *see* Dyfed.
Channel Islands — The Greffe, Royal Court House, St Peter Port, Guernsey.
— La Société Guernesiaise, La Couture House, La Couture, St Peter Port, Guernsey.

Channel Islands — The Judicial Greffe, Royal Square, St Helier, Jersey.
—   La Société Jersiaise Museum and Library, 9 Pier Road, St Helier, Jersey.
Cheshire — Record Office, The Castle, Chester CH1 2DN.
—   Chester City Record Office, Town Hall, Chester CH1 2HJ.
Cleveland — County Archives Department, Exchange House, 6 Marton Road, Middlesbrough
        TS1 1DB.
Clwyd — Record Office, Old Rectory, Hawarden, Deeside CH5 3NR *and* 46 Clwyd Street,
        Ruthin LL15 1HP.
Cornwall — Record Office, County Hall, Truro TR1 3AY.
—   Royal Institution of Cornwall, County Museum, River Street, Truro TR1 2SJ.
Coventry — City Record Office, Room 220, Second Floor, Broadgate House, Coventry CV1 1NG.
Cumbria — Record Office, The Castle, Carlisle CA3 8UR *and* County Offices, Kendal LA9
        4RQ, *and* 140 Duke Street, Barrow in Furness LA14 1XW.

Denbighshire — *see* Clwyd.
Derbyshire — Record Office, County Offices, Matlock DE4 3AG.
—   Derby Local Studies Library, Derby Central Library, Wardwick, Derby DE1 1HS.
Devon — Record Office, Castle Street, Exeter EX4 3PQ.
—   Exeter Cathedral Library and Archives, Bishop's Palace, Exeter EX1 1HX.
—   Exeter University Library, Prince of Wales Road, Exeter EX4 4PT.
—   West Devon Record Office, Unit 3, Clare Place, Coxside, Plymouth PL4 0JW.
Doncaster — Archives Department, King Edward Road, Balby, Doncaster DN4 0NA.
Dorset — Record Office, County Hall, Dorchester DT1 1XJ.
Dublin — *see* Ireland, Republic of.
Dudley — Archives and Local History Department, Central Library, St James's Road, Dudley
        DY1 1HR.
Dumfries and Galloway — Regional Council Library Service (Archives), Ewart Public Library,
        Catherine Street, Dumfries DG1 1JB.
Dundee — District Archive and Record Centre, City Chambers, City Square, Dundee DD1 3BY
        (including Tayside Regional Archives).
—   Dundee University Library, Archives Department, Dundee DD1 4HN.
Durham — County Record Office, County Hall, Durham DH1 5UL.
—   Dean and Chapter Library, The College, Durham DH1 3EH.
—   Durham University, Department of Palaeography and Diplomatic, Prior's Kitchen, The
        College, Durham DH1 3EQ.
—   Local History Section, Darlington Branch Library, Crown Street, Darlington DL1 1ND.
Dyfed — Archive Service, Carmarthenshire Record Office, County Hall, Carmarthen SA31 1JP,
        and Ceredigion Area Record Office, Swyddfa'r Sir, Marine Terrace, Aberystwyth, SY23
        2DE, *and* Pembrokeshire Record Office, The Castle, Haverfordwest SA61 2EF.
—   National Library of Wales, Department of Manuscripts and Records, Aberystwyth
        SY23 3BU.
—   Royal Commission on Ancient and Historical Monuments in Wales *and* National
        Monuments Record, Edleston House, Queen's Road, Aberystwyth SY23 2HP.
Edinburgh — District Archives, City Chambers, High Street, Edinburgh EH1 1YJ.
—   Edinburgh University Library, Special Collections Department, 30 George Square,
        Edinburgh EH8 9LJ.
—   General Register Office for Scotland, New Register House, Edinburgh EH1 3YT (births,
        marriages, deaths).
—   National Library of Scotland, George IV Bridge, Edinburgh EH1 1EW.
—   National Museum of Antiquities, Country Life Archive, York Buildings, Queen Street,
        Edinburgh EH2 1JD.
—   Royal Commission on the Ancient and Historical Monuments of Scotland *and* National
        Monuments Record of Scotland, 54 Melville Street, Edinburgh EH3 7HF.
—   School of Scottish Studies, 27–28 George Square, Edinburgh EH8 9LD.
—   Scottish Catholic Archives, Columba House, 16 Drummond Place, Edinburgh EH3 6PL
        (formerly Blair's College archives).

Edinburgh — Scottish Record Office *and* National Register of Archives, PO Box 36, H.M. General Register House, Edinburgh EH1 3YY, *and* West Register House, Charlotte Square, Edinburgh EH2 4DF.

Essex — Record Office, County Hall, Chelmsford CM1 1LX, *and* Southend Branch, Central Library, Victoria Avenue, Southend-on-Sea SS2 6EX.

Fife — St Andrews University, North Street, St Andrews KY16 9TR.

Flintshire — *see* Clwyd.

Gateshead — Central Library, Prince Consort Road, Gateshead NE8 4LN.

Glamorgan — Archive Service, Glamorgan Record Office, Mid-Glamorgan County Hall, Cathays Park, Cardiff CF1 3NE (for Mid, South and West Glamorgan).

— National Museum of Wales, Welsh Folk Museum, St Fagans, Cardiff CF5 6XB.

Glasgow — Business Archives Council of Scotland, Glasgow University Archives, The University, Glasgow G12 8QQ.

— City of Glasgow, Mitchell Library, Rare Books and Manuscripts Department, 201 North Street, Glasgow G3 7DN.

— Glasgow University Archives, The University, Glasgow G12 8QQ.

— Glasgow University Library, Department of Special Collections, Hillhead Street, Glasgow G12 8QE.

— *see also* Strathclyde.

Gloucestershire — Record Office, Worcester Street, Gloucester GL1 3WD.

Grampian — Regional Archives, Woodhill House, Ashgrove Road West, Aberdeen AB9 2LU.

Greater Manchester — *see* Manchester, Greater.

Gwent — County Record Office, County Hall, Cwmbran NP4 2XH.

Gwynedd — Archives Service, Caernarfon Area Record Office, County Offices, Shirehall Street, Caernarfon LL55 1 SH (archives located at Victoria Dock, Caernarfon LL55 1 SR) *and* Dolgellau Area Record Office, Cae Penarlâg, Dolgellau LL40 2YB *and* Llangefni Area Record Office, Shire Hall, Llangefni LL77 7TW.

— University College of North Wales Library, Department of Manuscripts, Bangor LL57 2DG.

Hampshire — Record Office, 20 Southgate Street, Winchester SO23 9EF.

— Portsmouth City Records Office, 3 Museum Road, Portsmouth PO1 2LE.

— Southampton City Record Office, Civic Centre, Southampton SO9 4XL.

— Southampton University Library, Southampton SO9 5NH.

Herefordshire and Worcester — Record Office, County Hall, Spetchley Road, Worcester WR2 1TN, *and* Hereford Record Office, The Old Barracks, Harold Street, Hereford HR1 2QX, *and* St Helen's Record Office, Fish Street, Worcester WR1 2HN.

Hertfordshire — Record Office, County Hall, Hertford SG13 8DE.

Highland — Regional Archive, Inverness Public Library, Farraline Park, Inverness IV1 1LS.

Humberside — County Record Office, County Hall, Beverley HU17 9BA.

— Hull University Brynmor Jones Library, Cottingham Road, Hull HU6 7RX.

— South Humberside Area Record Office, Town Hall Square, Grimsby DN31 1HX.

— Kingston upon Hull City Record Office, 79 Lowgate, Kingston upon Hull HU1 2AA.

Ireland, Northern — Public Record Office of Northern Ireland, 66 Balmoral Avenue, Belfast BT9 6NY.

— General Register Office, 49–55 Chichester Street, Belfast BT1 4HL (births, marriages, deaths).

Ireland, Republic of — Public Record Office of Ireland, Four Courts, Dublin 7.

— Chief Herald of Ireland, Genealogical Office, The Castle, Dublin.

— Cork Archives Institute, Christchurch, Cork.

— Dublin Corporation Archives, Dublin Public Libraries, Archives Division, City Hall, Dame Street, Dublin 2.

— Mid-West Regional Development Organisation, 104 Henry Street, Limerick.

— National Library of Ireland, Kildare Street, Dublin 2.

— Registrar General's Office, Custom House, Dublin.

— Trinity College Library, College Green, Dublin 2.

Ireland, Republic of — University College Dublin, Archives Department, 82 St Stephen's Green, Dublin, 2.

Isle of Man — Chief Registrar, General Registry, Finch Road, Douglas (births, marriages, deaths).
—   General Registry, Finch Road, Douglas (deeds, probate etc.).
—   Manx Museum Library, Kingswood Grove, Douglas.

Isle of Wight — County Record Office, 26 Hillside, Newport PO30 2EB.

Kent — Archives Office, County Hall, Maidstone ME14 1XQ, *and* South East Kent Branch, Folkestone Central Library, Grace Hill, Folkestone CT20 1HD *and* Ramsgate Branch, Ramsgate Library, Guildford Lawn, Ramsgate CT11 9AY.
—   Bromley, *see* London.
—   Canterbury Cathedral Archives and Library *and* City *and* Diocesan Record Office, The Precincts, Canterbury CT1 2EG.
—   Institute of Heraldic and Genealogical Studies, Northgate, Canterbury CT1 1BA.

Kirklees — West Yorkshire Archive Service, Kirklees, Central Library, Princess Alexandra Walk, Huddersfield HD2 2SU.

Knowsley — Library Information Services, Local Studies and Archives Collection, Knowsley Central Library, Derby Road, Huyton, Liverpool L36 9UJ.

Lancashire — Record Office, Bow Lane, Preston PR1 8ND.

Leeds — West Yorkshire Archive Service, Leeds, Chapeltown Road, Sheepscar, Leeds LS7 3AP.
—   Leeds University, Brotherton Library, Leeds LS2 9JT.
—   Yorkshire Archaeological Society, Claremont, Clarendon Road, Leeds LS2 9NZ.

Leicestershire — Record Office, 57 New Walk, Leicester LE1 7JB.
—   Leicester University Library, University Road, Leicester LE1 7RH.

Lincolnshire — Archives Office, The Castle, Lincoln LN1 3AB.

Liverpool — Record Office, City Libraries, William Brown Street, Liverpool L3 8EW.
—   Liverpool University Archives, PO Box 147, Senate House, Abercromby Square, Liverpool L69 3BX.
—   Liverpool University, Sydney Jones Library, PO Box 123, Liverpool L69 3DA.

London — Barking and Dagenham Public Libraries, Valence Reference Library, Becontree Avenue, Dagenham, Essex RM8 3HT.
—   Barnet Public Libraries, Local History Library, Hendon Catholic Social Centre, Egerton Gardens, Hendon NW4 4BE.
—   British Architectural Library, Royal Institute of British Architects, Manuscripts Collection, 66 Portland Place W1N 4AD.
—   British Library, Department of Manuscripts, Great Russell Street WC1B 3DG.
—   British Library of Political and Economic Science, 10 Portugal Street WC2A 2HD.
—   British Museum (Natural History), Cromwell Road SW7 5 BD.
—   British Records Association, Charterhouse, Charterhouse Square EC1M 6AU.
—   Bromley Public Libraries, Archives Section, Central Library, High Street, Bromley, Kent BR1 1EX.
—   Business Archives Council, 185 Tower Bridge Road, SE1 2UF.
—   Camden Public Libraries, Swiss Cottages Library, 88 Avenue Road NW3 3HA, *and* Holborn Library, 32–38 Theobalds Road WC1X 8PA.
—   Charity Commission for England and Wales, 14 Ryder Street, St James's SW1Y 6AH.
—   Church Commissioners, 1 Millbank SW1P 3JZ.
—   Church House Record Centre, Dean's Yard, SW1P 3NZ (information on records of Church of England).
—   Church of Jesus Christ of Latter-Day Saints, Branch Library, Hyde Park Chapel, 64 Exhibition Road SW7 2PA.
—   City of London Polytechnic, Fawcett Library, Old Castle Street E1 7NT.
—   Corporation of London Records Office, PO Box 270, Guildhall EC2P 2EJ.
—   Customs and Excise, *see* Her Majesty's Customs and Excise.
—   Dr. Williams's Library, 14 Gordon Square WC1H 0AG (nonconformist records).
—   Duchy of Cornwall Office, 10 Buckingham Gate SW1E 6LA.
—   Ealing Borough Libraries, Central Library, Walpole Park, Ealing W5 5EQ.

London – Greater London Record Office, 40 Northampton Road EC1R 0HB.
— Greenwich Local History Library and Archives, Woodlands, 90 Mycenae Road, Black-heath SE3 7SE.
— Guildhall Library, Aldermanbury EC2P 2EJ.
— Hackney Library Services, Archives Department, Rose Lipman Library, De Beauvoir Road N1 5SQ.
— Hammersmith and Fulham Public Libraries, Archives Department, Shepherd's Bush Library, 7 Uxbridge Road W12 8LJ.
— Haringey Libraries, Museum and Arts Department, Bruce Castle Museum, Lordship Lane N17 8NU.
— Her Majesty's Customs and Excise, Library Services, Room 428, King's Beam House, Mark Lane EC3R 7HE.
— House of Lords Record Office, House of Lords SW1A 0PW.
— Imperial College of Science and Technology Archives, Room 455, Sherfield Building, Imperial College SW7 2AZ.
— Imperial War Museum, Department of Documents, Lambeth Road SE1 6HZ.
— India Office Library and Records, Foreign and Commonwealth Office, 197 Blackfriars Road SE1 8NG.
— Institute of Geological Sciences Library, Exhibition Road SW7 2DE.
— Institution of Civil Engineers Library, Great George Street, Westminster SW1P 3AA.
— Institution of Electrical Engineers, Archives Department, Savoy Place WC2R 0BL.
— Islington Libraries Archives and Local History Collections, Finsbury Library, 245 St John Street, EC1 4NB, and Islington Central Library, 2 Fieldway Crescent N5 1PF.
— Kensington and Chelsea Public Libraries, Central Library, Phillimore Walk W8 7RX.
— Lambeth Archives Department, Minet Library, 52 Knatchbull Road SE5 9QY.
— Lambeth Palace Library, SE1 7JU.
— Lewisham Archives and Local History Department, The Manor House, Old Road, Lee SE13 5SY.
— Linnean Society of London, Burlington House, Piccadilly W1V 0LQ.
— London School of Economics see British Library of Political and Economic Science.
— Manorial Documents Register, Quality House, Quality Court, Chancery Lane WC2A 1HP.
— Museum of London, London Wall EC2Y 5HN.
— National Army Museum, Department of Records, Royal Hospital Road SW3 4HT.
— National Maritime Museum, Manuscripts Section, Greenwich SE10 9NF.
— National Register of Archives, Quality House, Quality Court, Chancery Lane WC2A 1HP.
— Newham Local Studies Library, Stratford Reference Library, Water Lane E15 4NJ.
— Office of Population Censuses and Surveys, General Register Office, St Catherine's House, 10 Kingsway WC2B 6JP (births, marriages), and Alexandra House, 31 Kingsway WC2B 6UF (deaths).
— Post Office Archives, Freeling House, 23 Glass Hill Street SE1 0BQ
— Principal Registry of the Family Division, Somerset House, Strand WC2R 1 LP (wills).
— Public Record Office, Ruskin Avenue, Kew, Richmond, Surrey TW9 4DU and Chancery Lane WC2A 1LR.
— Religious Society of Friends' Library, Friends House, Euston Road NW1 2BJ.
— Royal Air Force Museum, Department of Archives and Aviation Records, Aerodrome Road, Hendon, NW9 5LL.
— Royal Army Medical College, Muniment Room, Millbank SW1 4RJ.
— Royal Botanic Gardens, Library and Archives, Kew, Richmond, Surrey TW9 3AB.
— Royal College of Physicians of London, 11 St Andrew's Place, Regent's Park NW1 4 LE.
— Royal College of Surgeons of England, 35-43 Lincoln's Inn Fields WC2A 3PN.
— Royal Commission on Historical Manuscripts and National Register of Archives, Quality House, Quality Court, Chancery Lane WC2A 1HP.

London – Royal Commission on Historical Monuments, England *and* National Monuments
    Record, Fortress House, 23 Savile Row W1X 1AB.
—   Royal Institution of Great Britain, 21 Albemarle Street W1X 4BS.
—   Royal Society Library, 6 Carlton House Terrace SW1Y 5AG.
—   Science Museum Library, South Kensington SW7 5NH.
—   Society of Antiquaries of London, Burlington House W1V 0HS.
—   Society of Genealogists, 14 Charterhouse Buildings EC1M 7BA.
—   Southwark Local Studies Library, 211 Borough High Street SE1 1JA.
—   United Reformed Church History Society, 86 Tavistock Place WC1H 9RT.
—   University College London, Manuscripts Room, DMS Watson Library, Gower Street
    WC1E 6BT.
—   University of London Library, Senate House, Malet Street WC1E 7HU.
—   Victoria and Albert Museum Library, Cromwell Road SW7 2RL.
—   Waltham Forest Archives and Local History Collection, Vestry House Museum, Vestry
    Road, Walthamstow E17 9NH.
—   Wellcome Institute for the History of Medicine, 183 Euston Road NW1 2BP.
—   Westminster Abbey Muniment Room and Library SW1P 3PA.
—   Westminster City Libraries, Archives Department, Victoria Library, Buckingham Palace
    Road SW1W 9UD, *and* Local History Library, Marylebone Library, Marylebone Road
    NW1 5PS.
—   Westminster Diocesan Archives, Archbishop's House, Ambrosden Avenue, SW1P 1QJ
    (Roman Catholic records).
Man, Isle of – *see* Isle of Man.
Manchester – City Archives Department, Central Library, St Peter's Square, Manchester
    M2 5PD.
—   John Rylands University Library of Manchester, Deansgate, Manchester M3 3EH
    (includes Methodist archives).
—   North Western Museum of Science and Industry, 97 Grosvenor Street, Manchester
    M1 7HF.
Manchester, Greater – Greater Manchester Record Office, 56 Marshall Street, New Cross,
    Ancoats, Manchester M4 5FU.
Merionethshire – *see* Gwynedd.
Merseyside – County Archives Service, 64–66 Islington, Liverpool L3 8LG.
Monmouthshire – *see* Gwent.
Moray – District Record Office, Tolbooth, Forres, Moray IV36 0AB.
Nithsdale – District Council Archives, Municipal Chambers, Buccleuch Street, Dumfries
    DG1 2AD.
Norfolk – Record Office, Central Library, Norwich NR2 1NJ.
North Yorkshire – *see* Yorkshire, North.
Northamptonshire – Record Office, Delapré Abbey, Northampton NN4 9AW.
—   British Steel Corporation, Records Services Section, East Midlands Regional Records
    Centre, By-Pass Road, Irthlingborough, Wellingborough NN9 5QH.
—   Northampton Central Library, Abington Street, Northampton NN1 2BA.
Northumberland – Record Office, Melton Park, North Gosforth, Newcastle upon Tyne
    NE3 5QX, *and* Berwick-upon-Tweed Record Office, Council Offices, Wallace Green,
    Berwick-upon-Tweed TD15 1ED. *See also* Tyne and Wear.
Nottinghamshire – Record Office, County House, High Pavement, Nottingham NG1 1HR.
—   Nottingham University Manuscripts Department, University Library, University Park,
    Nottingham NG7 2RD.
Orkney – The Orkney Library, Archives Department, Laing Street, Kirkwall KW15 1NW.
Oxfordshire – County Record Office, County Hall, New Road, Oxford OX1 1ND.
—   Bodleian Library, Department of Western Manuscripts, Oxford OX1 3BG.
—   Oxford University Archives, Bodleian Library, Oxford OX1 3BG.
Pembrokeshire – *see* Dyfed.

Perth and Kinross — District Council Archive, Sandeman Library, 16 Kinnoull Street, Perth PH1 5ET.
—   Perth Museum and Art Gallery, George Street, Perth PH1 5LB.
Powys — County Council, County Libraries Headquarters, Cefnllys Road, Llandrindod Wells, Powys LD1 5LD.
Renfrew — District Libraries Archives Service, Old Library, Collier Street, Johnstone PA5 8AR.
Rotherham — Metropolitan Borough, Brian O'Malley Central Library and Arts Centre, Walker Place, Rotherham S65 1JH.
Salford — Archives Centre, 658/662 Liverpool Road, Irlam, Manchester M30 5AD.
Sandwell — Metropolitan Borough Council, Smethwick District Library, High Street, Smethwick, Warley, West Midlands B66 1AB.
Sheffield — City Libraries, Archive Division, Central Library, Surrey Street, Sheffield S1 1XZ.
—   Sheffield University Library, Western Bank, Sheffield S10 2TN.
Shetland — Archives, 44 King Harold Street, Lerwick ZE1 0EQ.
Shropshire — Record Office, Shire Hall, Abbey Foregate, Shrewsbury SY2 6ND.
Somerset Record Office, Obridge Road, Taunton TA2 7PU.
South Tyneside — Central Library, Local History Department, Catherine Street, South Shields NE33 2PE.
South Yorkshire — *see* Yorkshire, South.
Staffordshire — Record Office, County Buildings, Eastgate Street, Stafford ST16 2LZ.
—   Burton-on-Trent Library, Riverside, High Street, Burton-on-Trent DE14 1AH.
—   Keele University Library, Keele ST5 5BG.
—   Lichfield Joint Record Office, Public Library, Bird Street, Lichfield WS13 6PN.
—   William Salt Library, Eastgate Street, Stafford ST16 2LZ.
Stockport — Library of Local Studies, Central Library, Wellington Road South, Stockport SK1 3RS.
Suffolk — Record Office, Ipswich Branch, County Hall, Ipswich IP4 2JS, *and* Bury St Edmunds Branch, School Hall Street, Bury St Edmunds IP33 1RX.
Strathclyde — Regional Archives, 30 John Street, PO Box 27, City Chambers, Glasgow G2 1DU, *and* Ayrshire Subregion Archives Office, County Buildings, Ayr KA7 1DR.
Surrey — Record Office, County Hall, Penrhyn Road, Kingston upon Thames KT1 2DN, *and* Guildford Muniment Room, Castle Arch, Guildford GU1 3SX.
Sussex, East — East Sussex Record Office, Pelham House, St Andrews Lane, Lewes BN7 1UN.
Sussex, West — West Sussex Record Office, County Hall, West Street, Chichester PO19 1RN.
Tameside — Local Studies Library, Stalybridge Library, Trinity Street, Stalybridge SK15 2BN.
Tayside — Regional Archives, *see* Dundee.
Tyne and Wear — Archives Department, Blandford House, West Blandford Street, Newcastle upon Tyne NE1 4JA, *and* Local Studies Centre, Howard Street, North Shields NE30 1LY.
Wakefield — District Library Headquarters, Balne Lane, Wakefield WF2 0DQ.
Wales, National Library of — *see* Dyfed.
Wales, National Museum of — *see* Glamorgan, South.
Walsall — Archives Service, Central Library, Lichfield Street, Walsall WS1 1TR.
Warwickshire — Warwick County Record Office, Priory Park, Cape Road, Warwick CV34 4JS.
—   Shakespeare Birthplace Trust Records Office, Henley Street, Stratford-upon-Avon CV37 6QW.
—   Warwick University Modern Records Centre, University Library, Coventry CV4 7AL.
West Yorkshire — *see* Yorkshire, West.
Western Isles — Island Council, Sandwick Road, Stornoway, Lewis PA87 2BW.
Westmorland — *see* Cumbria.
Wigan — Record Office, Town Hall, Leigh WN7 2DY.
Wight, Isle of — *see* Isle of Wight.
Wiltshire — Record Office, County Hall, Trowbridge BA14 8JG.
Wirral — Archive Service, Reference and Information Services, Birkenhead Central Library, Borough Road, Birkenhead L41 2XB.

Wolverhampton — Borough Archives, Central Library, Snow Hill, Wolverhampton WV1 3AX.

Worcestershire — *see* Hereford and Worcester.

Yorkshire, East — *see* Humberside.

Yorkshire, North — North Yorkshire County Record Office, County Hall, Northallerton DL7 8SG.

—   York City Archives Department, Art Gallery Building, Exhibition Square, York YO1 2EW.

—   York Minster Library, Dean's Yard, York YO1 2JD.

—   York University, Borthwick Institute of Historical Research, St Anthony's Hall, Peasholme Green, York YO1 2PW.

Yorkshire, South — South Yorkshire County Record Office, Cultural Activities Centre, Ellin Street, Sheffield S1 4PL.

Yorkshire, West — West Yorkshire Archive Service, Headquarters, Registry of Deeds, Newstead Road, Wakefield WF1 2DE, *see also* Bradford, Calderdale, Kirklees, Leeds, Wakefield.

INDEX

two or more relevant entries on the page